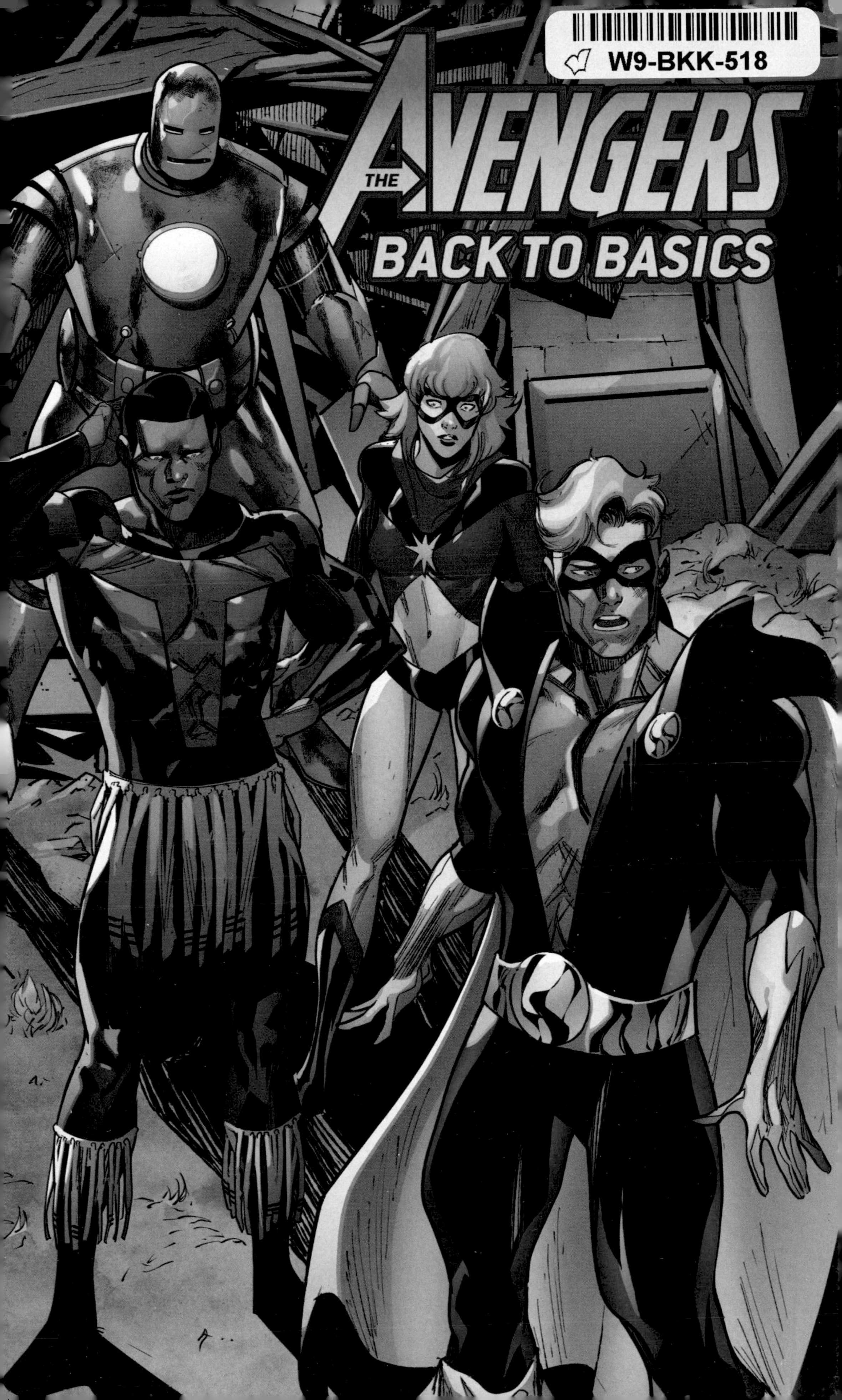
THE AVENGERS
BACK TO BASICS

RECENTLY, THE AVENGERS EXPANDED THEIR RANKS. AMONG THE NEWEST MEMBERS IS THE INHUMAN POLYMORPH KAMALA KHAN, A.K.A. MS. MARVEL (AND THE BIGGEST NERD IN JERSEY CITY). WHEN SHE'S NOT DEFENDING HER HOMETOWN OR SAVING THE WORLD WITH THE CHAMPIONS, SHE'S READING UP ON SUPER HERO HISTORY. AND WITH A LITTLE GIFT FROM THE VISION — A VIRTUAL REALITY VISOR — SHE CAN WATCH AND JOIN ANY AVENGERS' BATTLE AS THOUGH SHE'D BEEN THERE HERSELF.

YOU'RE ABOUT TO SEE AVENGERS HISTORY THROUGH A WHOLE NEW LENS...

AVENGERS CREATED BY **STAN LEE & JACK KIRBY**

COLLECTION EDITOR **MARK D. BEAZLEY** ▪ ASSISTANT EDITOR **CAITLIN O'CONNELL**
ASSOCIATE MANAGING EDITOR **KATERI WOODY** ▪ SENIOR EDITOR, SPECIAL PROJECTS **JENNIFER GRÜNWALD**
VP PRODUCTION & SPECIAL PROJECTS **JEFF YOUNGQUIST** ▪ SVP PRINT, SALES & MARKETING **DAVID GABRIEL**
BOOK DESIGNER **JAY BOWEN**

EDITOR IN CHIEF **C.B. CEBULSKI** ▪ CHIEF CREATIVE OFFICER **JOE QUESADA**
PRESIDENT **DAN BUCKLEY** ▪ EXECUTIVE PRODUCER **ALAN FINE**

AVENGERS: BACK TO BASICS. First printing 2018. ISBN 978-1-302-91263-5. Published by MARVEL WORLDWIDE, INC., a subsidiary of MARVEL ENTERTAINMENT, LLC. OFFICE OF PUBLICATION: 135 West 50th Street, New York, NY 10020. **Printed in Canada.** DAN BUCKLEY, President, Marvel Entertainment; JOHN NEE, Publisher; JOE QUESADA, Chief Creative Officer; TOM BREVOORT, SVP of Publishing; DAVID BOGART, SVP of Business Affairs & Operations, Publishing & Partnership; DAVID GABRIEL, SVP of Sales & Marketing, Publishing; JEFF YOUNGQUIST, VP of Production & Special Projects; DAN CARR, Executive Director of Publishing Technology; ALEX MORALES, Director of Publishing Operations; DAN EDINGTON, Managing Editor; SUSAN CRESPI, Production Manager; STAN LEE, Chairman Emeritus. For information regarding advertising in Marvel Comics or on Marvel.com, please contact Vit DeBellis, Custom Solutions & Integrated Advertising Manager, at vdebellis@marvel.com. For Marvel subscription inquiries, please call 888-511-5480. **Manufactured between 6/29/2018 and 7/31/2018 by SOLISCO PRINTERS, SCOTT, QC, CANADA.**

10 9 8 7 6 5 4 3 2 1

AND THERE CAME A DAY, A DAY UNLIKE ANY OTHER, WHEN EARTH'S MIGHTIEST HEROES FOUND THEMSELVES UNITED AGAINST A COMMON THREAT. ON THAT DAY, THE AVENGERS WERE BORN — TO FIGHT THE FOES NO SINGLE SUPER HERO COULD WITHSTAND!

THE AVENGERS
BACK TO BASICS

PETER DAVID
WRITER

BRIAN LEVEL (#1-2, #5-6) & **JUANAN RAMÍREZ** (#3-4)
ARTISTS

JORDAN BOYD (#1-2, #5-6) & **ERICK ARCINIEGA** (#3-4)
COLOR ARTISTS

COMICRAFT's JIMMY BETANCOURT
LETTERER

NICK ROCHE & CHRIS O'HALLORAN
COVER ARTISTS

SARAH BRUNSTAD
EDITOR

TOM BREVOORT
EXECUTIVE EDITOR

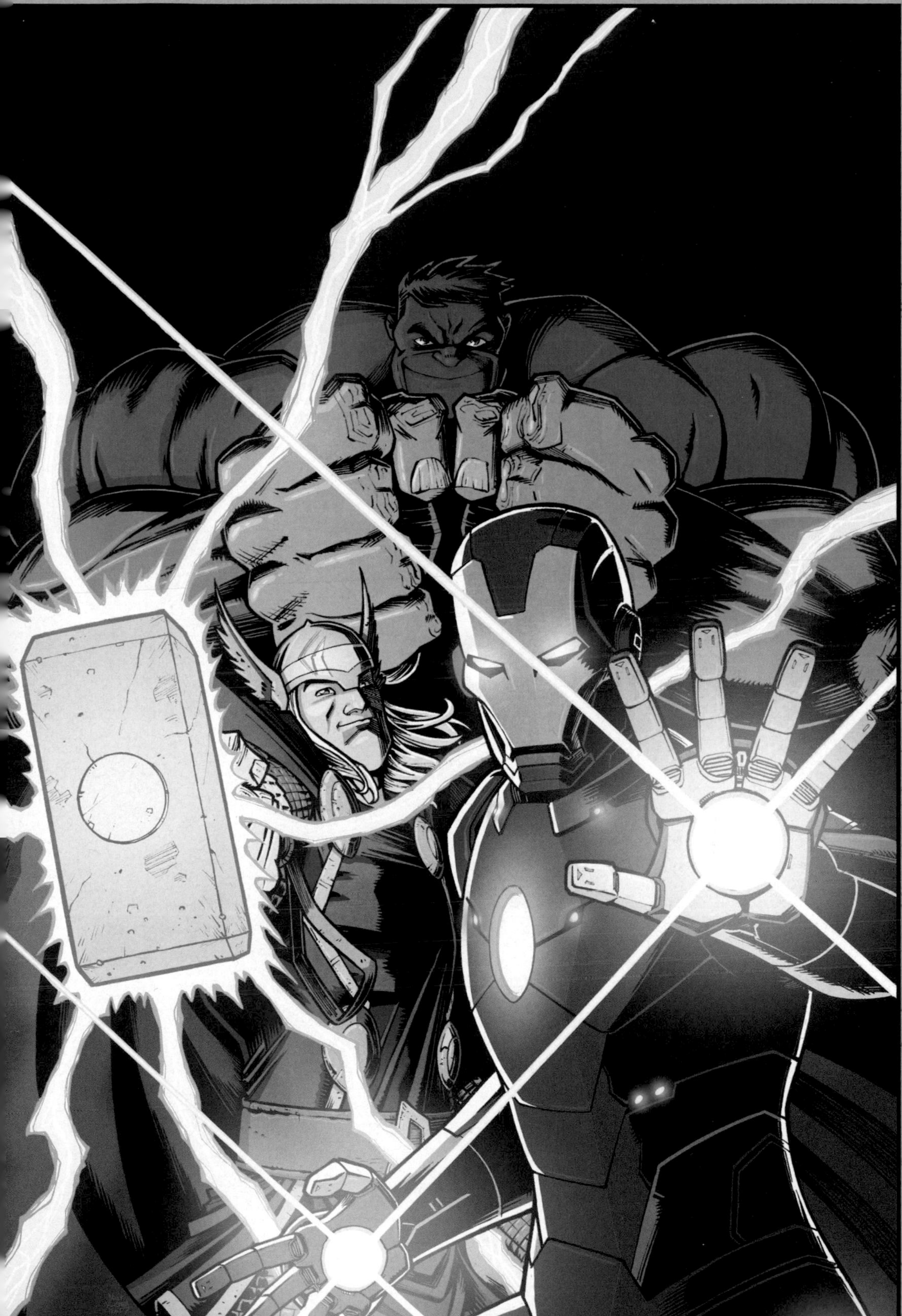

1

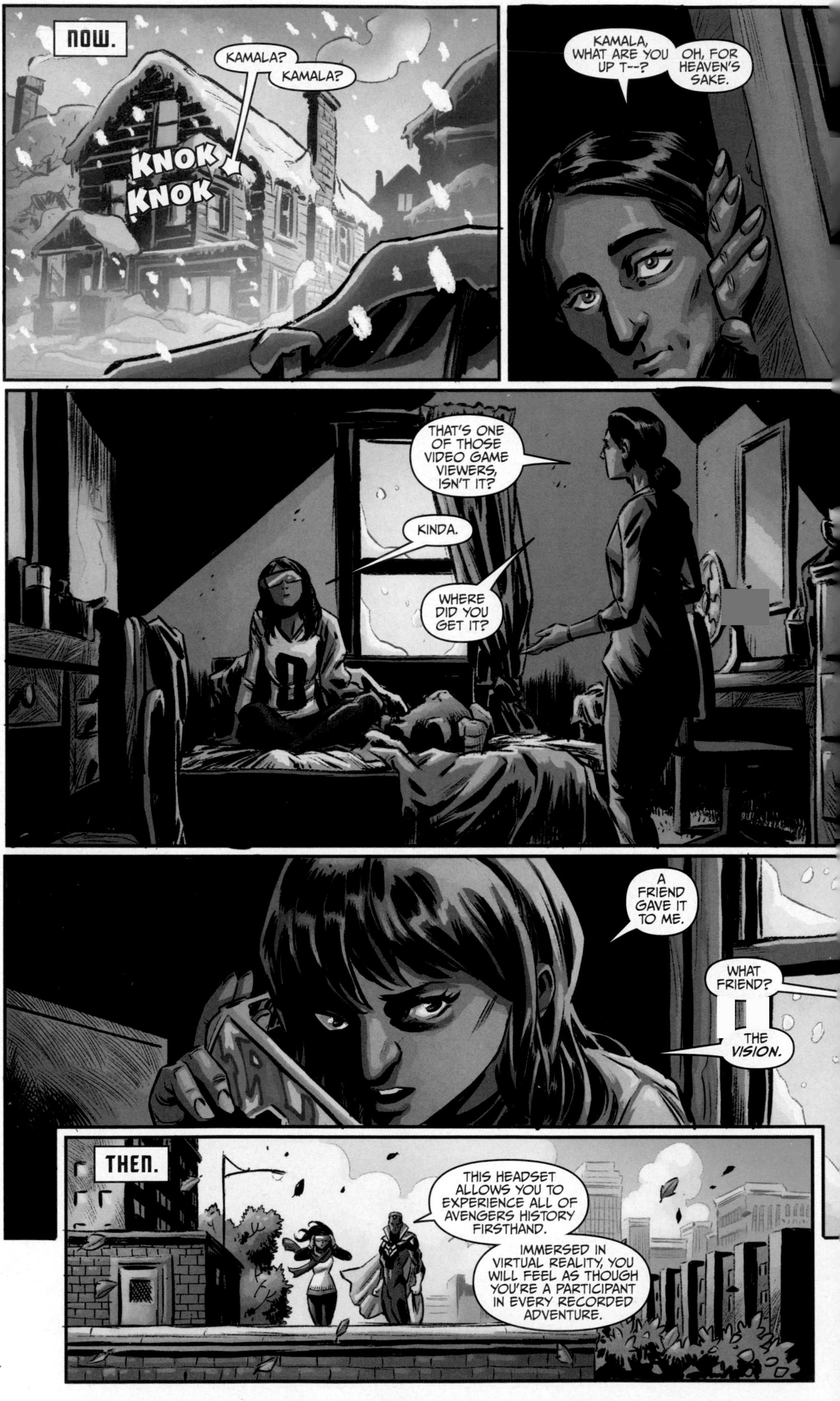
NOW.
KAMALA?
KAMALA?
KNOK KNOK
KAMALA, WHAT ARE YOU UP T--?
OH, FOR HEAVEN'S SAKE.
THAT'S ONE OF THOSE VIDEO GAME VIEWERS, ISN'T IT?
KINDA.
WHERE DID YOU GET IT?
A FRIEND GAVE IT TO ME.
WHAT FRIEND?
THE *VISION.*
THEN.
THIS HEADSET ALLOWS YOU TO EXPERIENCE ALL OF AVENGERS HISTORY FIRSTHAND.
IMMERSED IN VIRTUAL REALITY, YOU WILL FEEL AS THOUGH YOU'RE A PARTICIPANT IN EVERY RECORDED ADVENTURE.

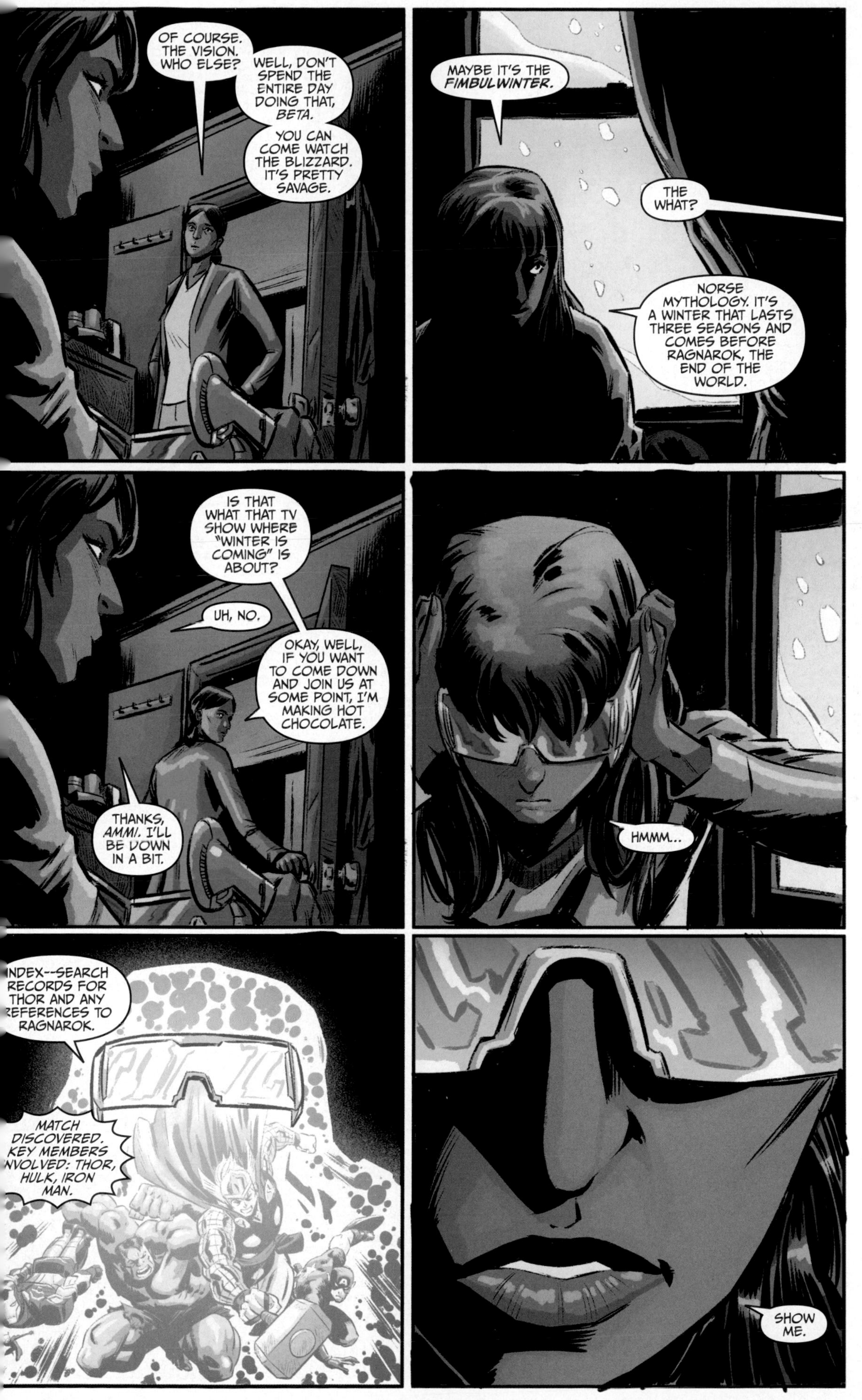

OF COURSE. THE VISION. WHO ELSE?
WELL, DON'T SPEND THE ENTIRE DAY DOING THAT, *BETA.*
YOU CAN COME WATCH THE BLIZZARD. IT'S PRETTY SAVAGE.
MAYBE IT'S THE *FIMBULWINTER.*
THE WHAT?
NORSE MYTHOLOGY. IT'S A WINTER THAT LASTS THREE SEASONS AND COMES BEFORE RAGNAROK, THE END OF THE WORLD.
IS THAT WHAT THAT TV SHOW WHERE "WINTER IS COMING" IS ABOUT?
UH, NO.
OKAY, WELL, IF YOU WANT TO COME DOWN AND JOIN US AT SOME POINT, I'M MAKING HOT CHOCOLATE.
THANKS, *AMMI.* I'LL BE DOWN IN A BIT.
HMMM...
INDEX--SEARCH RECORDS FOR THOR AND ANY REFERENCES TO RAGNAROK.
MATCH DISCOVERED. KEY MEMBERS INVOLVED: THOR, HULK, IRON MAN.
SHOW ME.

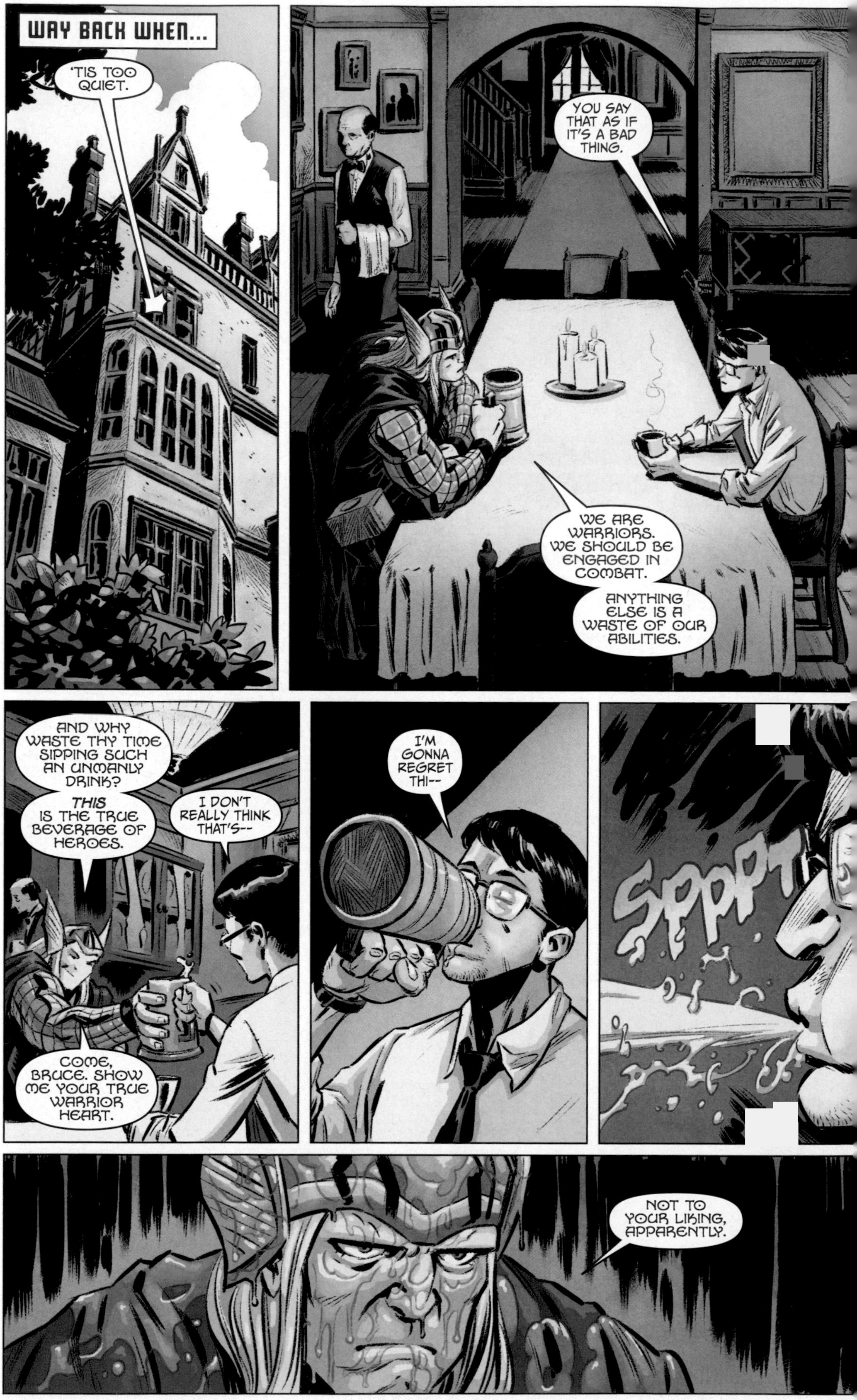
WAY BACK WHEN...
'TIS TOO QUIET.
YOU SAY THAT AS IF IT'S A BAD THING.
WE ARE WARRIORS. WE SHOULD BE ENGAGED IN COMBAT.
ANYTHING ELSE IS A WASTE OF OUR ABILITIES.
AND WHY WASTE THY TIME SIPPING SUCH AN UNMANLY DRINK?
THIS IS THE TRUE BEVERAGE OF HEROES.
I DON'T REALLY THINK THAT'S--
COME, BRUCE. SHOW ME YOUR TRUE WARRIOR HEART.
I'M GONNA REGRET THI--
SPPPT
NOT TO YOUR LIKING, APPARENTLY.

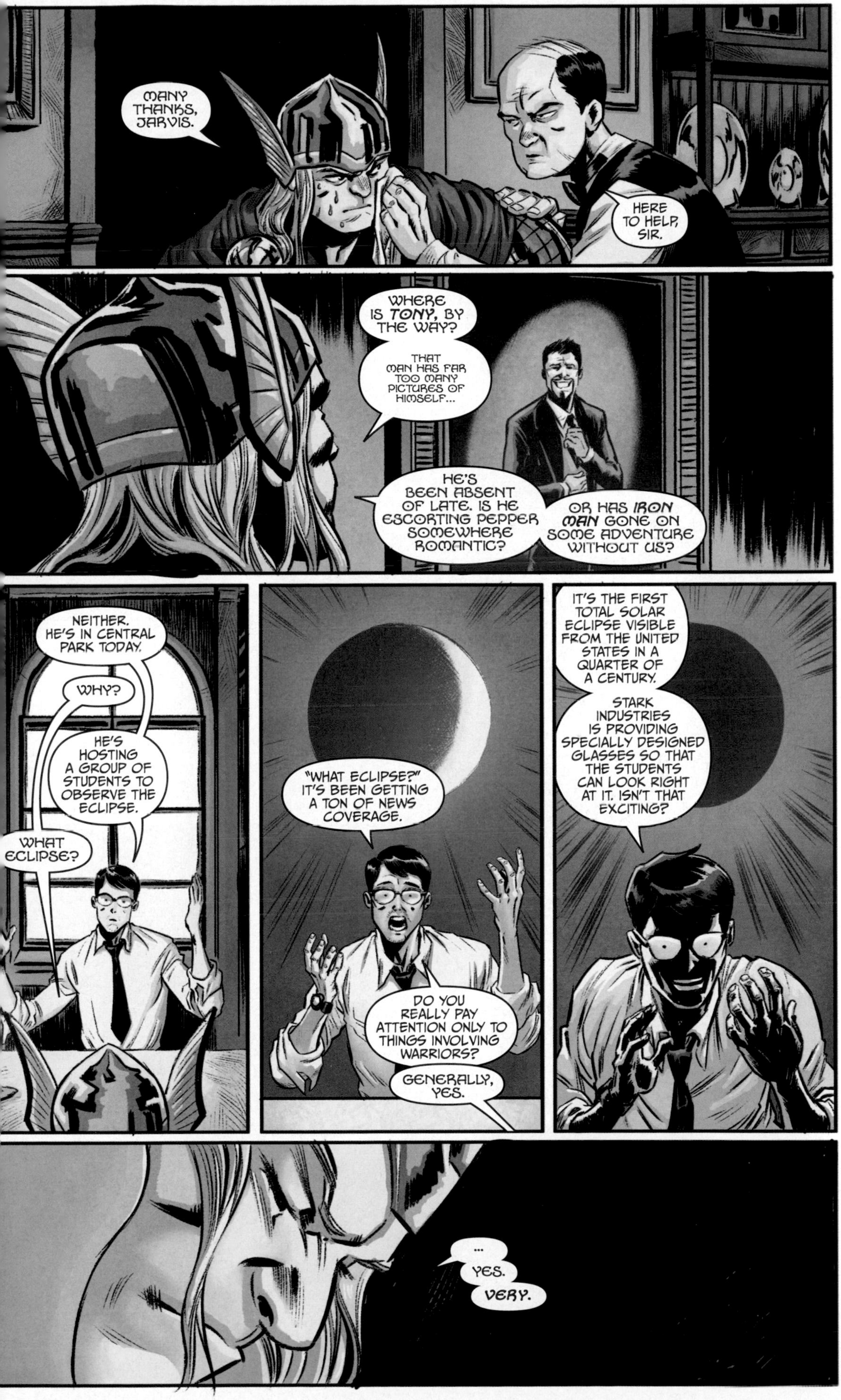
MANY THANKS, JARVIS.
HERE TO HELP, SIR.
WHERE IS TONY, BY THE WAY?
THAT MAN HAS FAR TOO MANY PICTURES OF HIMSELF...
HE'S BEEN ABSENT OF LATE. IS HE ESCORTING PEPPER SOMEWHERE ROMANTIC?
OR HAS IRON MAN GONE ON SOME ADVENTURE WITHOUT US?
NEITHER. HE'S IN CENTRAL PARK TODAY.
WHY?
HE'S HOSTING A GROUP OF STUDENTS TO OBSERVE THE ECLIPSE.
WHAT ECLIPSE?
"WHAT ECLIPSE?" IT'S BEEN GETTING A TON OF NEWS COVERAGE.
DO YOU REALLY PAY ATTENTION ONLY TO THINGS INVOLVING WARRIORS?
GENERALLY, YES.
IT'S THE FIRST TOTAL SOLAR ECLIPSE VISIBLE FROM THE UNITED STATES IN A QUARTER OF A CENTURY.
STARK INDUSTRIES IS PROVIDING SPECIALLY DESIGNED GLASSES SO THAT THE STUDENTS CAN LOOK RIGHT AT IT. ISN'T THAT EXCITING?
...
YES.
VERY.

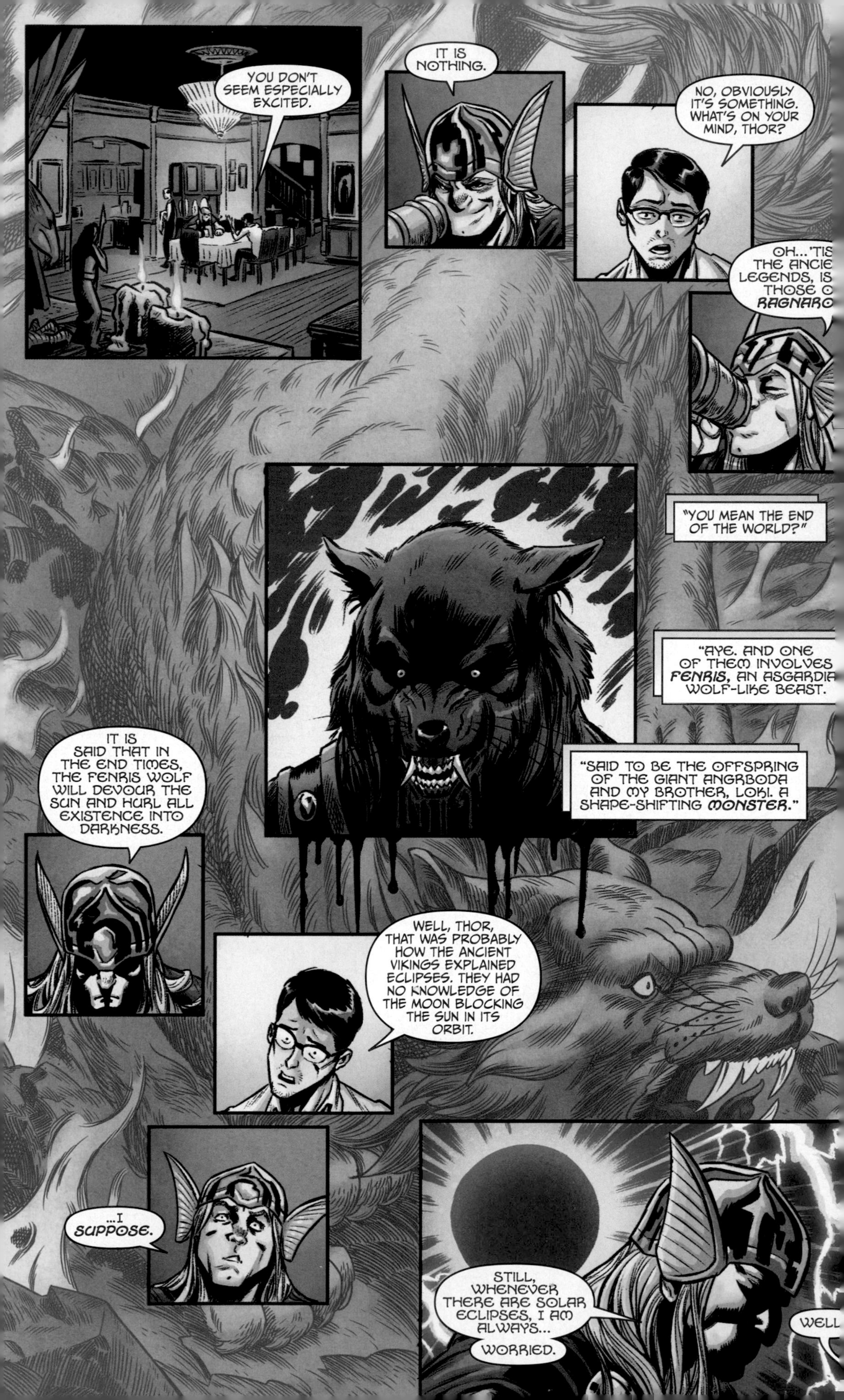
YOU DON'T SEEM ESPECIALLY EXCITED.
IT IS NOTHING.
NO, OBVIOUSLY IT'S SOMETHING. WHAT'S ON YOUR MIND, THOR?
OH... 'TIS THE ANCIE LEGENDS, IS THOSE O RAGNARO
"YOU MEAN THE END OF THE WORLD?"
"AYE. AND ONE OF THEM INVOLVES FENRIS, AN ASGARDIA WOLF-LIKE BEAST.
"SAID TO BE THE OFFSPRING OF THE GIANT ANGRBODA AND MY BROTHER, LOKI. A SHAPE-SHIFTING MONSTER."
IT IS SAID THAT IN THE END TIMES, THE FENRIS WOLF WILL DEVOUR THE SUN AND HURL ALL EXISTENCE INTO DARKNESS.
WELL, THOR, THAT WAS PROBABLY HOW THE ANCIENT VIKINGS EXPLAINED ECLIPSES. THEY HAD NO KNOWLEDGE OF THE MOON BLOCKING THE SUN IN ITS ORBIT.
...I SUPPOSE.
STILL, WHENEVER THERE ARE SOLAR ECLIPSES, I AM ALWAYS...
WORRIED.
WELL

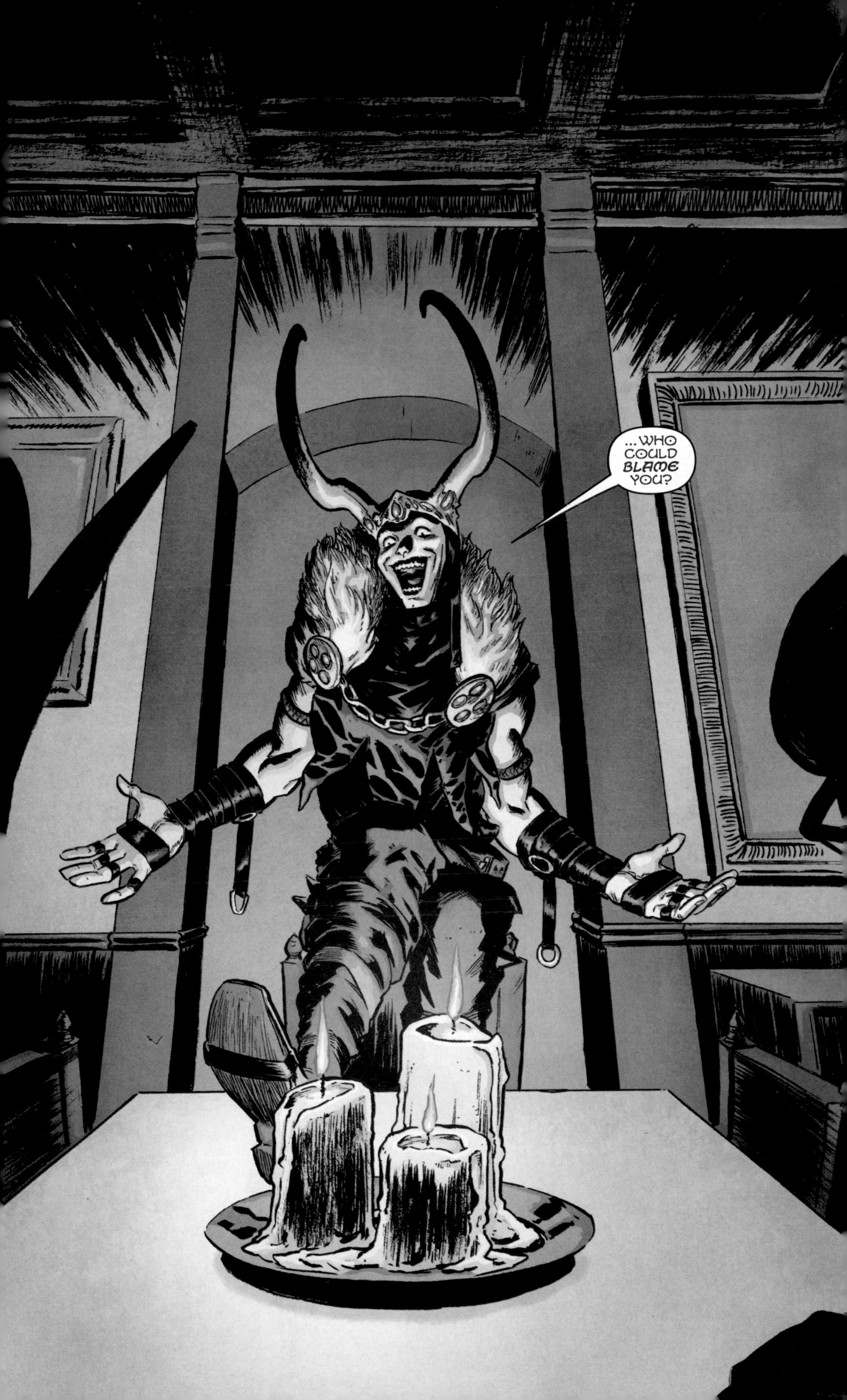
...WHO COULD BLAME YOU?

CENTRAL PARK.

CAN WE KEEP THESE, MISS POTTS?

ABSOLUTELY. KEEP THEM FOR THE NEXT ONE!

WHEN'S THAT GONNA BE?

NOT FOR A WHILE.

YOU PROMISED YOU'D BE HELPING, TONY.

I AM. I'M LENDING MY MANLY PRESENCE TO THE FESTIVITIES.

THE END IS NIGH

IS THAT SO? AND WHAT PURPOSE IS THAT SERVING, EXACTLY?

I THINK IT'S PRETTY MUCH SELF-EXPLANATORY.

KATIE? KATIE!!!

PROBLEM HERE?

THE END IS NIGH

OH! MR. STARK. I'M SURE IT'S NOTHING.

SURE WHAT'S NOTHING?

MY T.A., KATIE MILLER. SHE SEEMS TO HAVE WANDERED OFF.

SHE SAID SHE SPOTTED TORCHES IN THE WOODS AND WENT TO INVESTIGATE.

THE END IS NIGH

TORCHES?! HOW ABOUT I CHECK IT OUT?

OH, WOULD YOU? THAT'D BE SO KIND.

SHE WENT RIGHT OVER THERE.

AS YOU SAID, I'M SURE IT'S NOTHING.

OH, YES. NOTHING AT ALL.

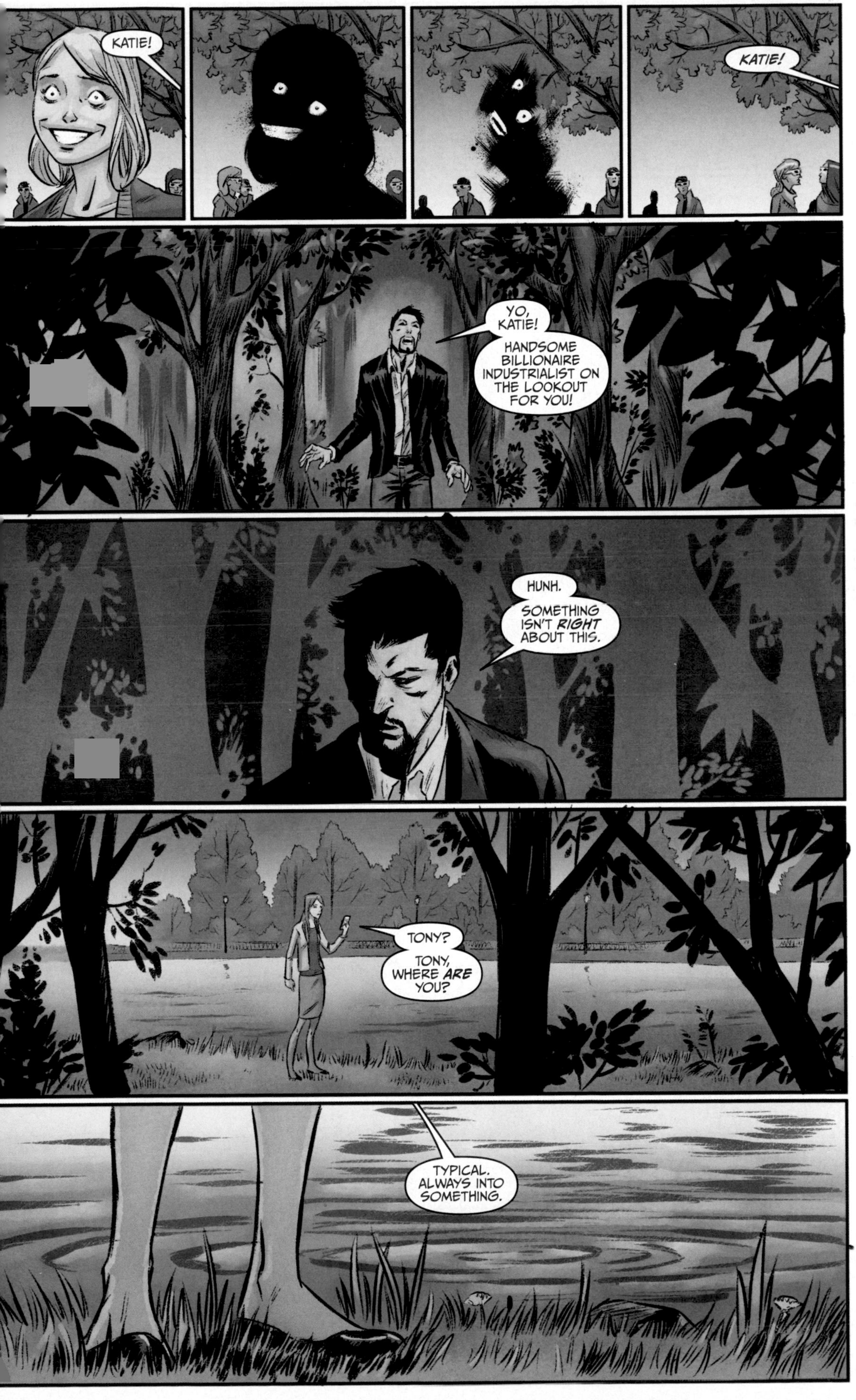
KATIE!
KATIE!
YO, KATIE!
HANDSOME BILLIONAIRE INDUSTRIALIST ON THE LOOKOUT FOR YOU!
HUNH.
SOMETHING ISN'T *RIGHT* ABOUT THIS.
TONY?
TONY, WHERE *ARE* YOU?
TYPICAL. ALWAYS INTO SOMETHING.

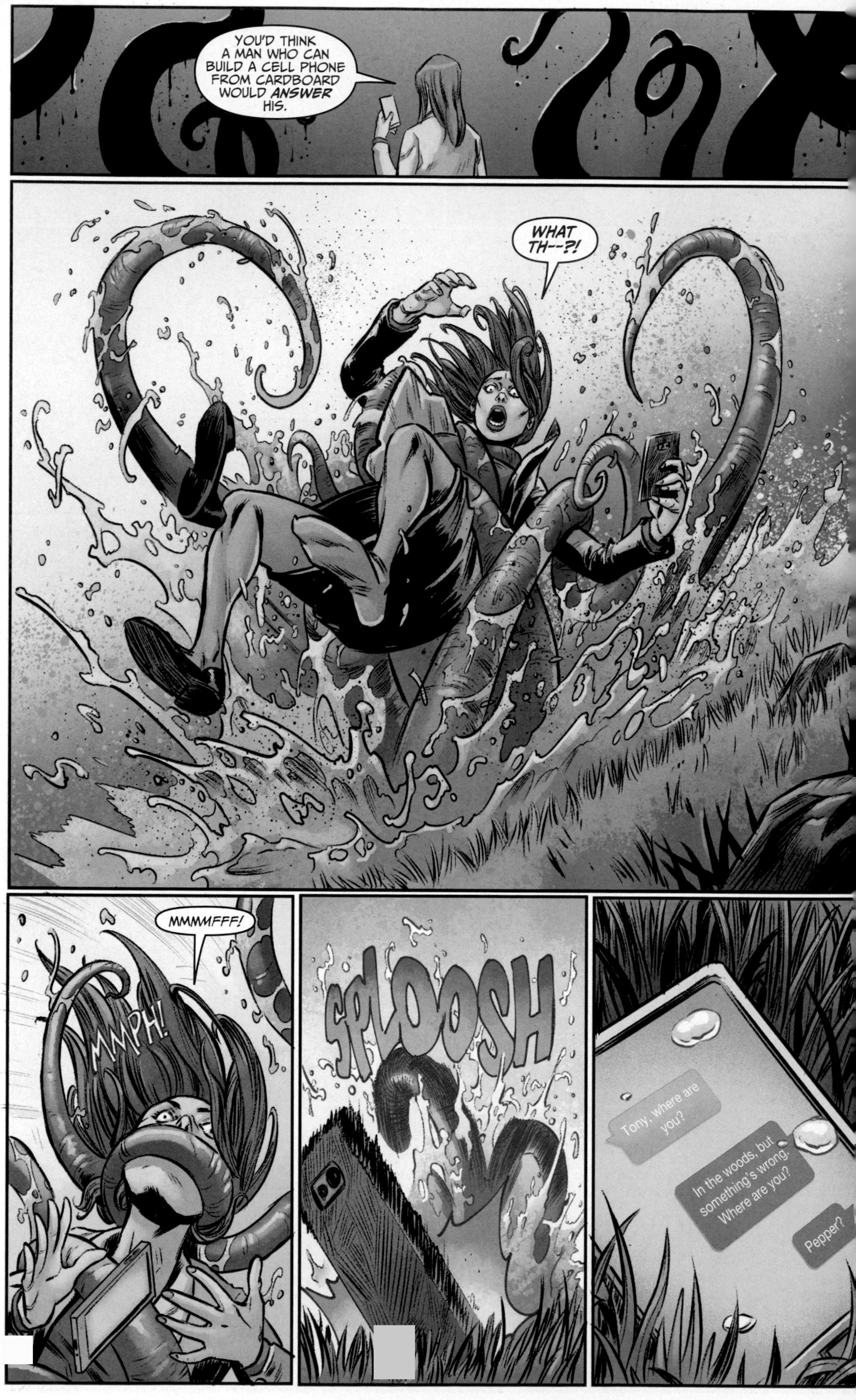
YOU'D THINK A MAN WHO CAN BUILD A CELL PHONE FROM CARDBOARD WOULD ANSWER HIS.
WHAT TH--?!
MMMMFFF!
MMPH!
SPLOOSH
Tony, where are you?
In the woods, but something's wrong. Where are you?
Pepper?

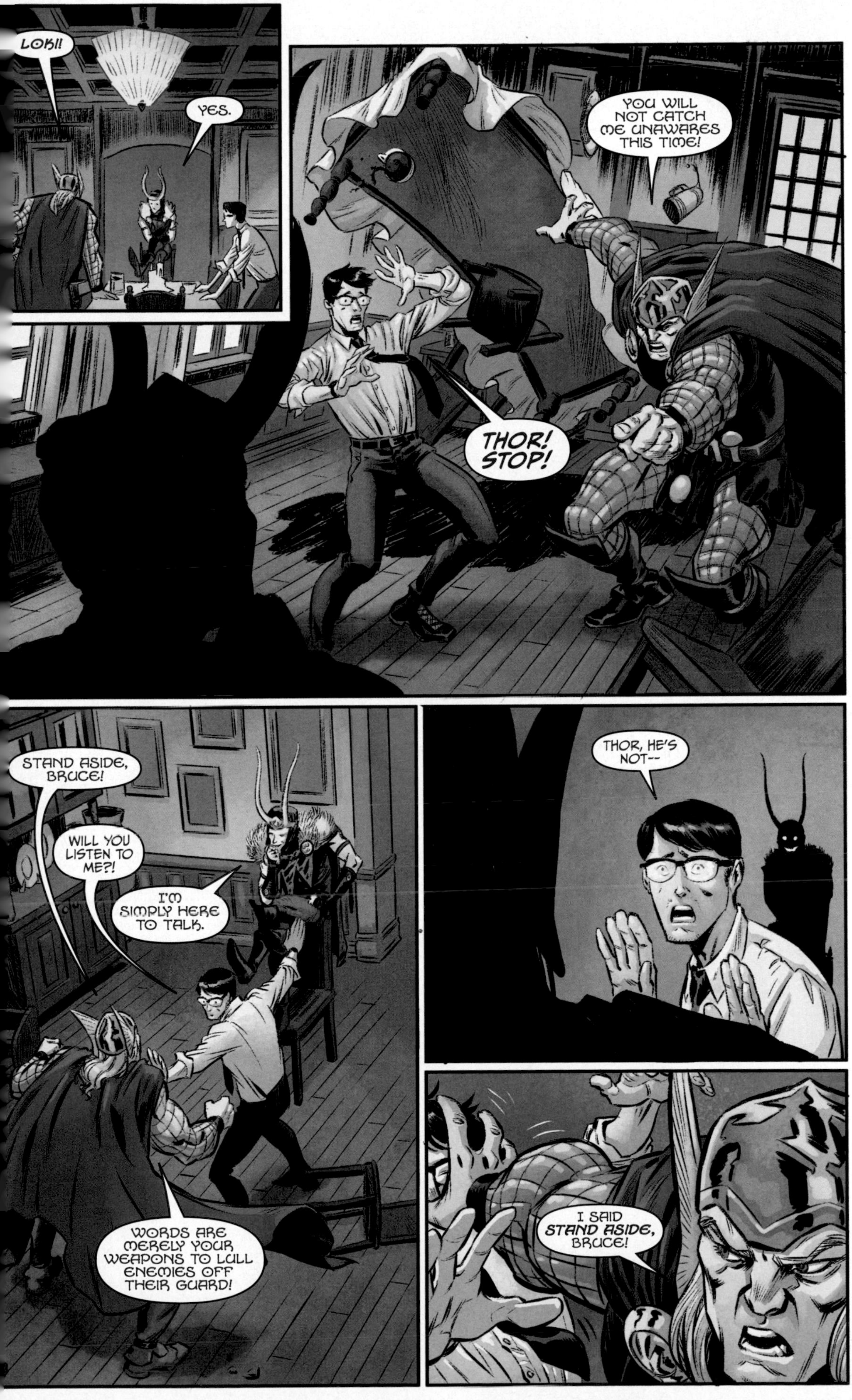
LOKI!
YES.
YOU WILL NOT CATCH ME UNAWARES THIS TIME!
THOR! STOP!
STAND ASIDE, BRUCE!
WILL YOU LISTEN TO ME?!
I'M SIMPLY HERE TO TALK.
WORDS ARE MERELY YOUR WEAPONS TO LULL ENEMIES OFF THEIR GUARD!
THOR, HE'S NOT--
I SAID STAND ASIDE, BRUCE!

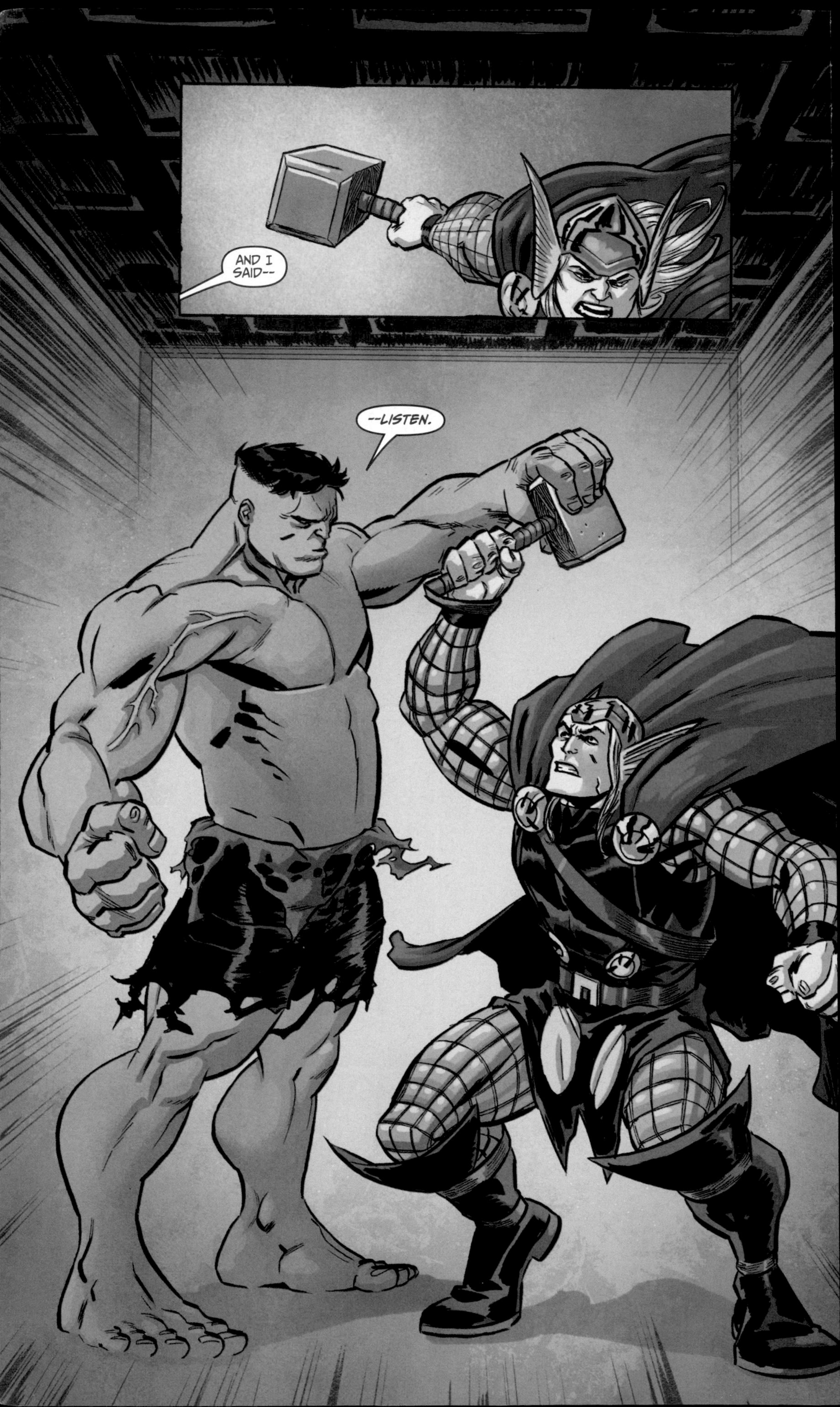
AND I SAID--
--LISTEN.

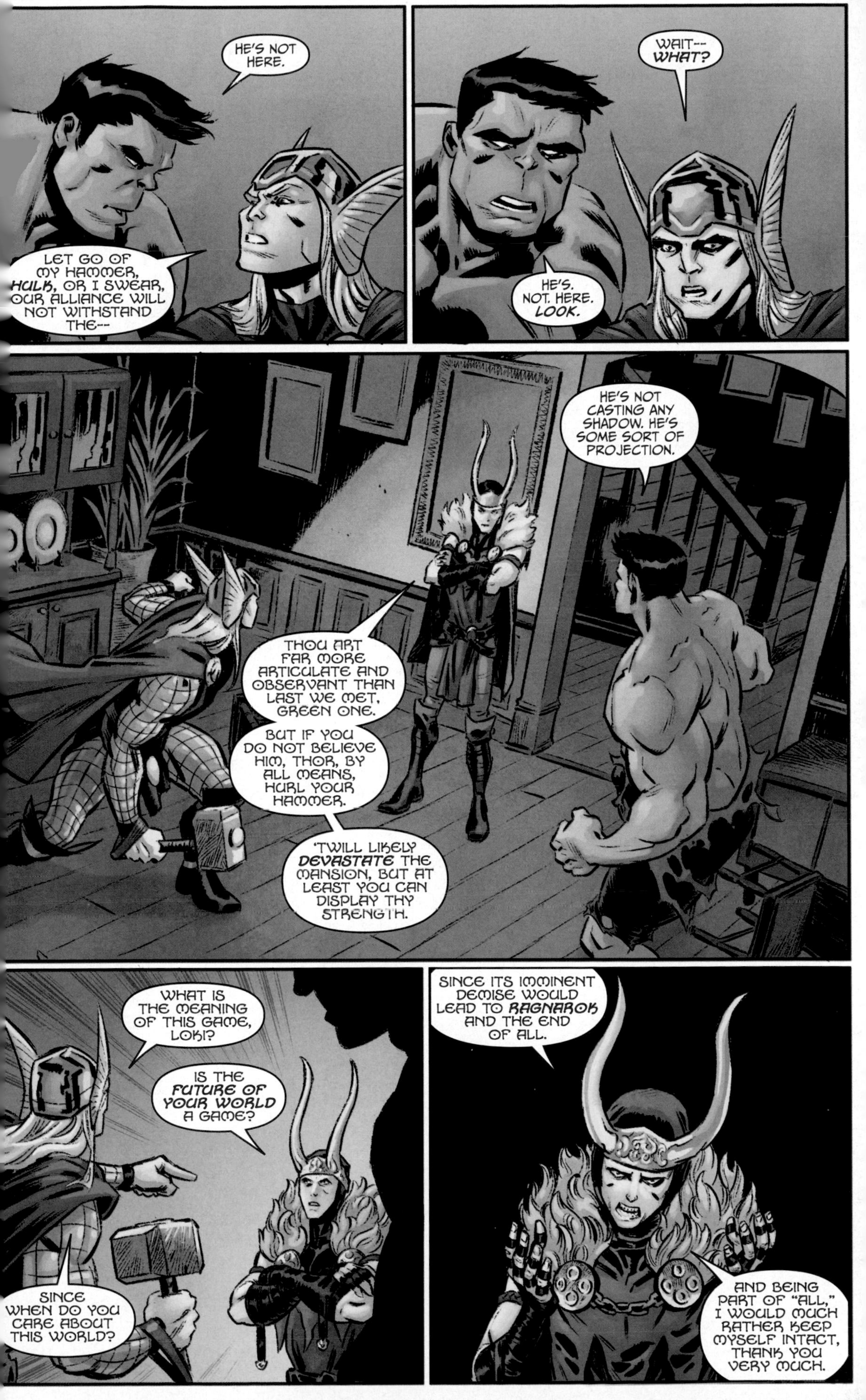
HE'S NOT HERE.
LET GO OF MY HAMMER, HULK, OR I SWEAR, OUR ALLIANCE WILL NOT WITHSTAND THE--
WAIT-- WHAT?
HE'S. NOT. HERE. LOOK.
HE'S NOT CASTING ANY SHADOW. HE'S SOME SORT OF PROJECTION.
THOU ART FAR MORE ARTICULATE AND OBSERVANT THAN LAST WE MET, GREEN ONE.
BUT IF YOU DO NOT BELIEVE HIM, THOR, BY ALL MEANS, HURL YOUR HAMMER.
'TWILL LIKELY DEVASTATE THE MANSION, BUT AT LEAST YOU CAN DISPLAY THY STRENGTH.
WHAT IS THE MEANING OF THIS GAME, LOKI?
IS THE FUTURE OF YOUR WORLD A GAME?
SINCE WHEN DO YOU CARE ABOUT THIS WORLD?
SINCE ITS IMMINENT DEMISE WOULD LEAD TO RAGNAROK AND THE END OF ALL.
AND BEING PART OF "ALL," I WOULD MUCH RATHER KEEP MYSELF INTACT, THANK YOU VERY MUCH.

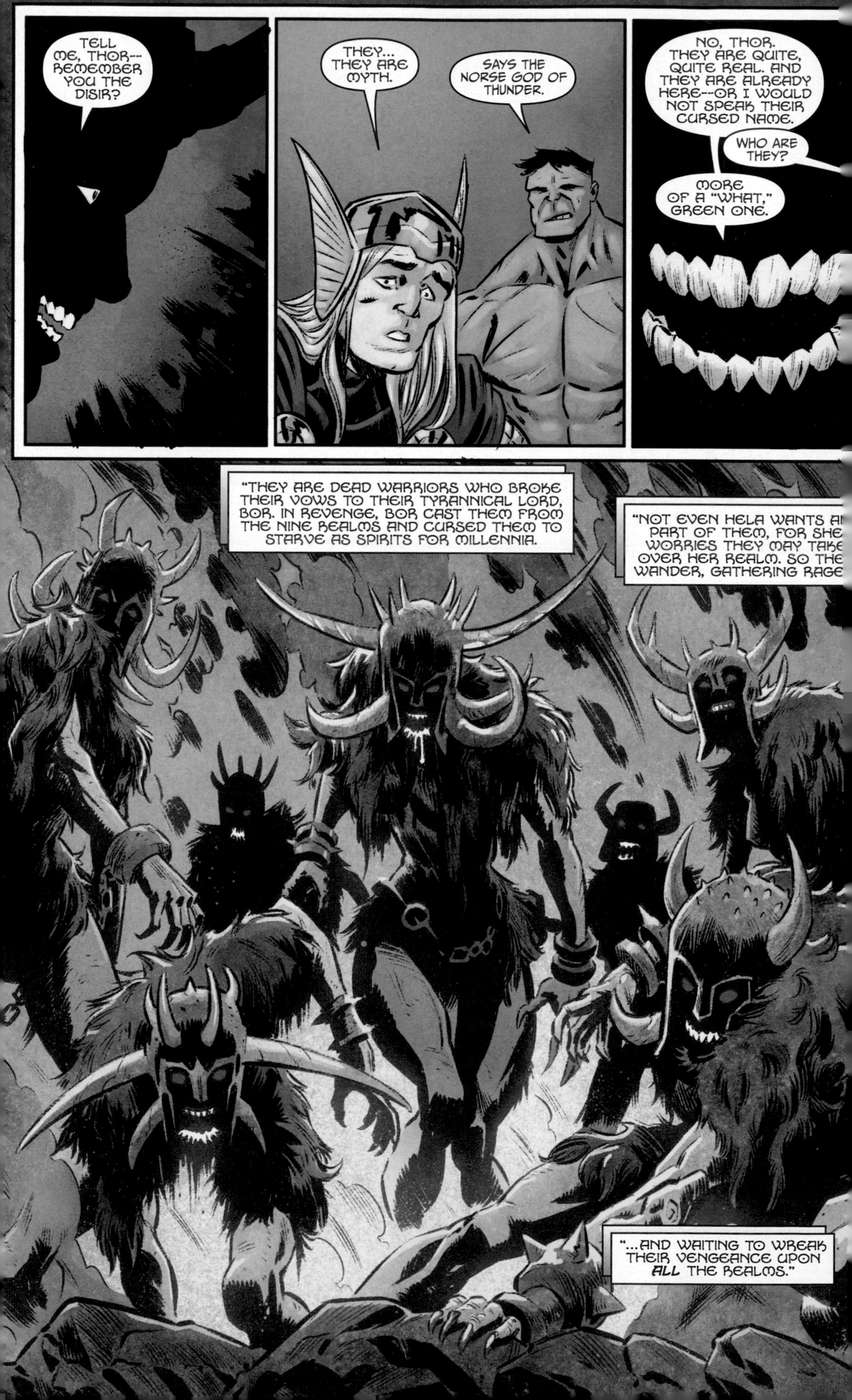

TELL ME, THOR-- REMEMBER YOU THE DISIR?
THEY... THEY ARE MYTH.
SAYS THE NORSE GOD OF THUNDER.
NO, THOR. THEY ARE QUITE, QUITE REAL. AND THEY ARE ALREADY HERE--OR I WOULD NOT SPEAK THEIR CURSED NAME.
WHO ARE THEY?
MORE OF A "WHAT," GREEN ONE.
"THEY ARE DEAD WARRIORS WHO BROKE THEIR VOWS TO THEIR TYRANNICAL LORD, BOR. IN REVENGE, BOR CAST THEM FROM THE NINE REALMS AND CURSED THEM TO STARVE AS SPIRITS FOR MILLENNIA.
"NOT EVEN HELA WANTS AN PART OF THEM, FOR SHE WORRIES THEY MAY TAKE OVER HER REALM. SO THE WANDER, GATHERING RAGE
"...AND WAITING TO WREAK THEIR VENGEANCE UPON ALL THE REALMS."

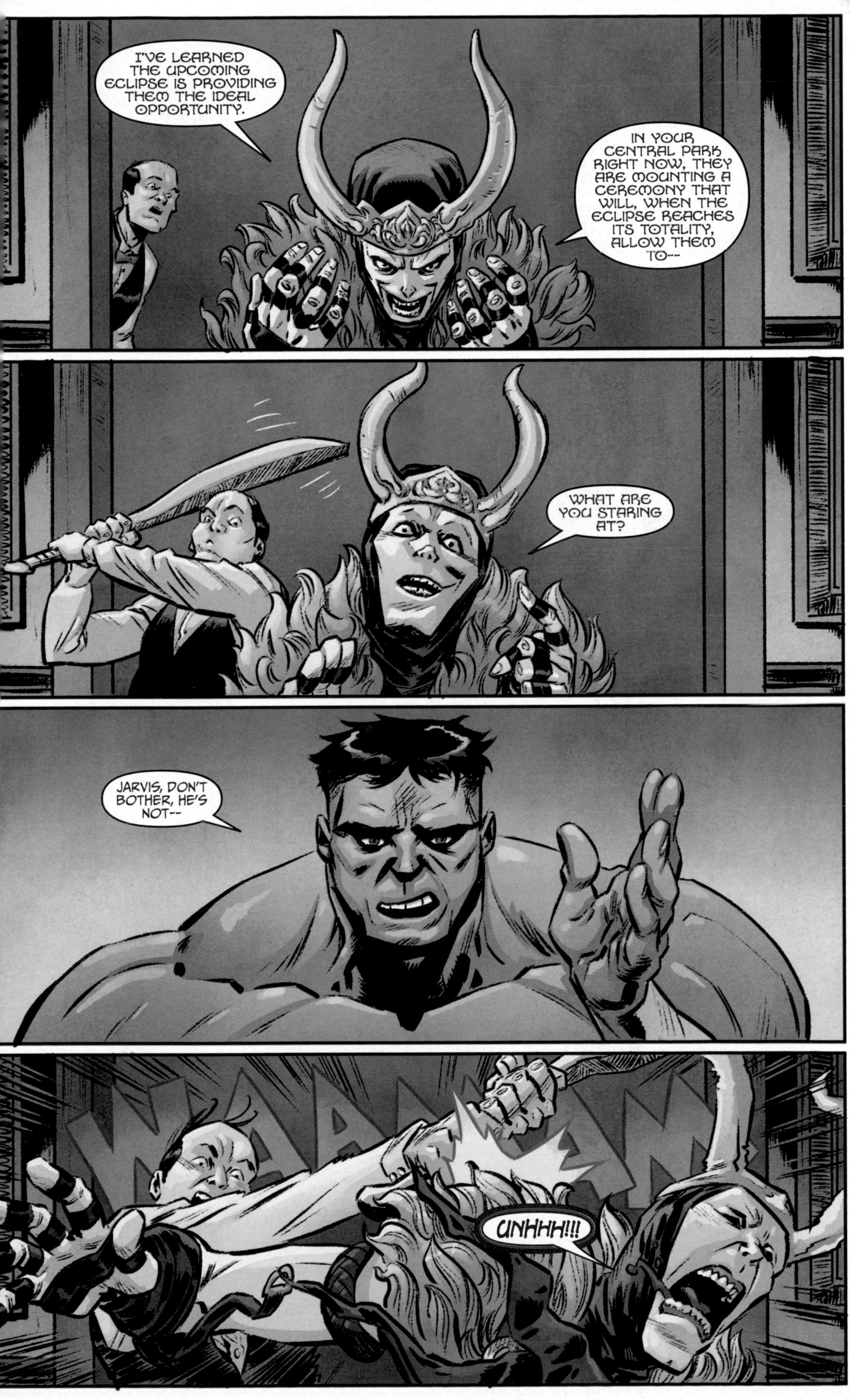

I'VE LEARNED THE UPCOMING ECLIPSE IS PROVIDING THEM THE IDEAL OPPORTUNITY.
IN YOUR CENTRAL PARK RIGHT NOW, THEY ARE MOUNTING A CEREMONY THAT WILL, WHEN THE ECLIPSE REACHES ITS TOTALITY, ALLOW THEM TO--
WHAT ARE YOU STARING AT?
JARVIS, DON'T BOTHER, HE'S NOT--
UNHHH!!!

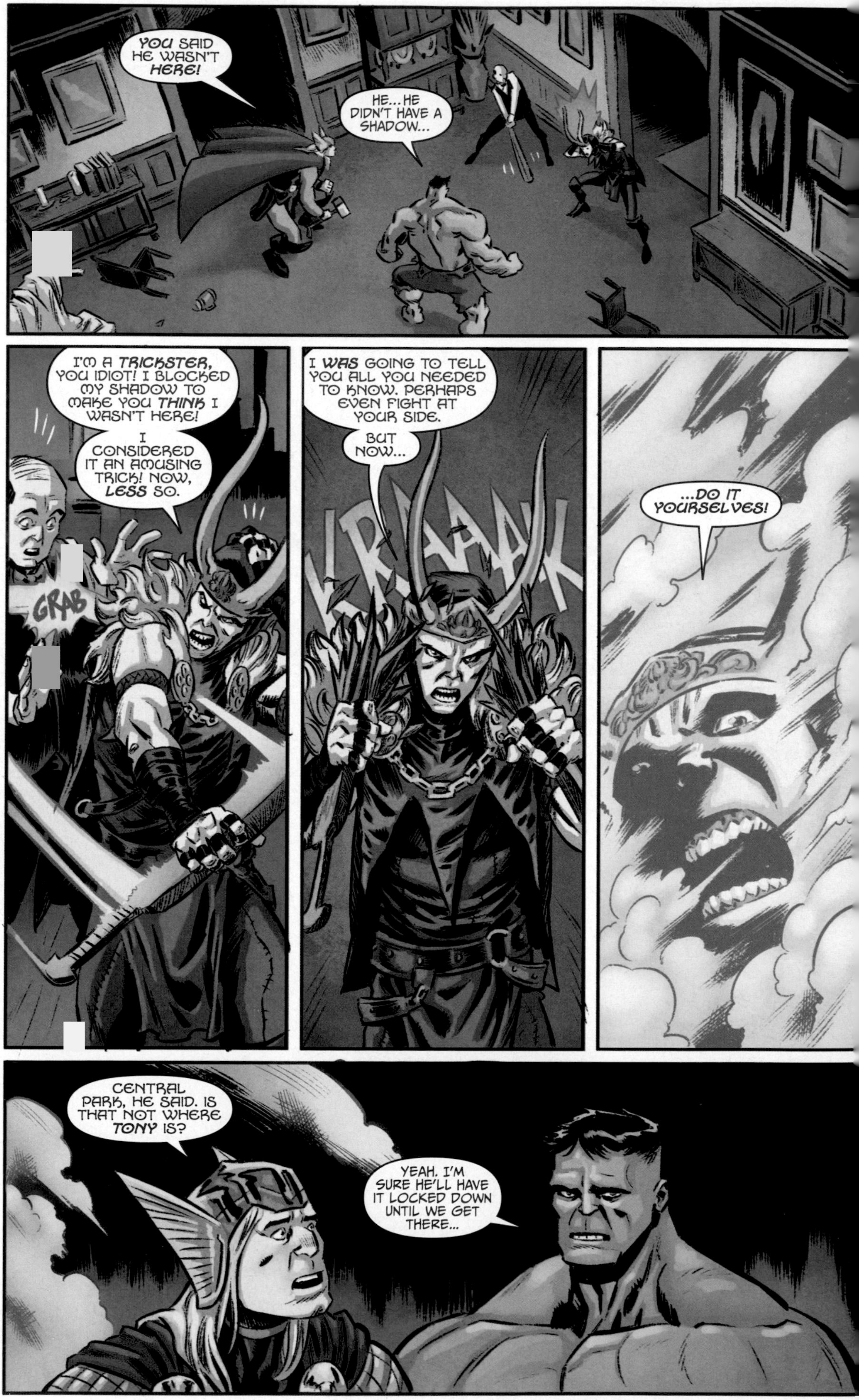
YOU SAID HE WASN'T HERE!
HE...HE DIDN'T HAVE A SHADOW...
I'M A TRICKSTER, YOU IDIOT! I BLOCKED MY SHADOW TO MAKE YOU THINK I WASN'T HERE!
I CONSIDERED IT AN AMUSING TRICK! NOW, LESS SO.
GRAB
I WAS GOING TO TELL YOU ALL YOU NEEDED TO KNOW. PERHAPS EVEN FIGHT AT YOUR SIDE.
BUT NOW...
...DO IT YOURSELVES!
CENTRAL PARK, HE SAID. IS THAT NOT WHERE TONY IS?
YEAH. I'M SURE HE'LL HAVE IT LOCKED DOWN UNTIL WE GET THERE...

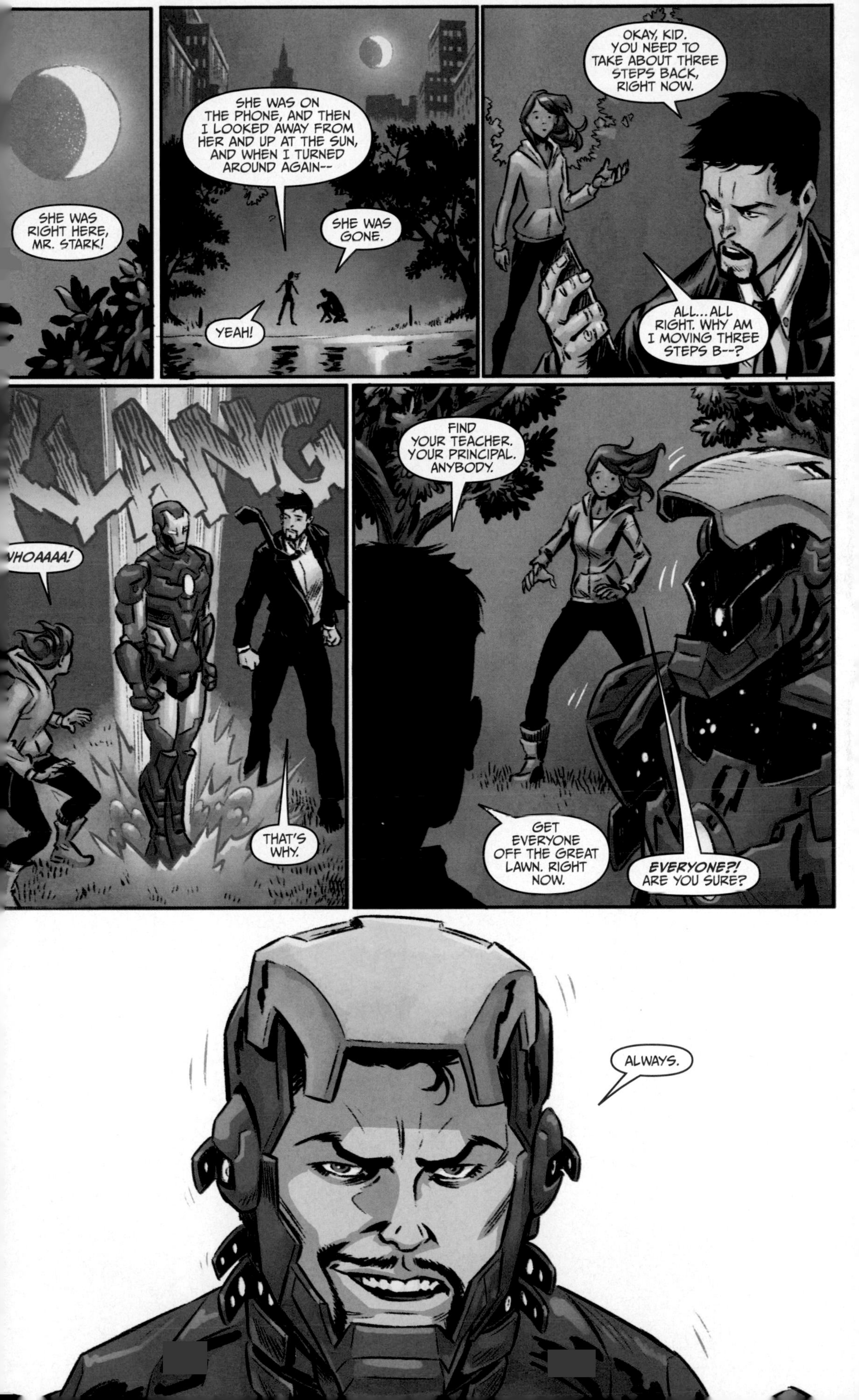

SHE WAS RIGHT HERE, MR. STARK!
SHE WAS ON THE PHONE, AND THEN I LOOKED AWAY FROM HER AND UP AT THE SUN, AND WHEN I TURNED AROUND AGAIN--
SHE WAS GONE.
YEAH!
OKAY, KID. YOU NEED TO TAKE ABOUT THREE STEPS BACK, RIGHT NOW.
ALL...ALL RIGHT. WHY AM I MOVING THREE STEPS B--?
WHOAAAA!
THAT'S WHY.
FIND YOUR TEACHER. YOUR PRINCIPAL. ANYBODY.
GET EVERYONE OFF THE GREAT LAWN. RIGHT NOW.
EVERYONE?! ARE YOU SURE?
ALWAYS.

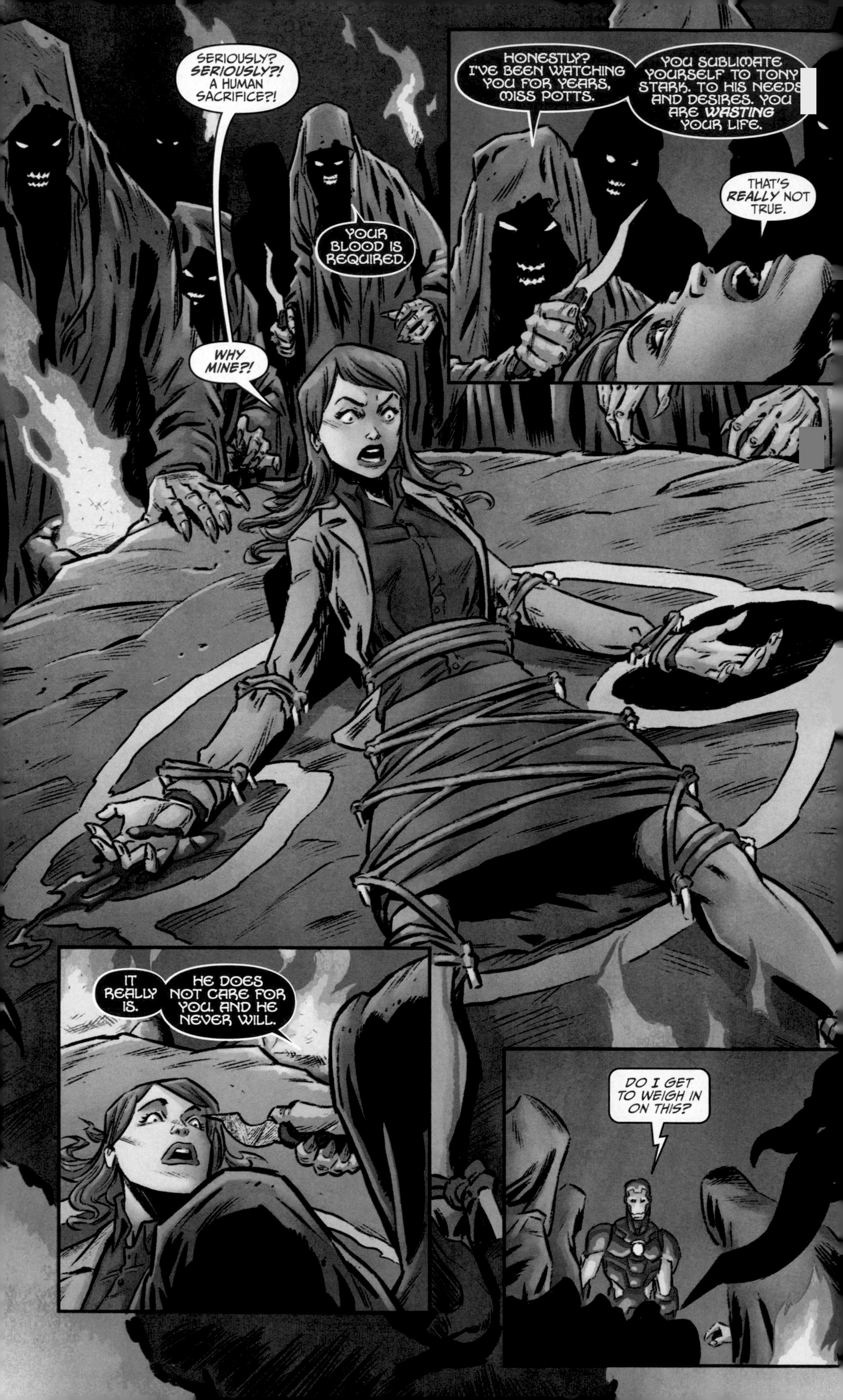
SERIOUSLY? SERIOUSLY?! A HUMAN SACRIFICE?!
YOUR BLOOD IS REQUIRED.
WHY MINE?!
HONESTLY? I'VE BEEN WATCHING YOU FOR YEARS, MISS POTTS.
YOU SUBLIMATE YOURSELF TO TONY STARK. TO HIS NEEDS AND DESIRES. YOU ARE WASTING YOUR LIFE.
THAT'S REALLY NOT TRUE.
IT REALLY IS.
HE DOES NOT CARE FOR YOU. AND HE NEVER WILL.
DO I GET TO WEIGH IN ON THIS?

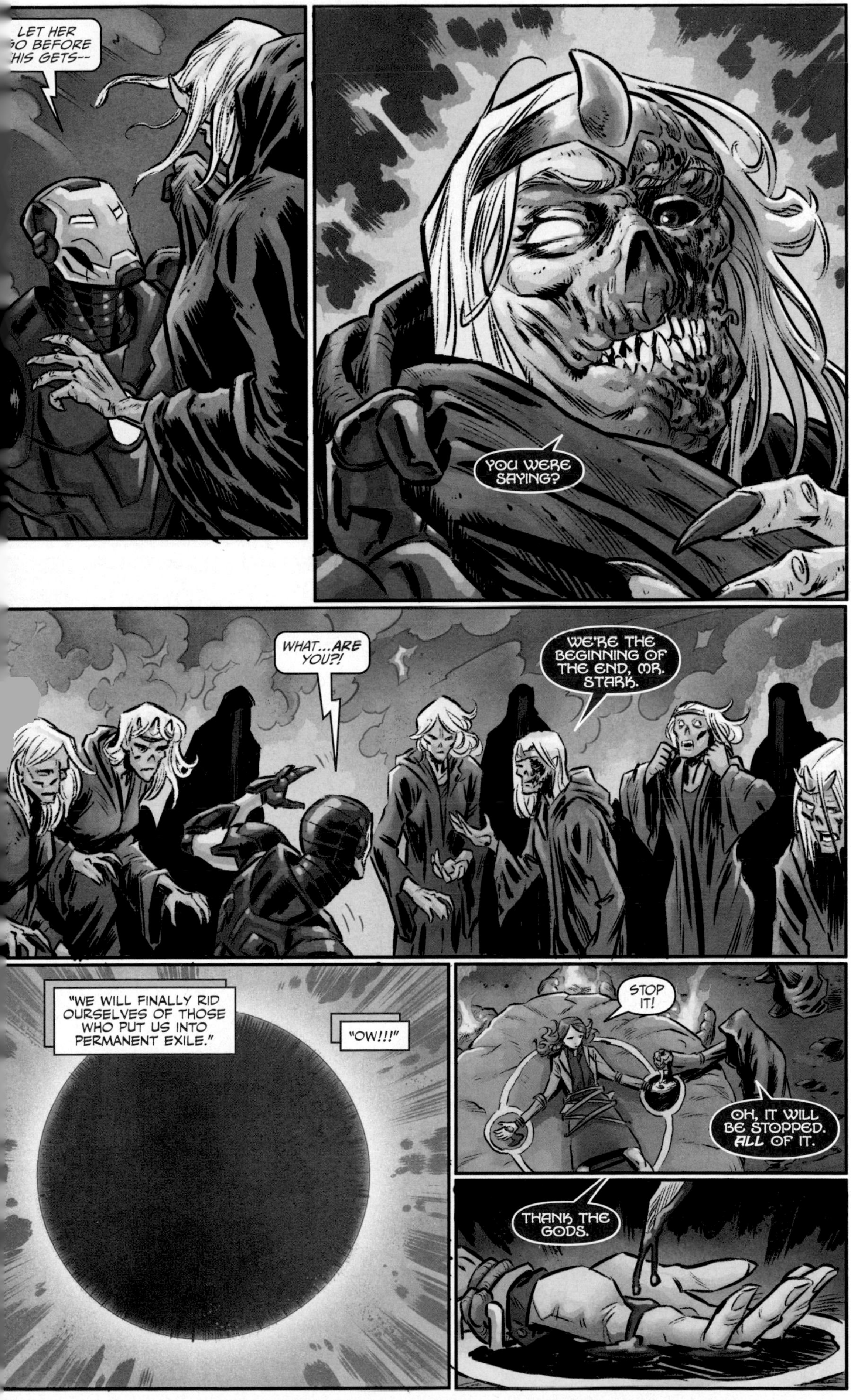
LET HER GO BEFORE THIS GETS--
YOU WERE SAYING?
WHAT...ARE YOU?!
WE'RE THE BEGINNING OF THE END, MR. STARK.
"WE WILL FINALLY RID OURSELVES OF THOSE WHO PUT US INTO PERMANENT EXILE."
"OW!!!"
STOP IT!
OH, IT WILL BE STOPPED. ALL OF IT.
THANK THE GODS.

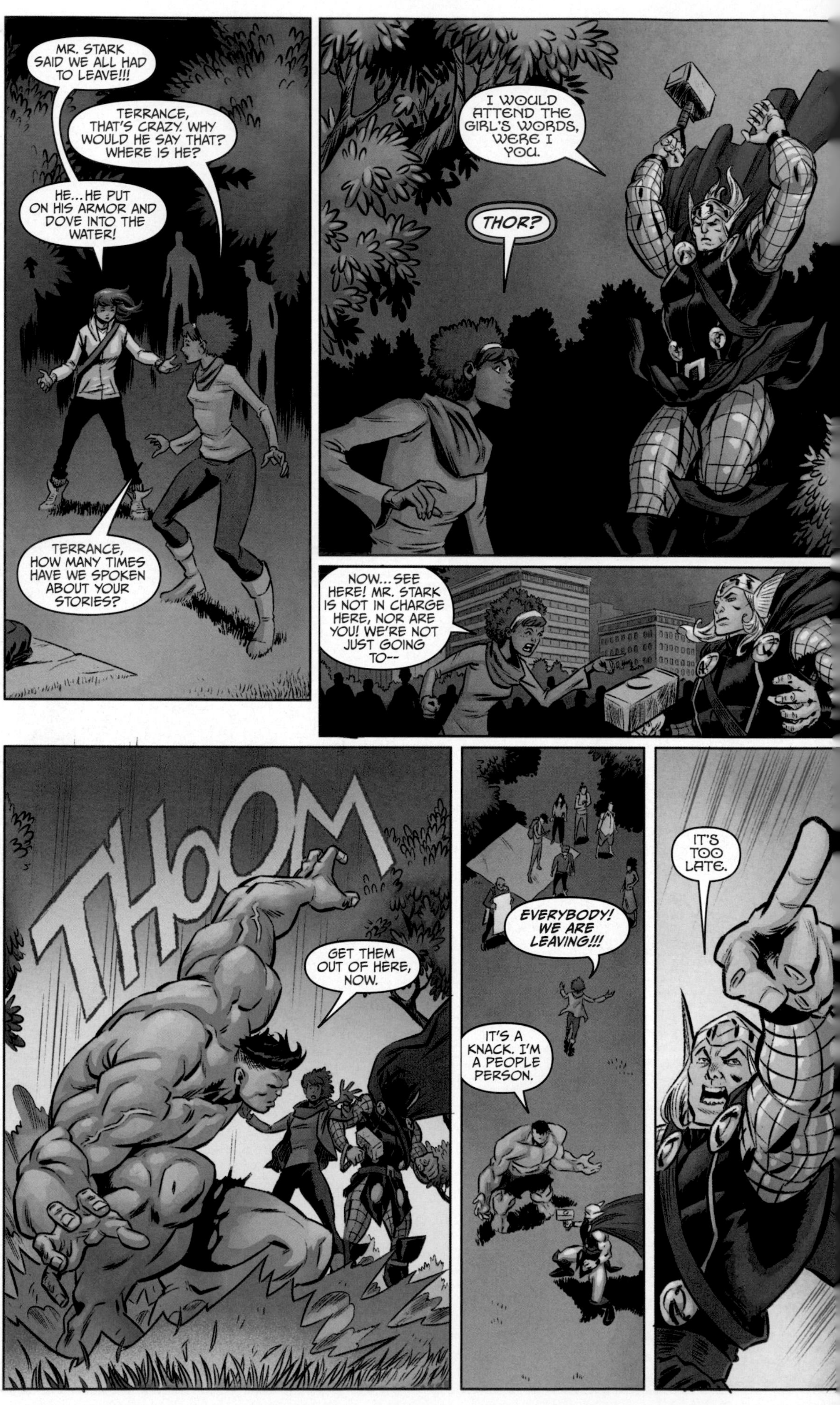

MR. STARK SAID WE ALL HAD TO LEAVE!!!
TERRANCE, THAT'S CRAZY. WHY WOULD HE SAY THAT? WHERE IS HE?
HE...HE PUT ON HIS ARMOR AND DOVE INTO THE WATER!
TERRANCE, HOW MANY TIMES HAVE WE SPOKEN ABOUT YOUR STORIES?
I WOULD ATTEND THE GIRL'S WORDS, WERE I YOU.
THOR?
NOW...SEE HERE! MR. STARK IS NOT IN CHARGE HERE, NOR ARE YOU! WE'RE NOT JUST GOING TO--
THOOM
GET THEM OUT OF HERE, NOW.
EVERYBODY! WE ARE LEAVING!!!
IT'S A KNACK. I'M A PEOPLE PERSON.
IT'S TOO LATE.

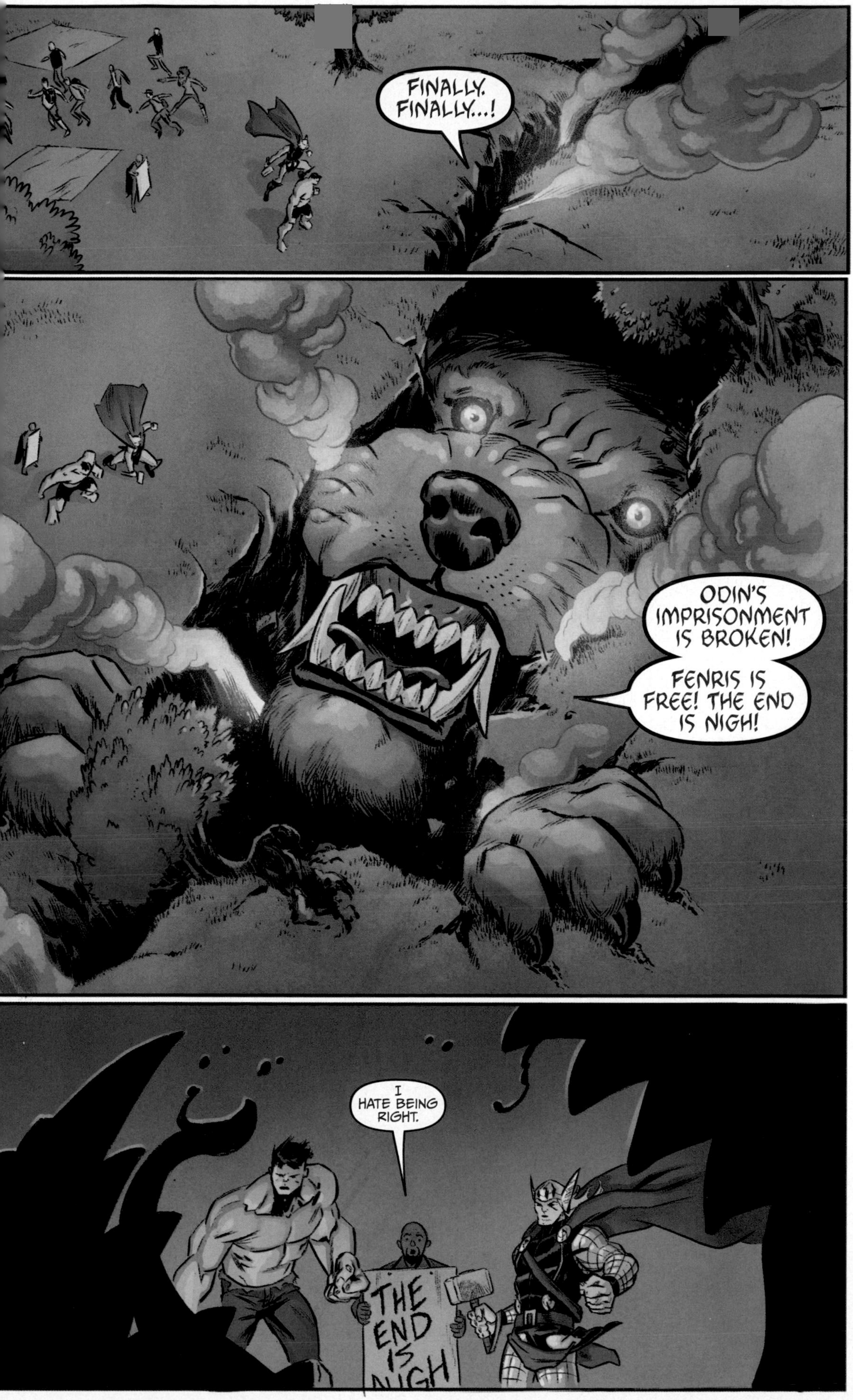
FINALLY. FINALLY...!
ODIN'S IMPRISONMENT IS BROKEN!
FENRIS IS FREE! THE END IS NIGH!
I HATE BEING RIGHT.
THE END IS NIGH

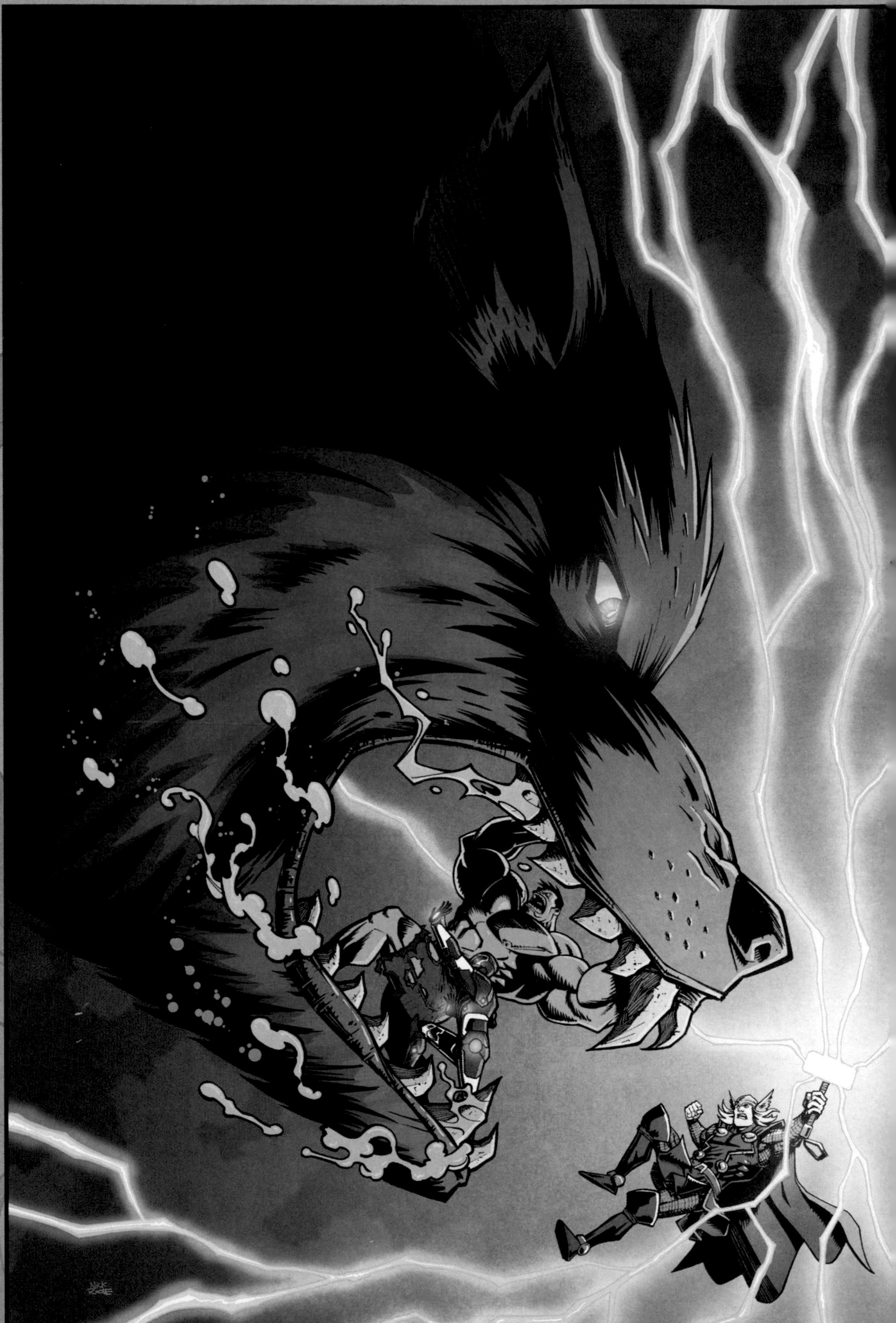

2

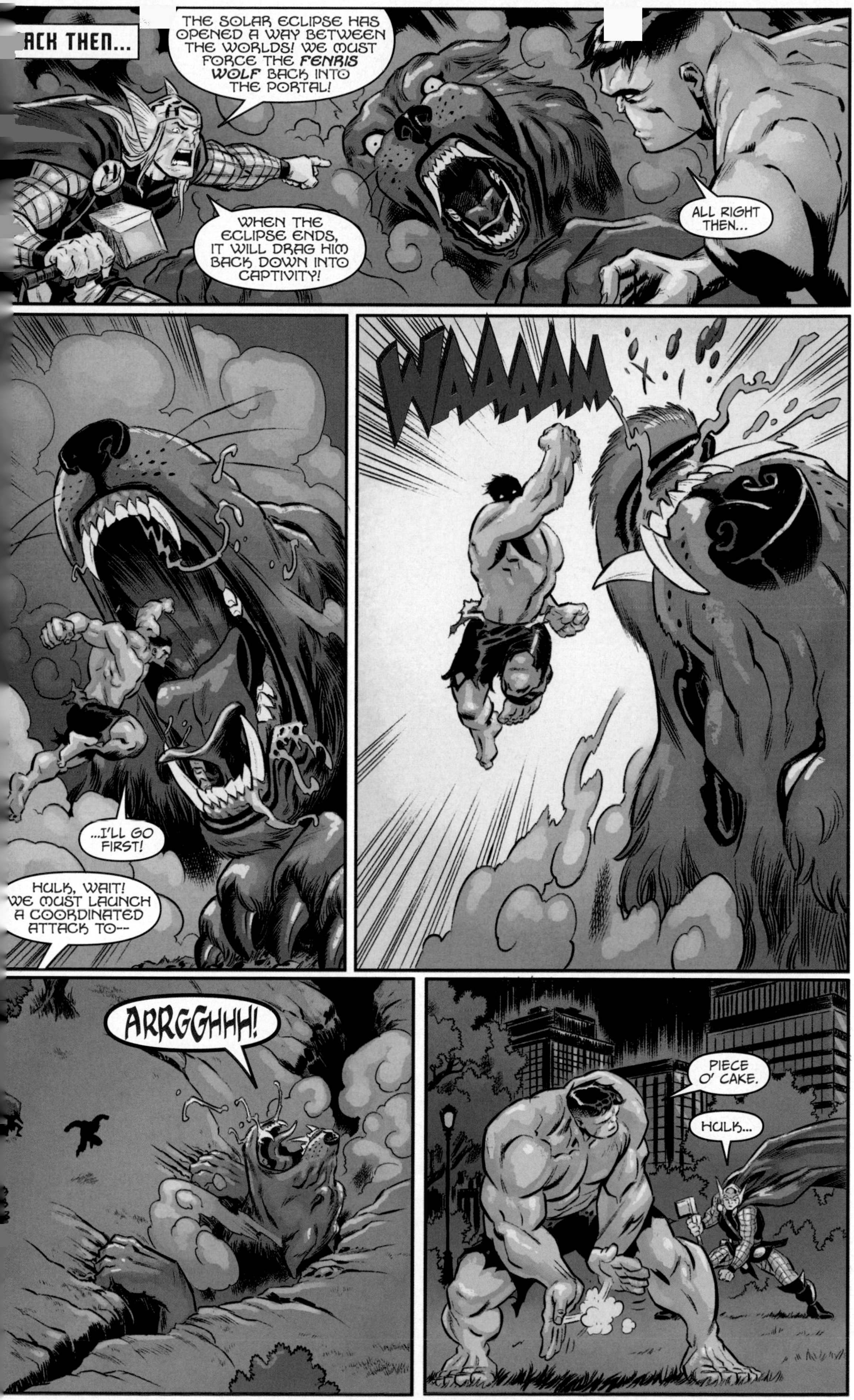

…ACK THEN...
THE SOLAR ECLIPSE HAS OPENED A WAY BETWEEN THE WORLDS! WE MUST FORCE THE FENRIS WOLF BACK INTO THE PORTAL!
WHEN THE ECLIPSE ENDS, IT WILL DRAG HIM BACK DOWN INTO CAPTIVITY!
ALL RIGHT THEN...
...I'LL GO FIRST!
HULK, WAIT! WE MUST LAUNCH A COORDINATED ATTACK TO--
WAAAAM
ARRGGHHH!
PIECE O' CAKE.
HULK...

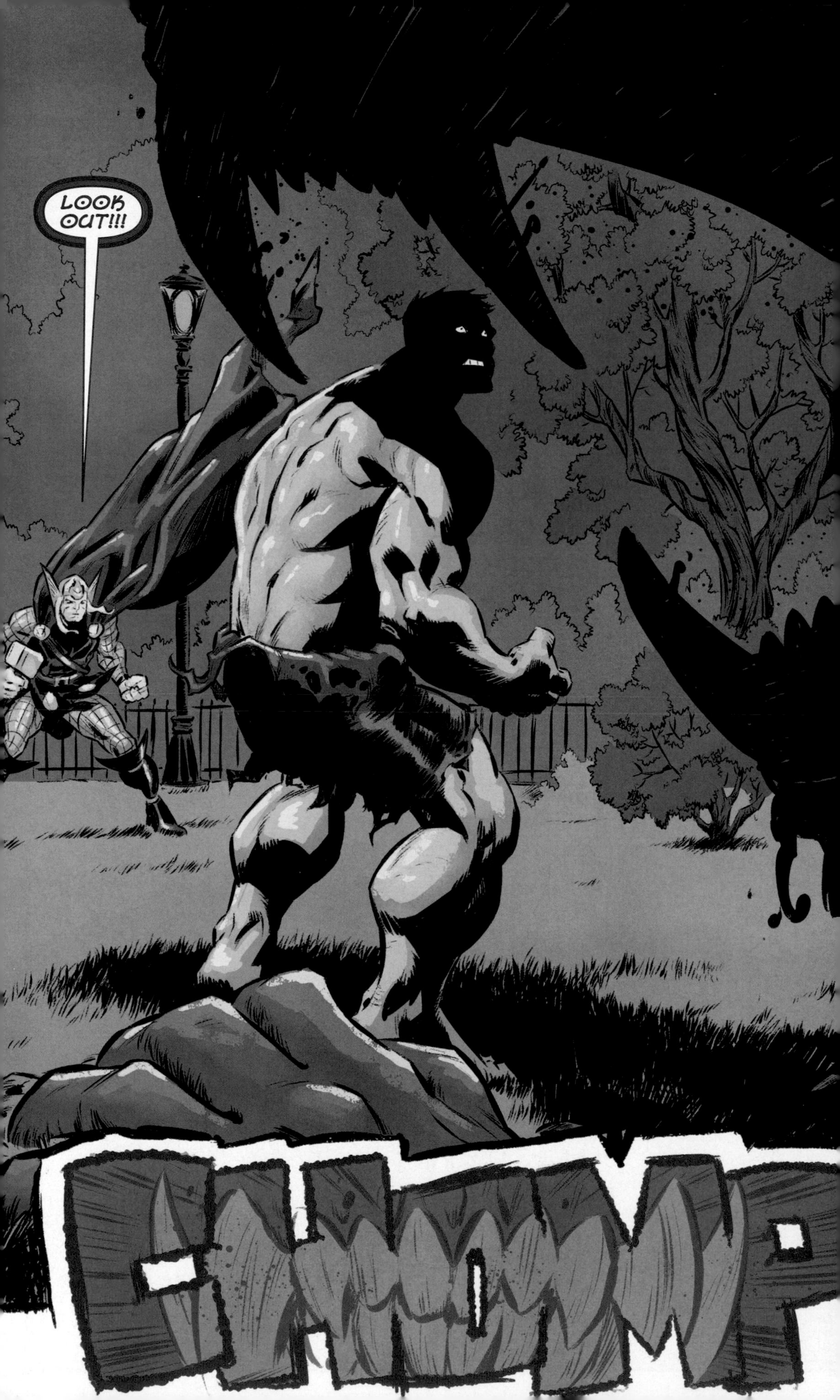
LOOK OUT!!!
CHOMP

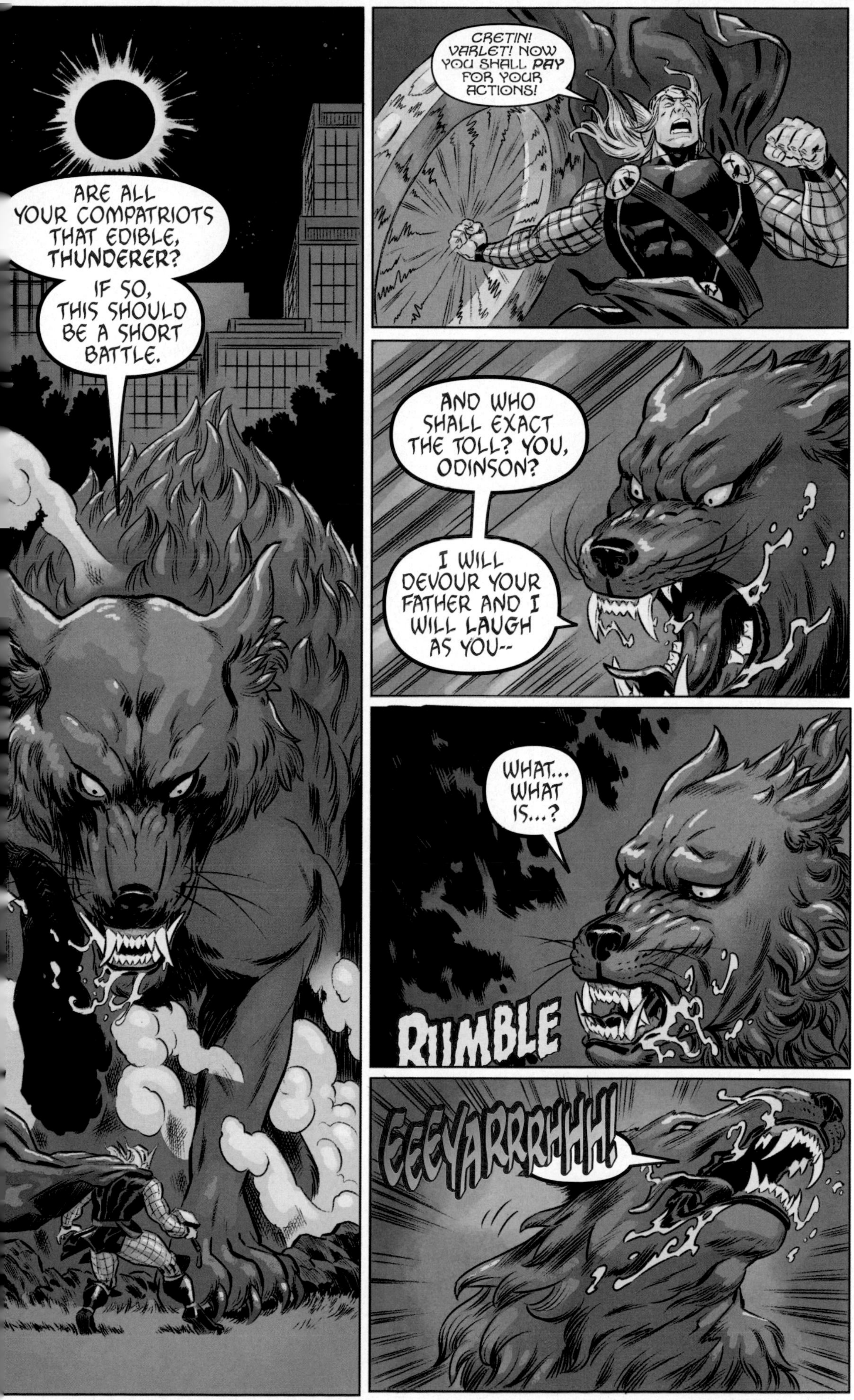
ARE ALL YOUR COMPATRIOTS THAT EDIBLE, THUNDERER?
IF SO, THIS SHOULD BE A SHORT BATTLE.
CRETIN! VARLET! NOW YOU SHALL PAY FOR YOUR ACTIONS!
AND WHO SHALL EXACT THE TOLL? YOU, ODINSON?
I WILL DEVOUR YOUR FATHER AND I WILL LAUGH AS YOU--
WHAT... WHAT IS...?
RUMBLE
EEEYARRRRHHH!

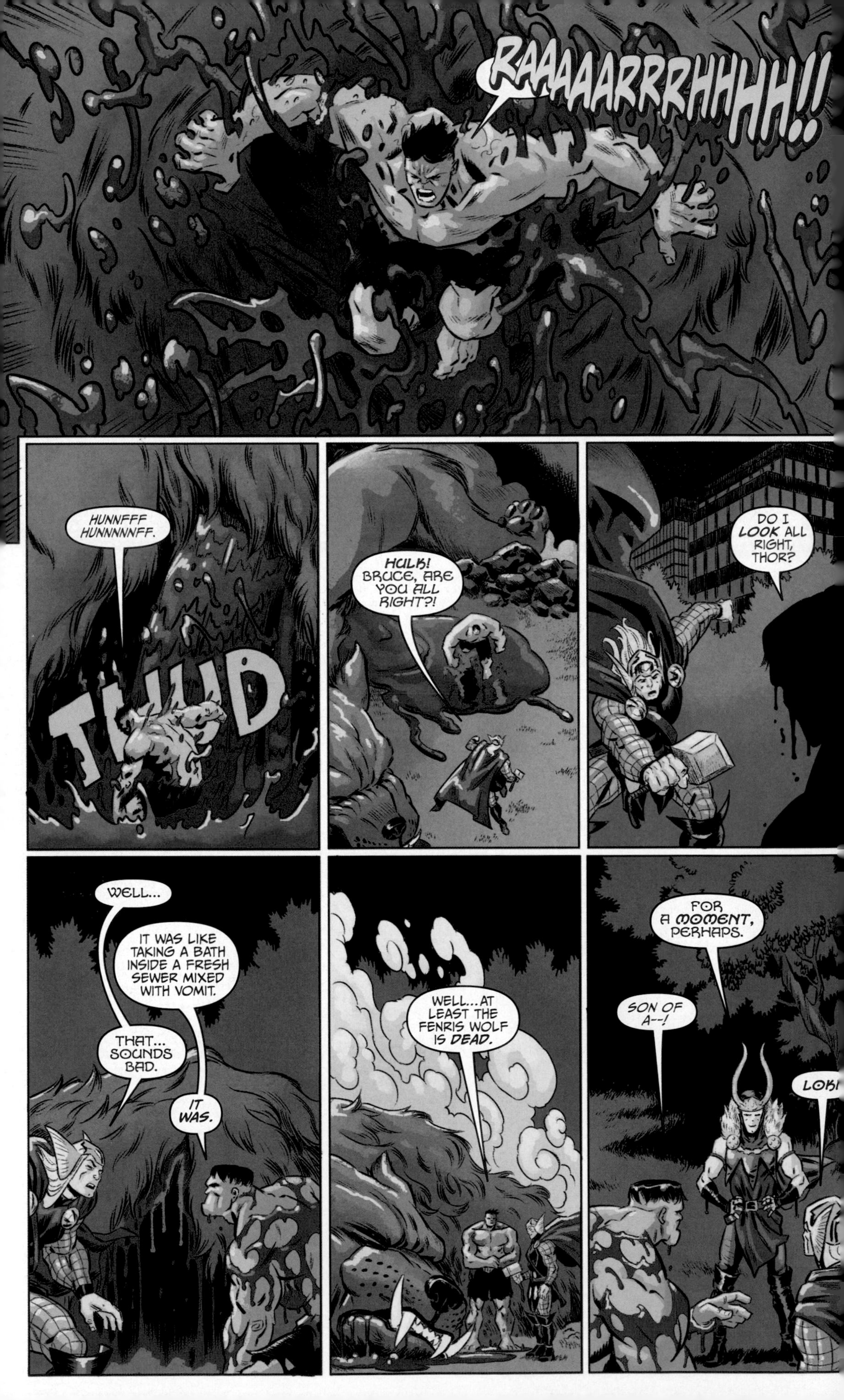
RAAAAARRRHHHH!!
HUNNFFF HUNNNNNFF.
THUD
HULK! BRUCE, ARE YOU ALL RIGHT?!
DO I LOOK ALL RIGHT, THOR?
WELL...
IT WAS LIKE TAKING A BATH INSIDE A FRESH SEWER MIXED WITH VOMIT.
THAT... SOUNDS BAD.
IT WAS.
WELL...AT LEAST THE FENRIS WOLF IS DEAD.
FOR A MOMENT, PERHAPS.
SON OF A--!
LOKI

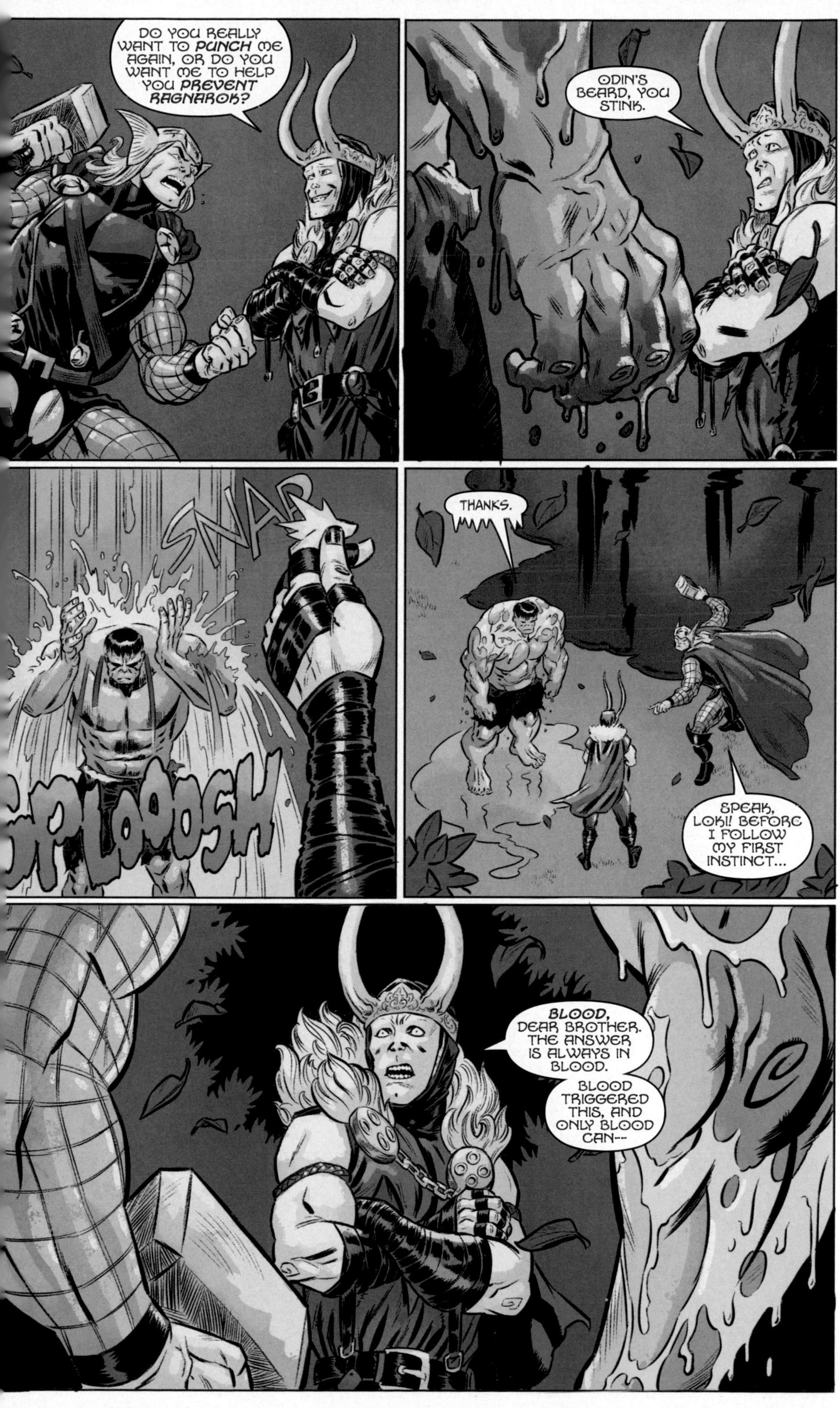
DO YOU REALLY WANT TO PUNCH ME AGAIN, OR DO YOU WANT ME TO HELP YOU PREVENT RAGNAROK?
ODIN'S BEARD, YOU STINK.
SNAP
SPLOOOSH
THANKS.
SPEAK, LOKI! BEFORE I FOLLOW MY FIRST INSTINCT...
BLOOD, DEAR BROTHER. THE ANSWER IS ALWAYS IN BLOOD.
BLOOD TRIGGERED THIS, AND ONLY BLOOD CAN--

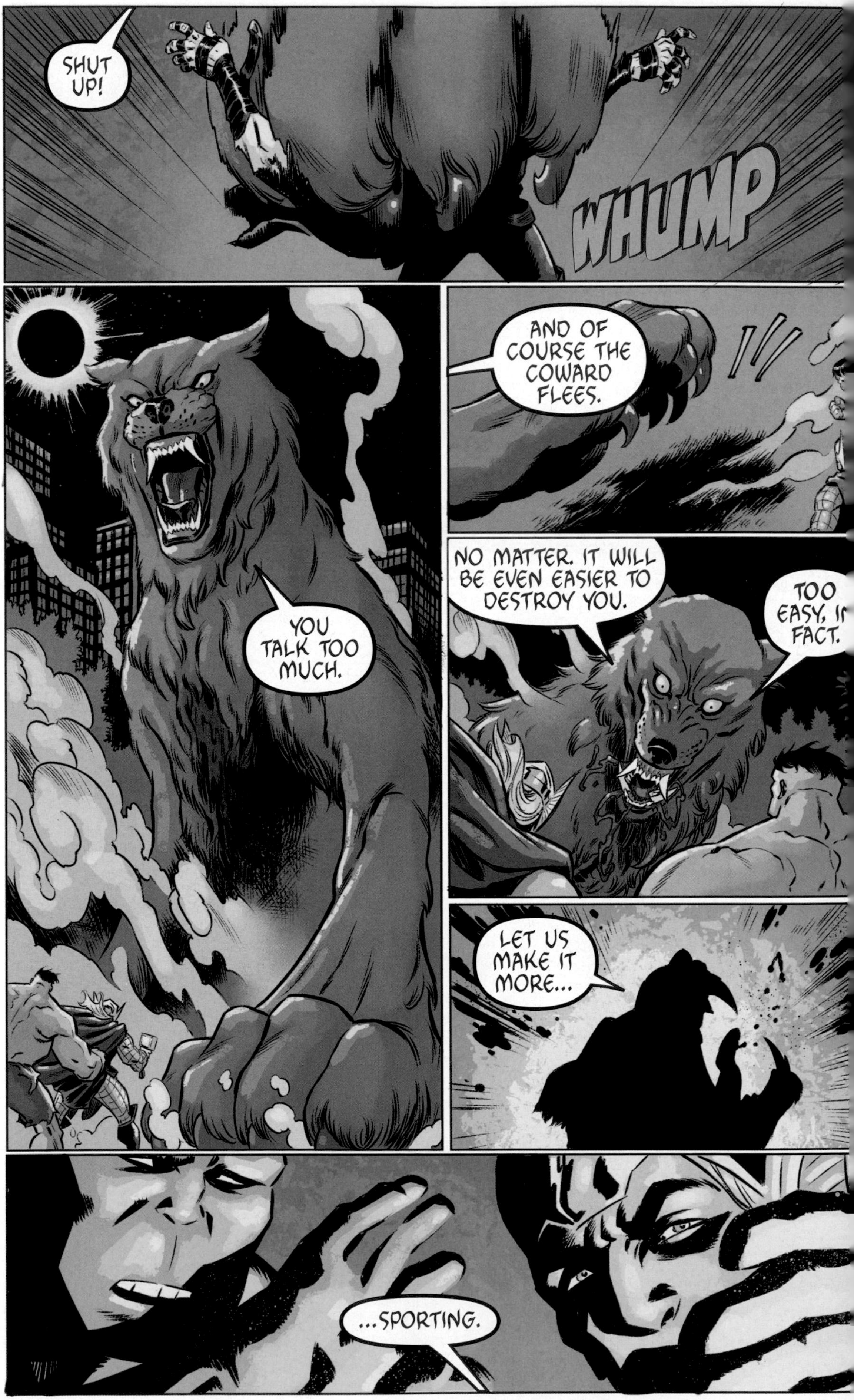
SHUT UP!
WHUMP
YOU TALK TOO MUCH.
AND OF COURSE THE COWARD FLEES.
NO MATTER. IT WILL BE EVEN EASIER TO DESTROY YOU.
TOO EASY, IN FACT.
LET US MAKE IT MORE...
...SPORTING.

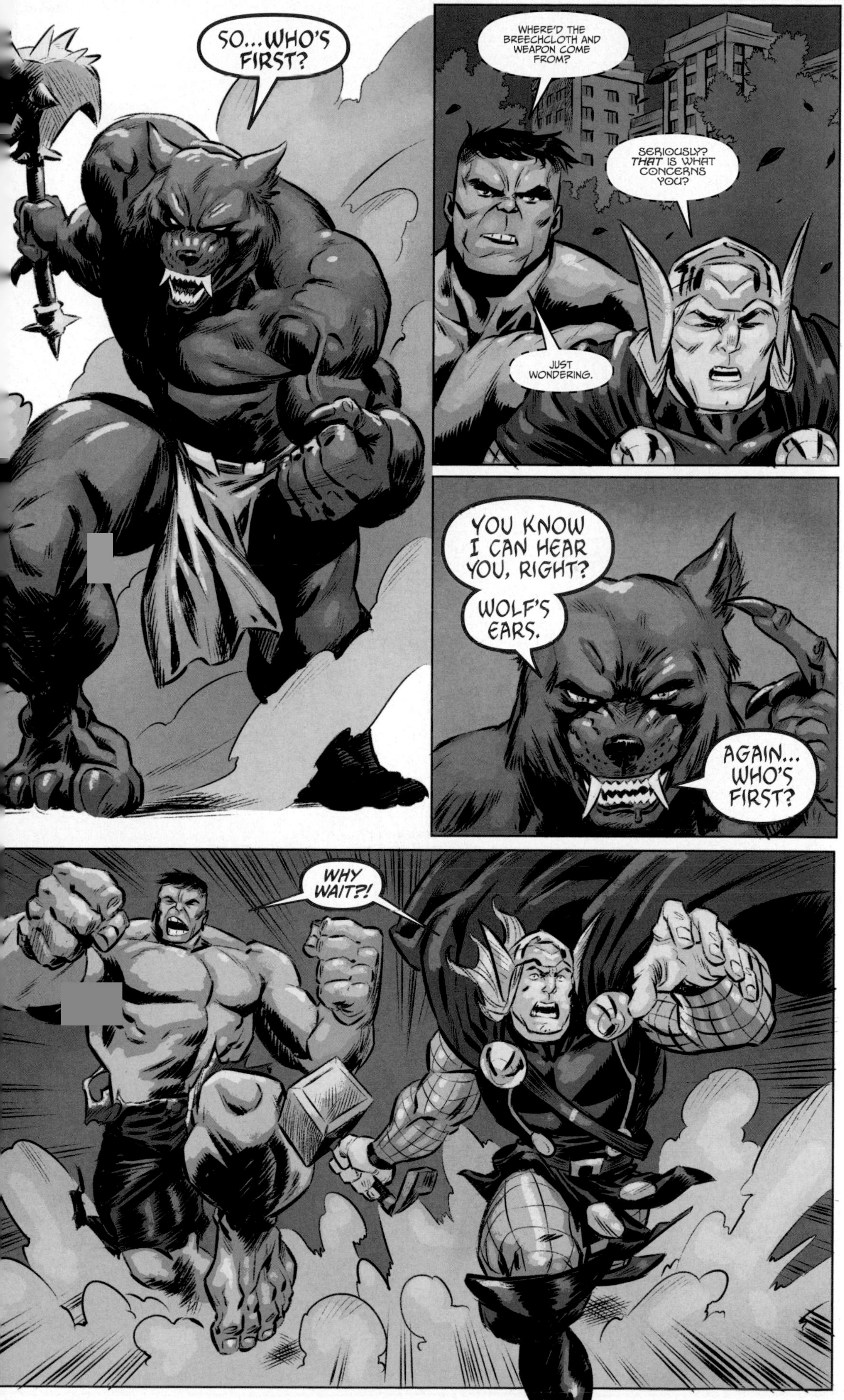
SO...WHO'S FIRST?
WHERE'D THE BREECHCLOTH AND WEAPON COME FROM?
SERIOUSLY? *THAT* IS WHAT CONCERNS YOU?
JUST WONDERING.
YOU KNOW I CAN HEAR YOU, RIGHT?
WOLF'S EARS.
AGAIN... WHO'S FIRST?
WHY WAIT?!

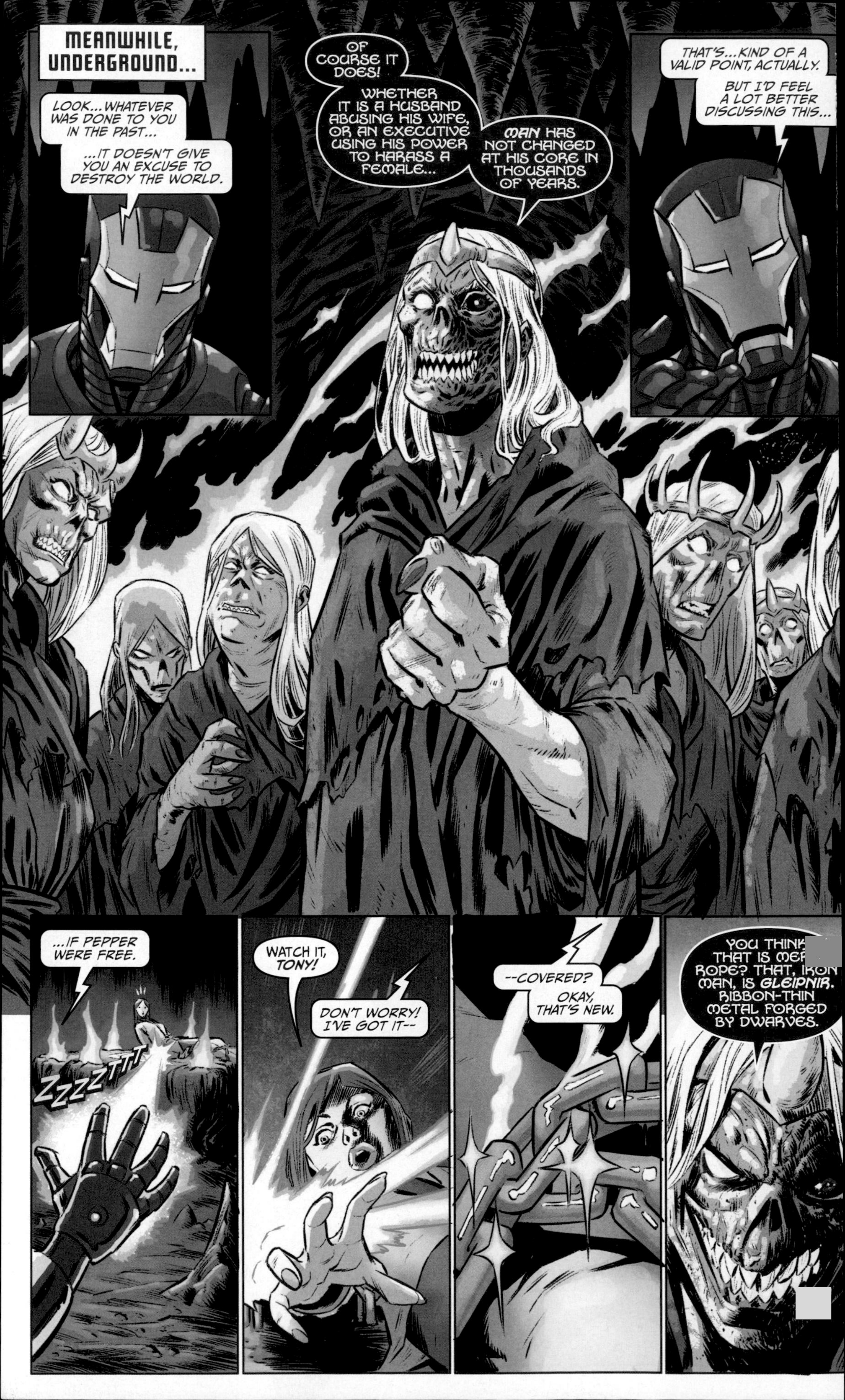

MEANWHILE, UNDERGROUND...
LOOK...WHATEVER WAS DONE TO YOU IN THE PAST...
...IT DOESN'T GIVE YOU AN EXCUSE TO DESTROY THE WORLD.
OF COURSE IT DOES!
WHETHER IT IS A HUSBAND ABUSING HIS WIFE, OR AN EXECUTIVE USING HIS POWER TO HARASS A FEMALE...
MAN HAS NOT CHANGED AT HIS CORE IN THOUSANDS OF YEARS.
THAT'S...KIND OF A VALID POINT, ACTUALLY.
BUT I'D FEEL A LOT BETTER DISCUSSING THIS...
...IF PEPPER WERE FREE.
ZZZZTTT
WATCH IT, TONY!
DON'T WORRY! I'VE GOT IT--
--COVERED? OKAY, THAT'S NEW.
YOU THINK THAT IS ROPE? THAT, IRON MAN, IS GLEIPNIR. RIBBON-THIN METAL FORGED BY DWARVES.

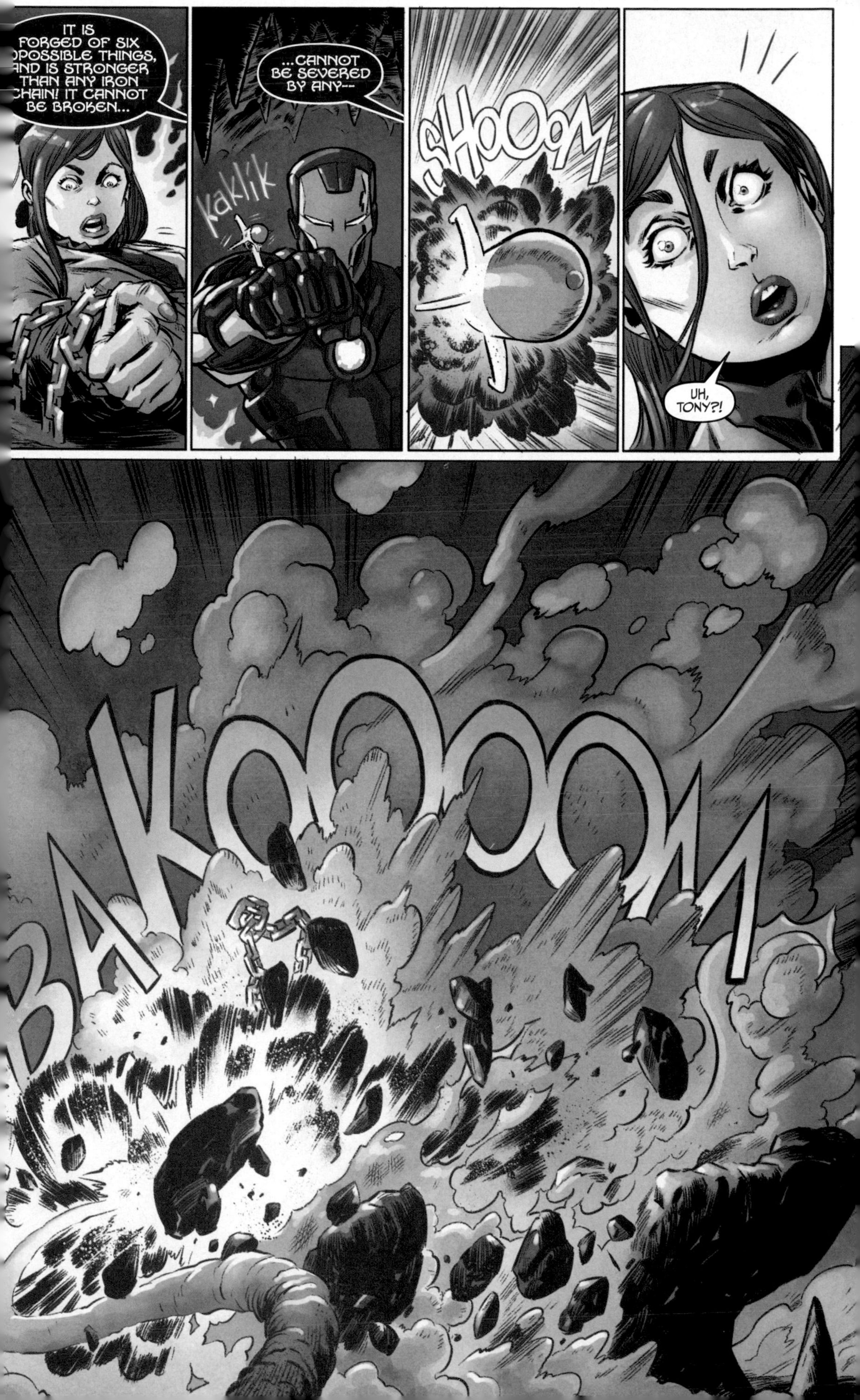
IT IS FORGED OF SIX IMPOSSIBLE THINGS, AND IS STRONGER THAN ANY IRON CHAIN! IT CANNOT BE BROKEN...
KAKLIK
...CANNOT BE SEVERED BY ANY--
SHOOOM
UH, TONY?!
BAKOOOOM

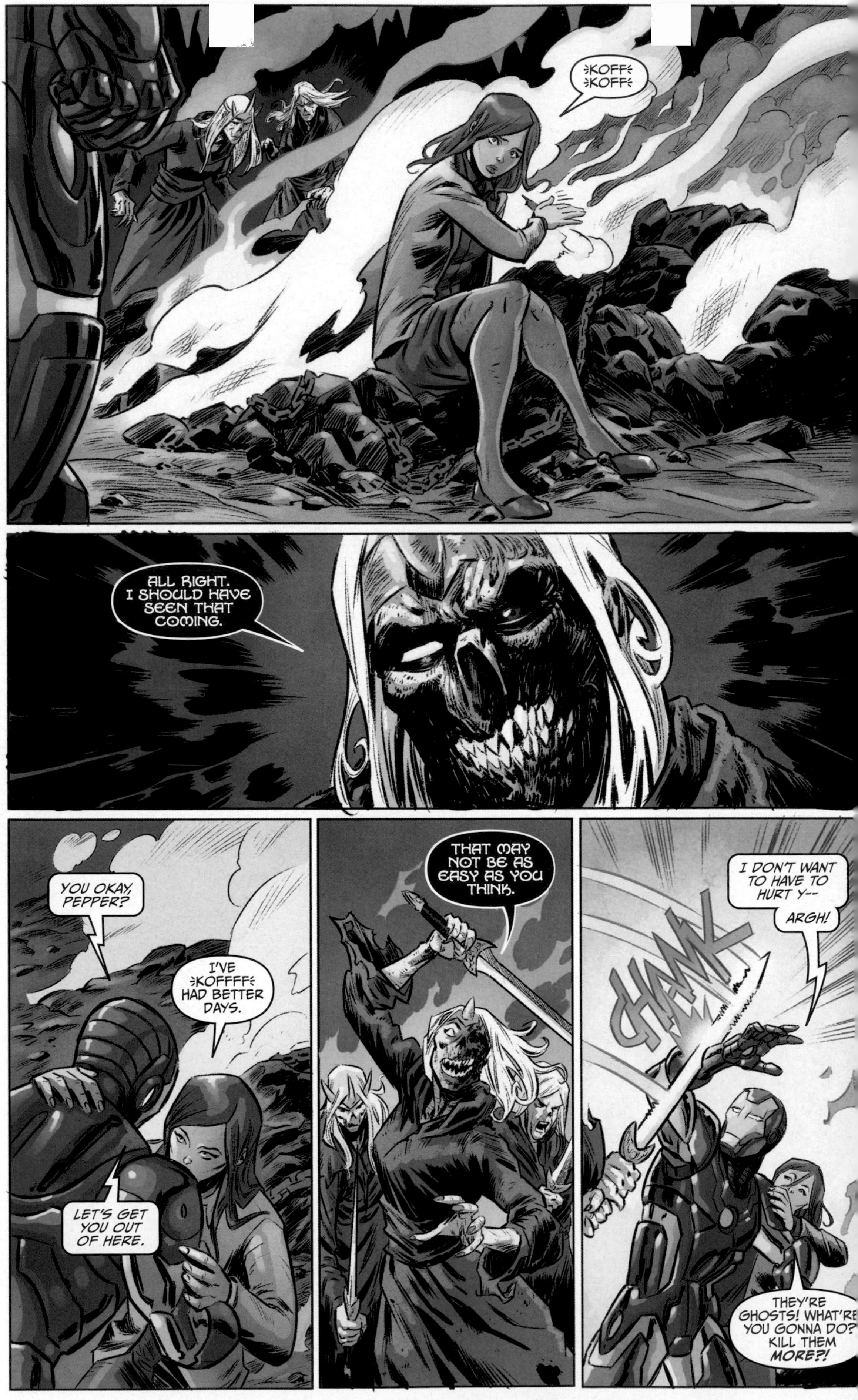

KOFF *KOFF*
ALL RIGHT. I SHOULD HAVE SEEN THAT COMING.
YOU OKAY, PEPPER?
I'VE *KOFFFF* HAD BETTER DAYS.
LET'S GET YOU OUT OF HERE.
THAT MAY NOT BE AS EASY AS YOU THINK.
CHAK
I DON'T WANT TO HAVE TO HURT Y--
ARGH!
THEY'RE GHOSTS! WHAT'RE YOU GONNA DO? KILL THEM MORE?!

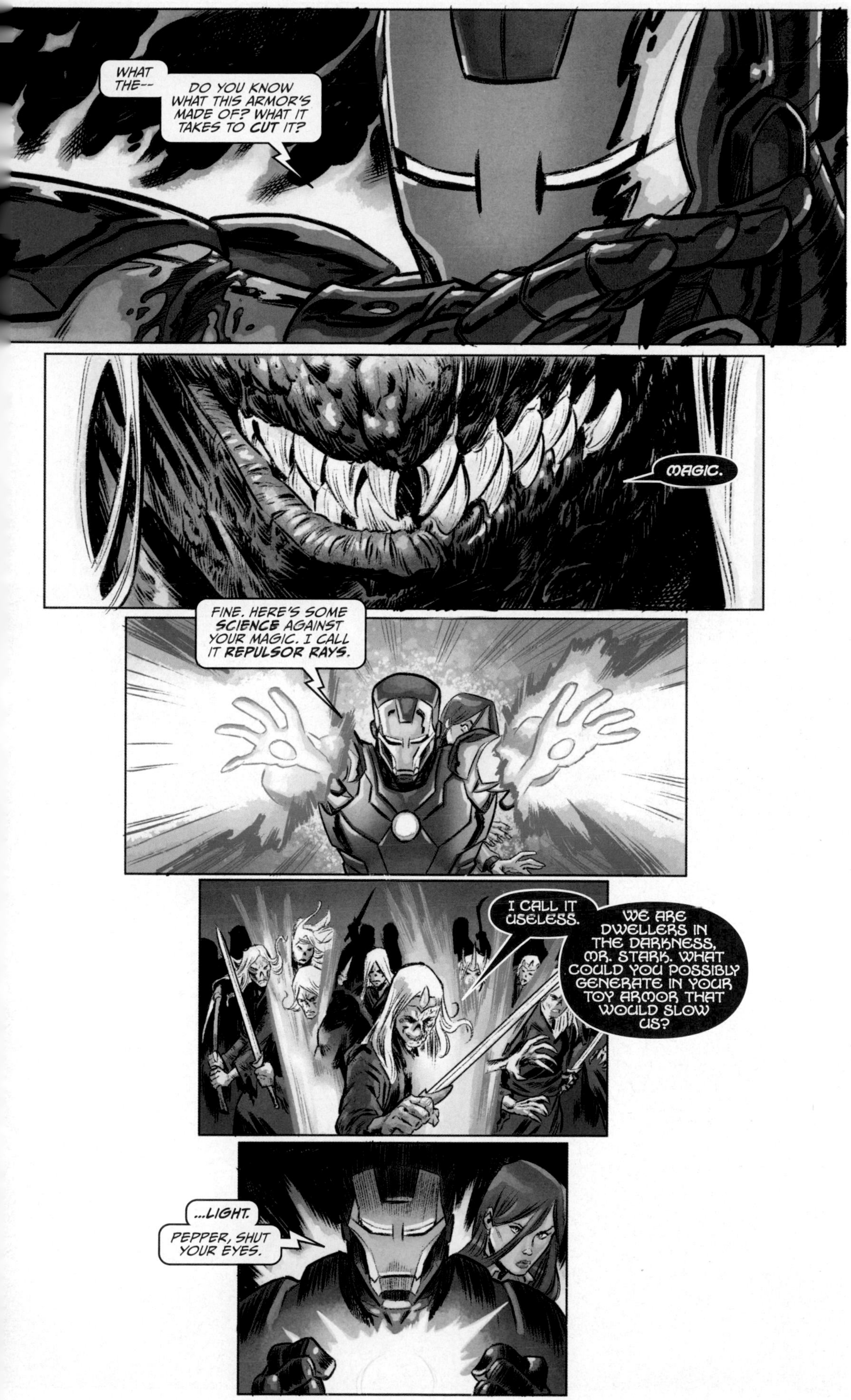

WHAT THE--
DO YOU KNOW WHAT THIS ARMOR'S MADE OF? WHAT IT TAKES TO CUT IT?
MAGIC.
FINE. HERE'S SOME SCIENCE AGAINST YOUR MAGIC. I CALL IT REPULSOR RAYS.
I CALL IT USELESS.
WE ARE DWELLERS IN THE DARKNESS, MR. STARK. WHAT COULD YOU POSSIBLY GENERATE IN YOUR TOY ARMOR THAT WOULD SLOW US?
...LIGHT.
PEPPER, SHUT YOUR EYES.

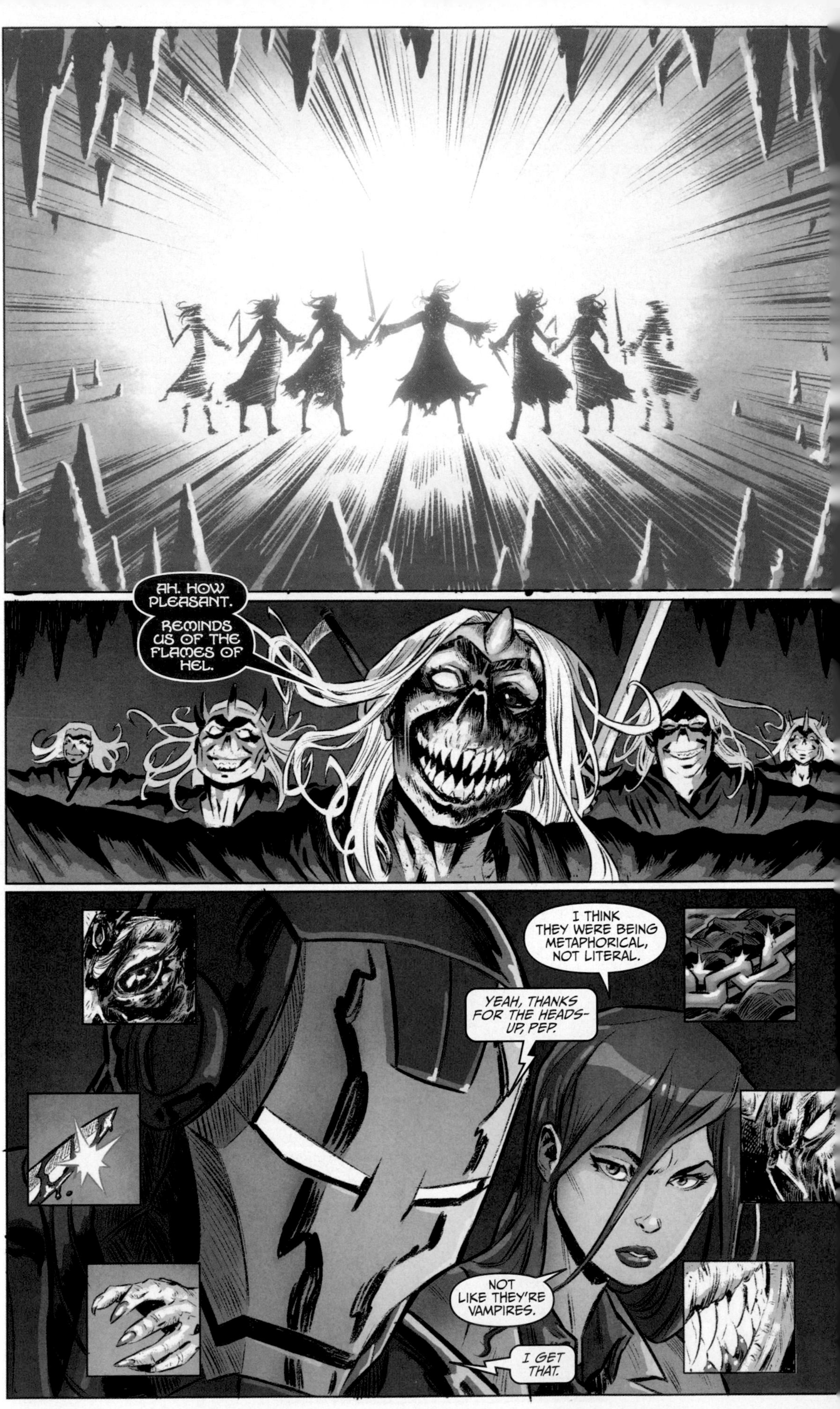

AH. HOW PLEASANT.
REMINDS US OF THE FLAMES OF HEL.
I THINK THEY WERE BEING METAPHORICAL, NOT LITERAL.
YEAH, THANKS FOR THE HEADS-UP, PEP.
NOT LIKE THEY'RE VAMPIRES.
I GET THAT.

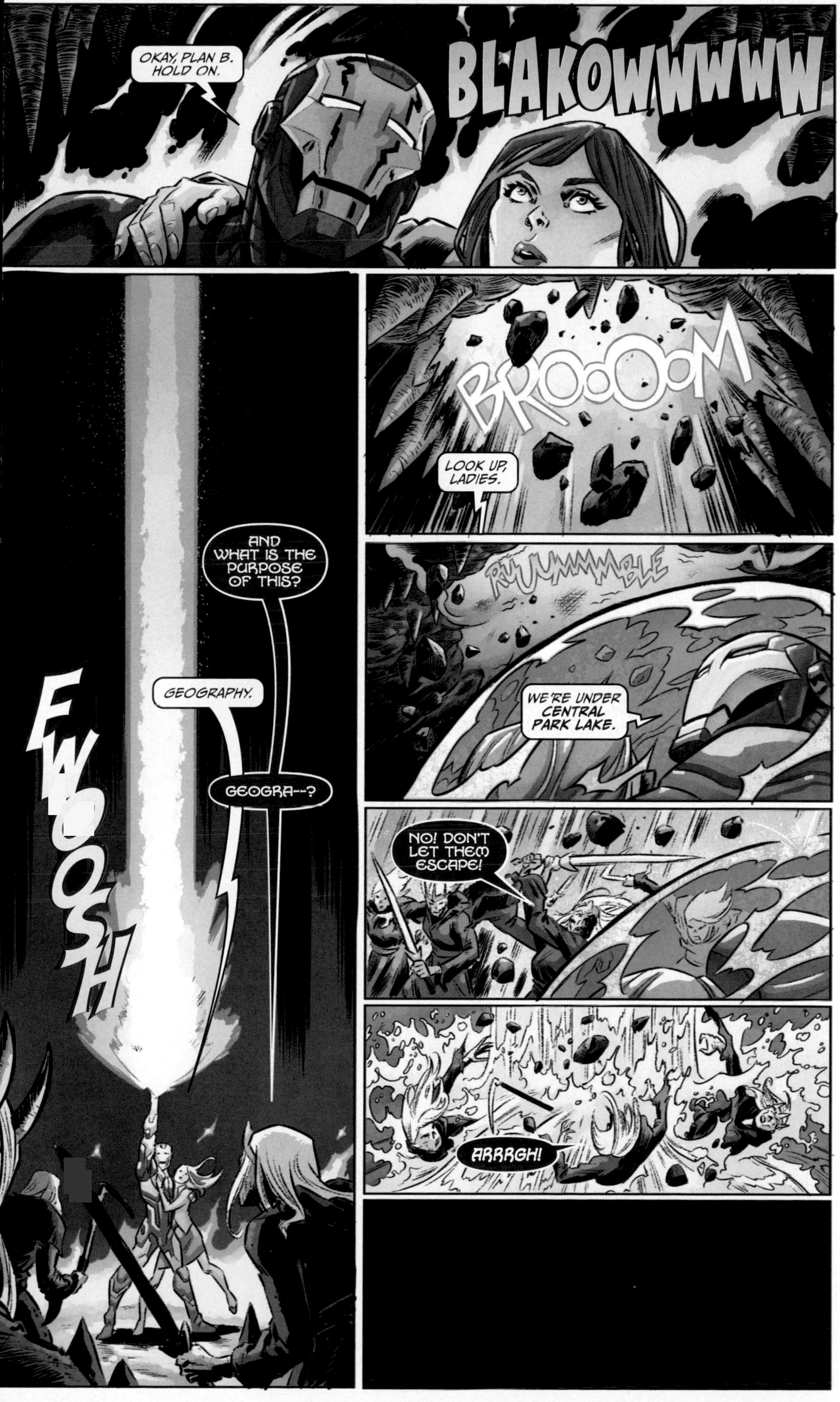
OKAY, PLAN B. HOLD ON.
BLAKOWWWWW
AND WHAT IS THE PURPOSE OF THIS?
GEOGRAPHY.
GEOGRA--?
FWOOSH
BROOOOM
LOOK UP, LADIES.
RUUMMMBLE
WE'RE UNDER CENTRAL PARK LAKE.
NO! DON'T LET THEM ESCAPE!
ARRRGH!

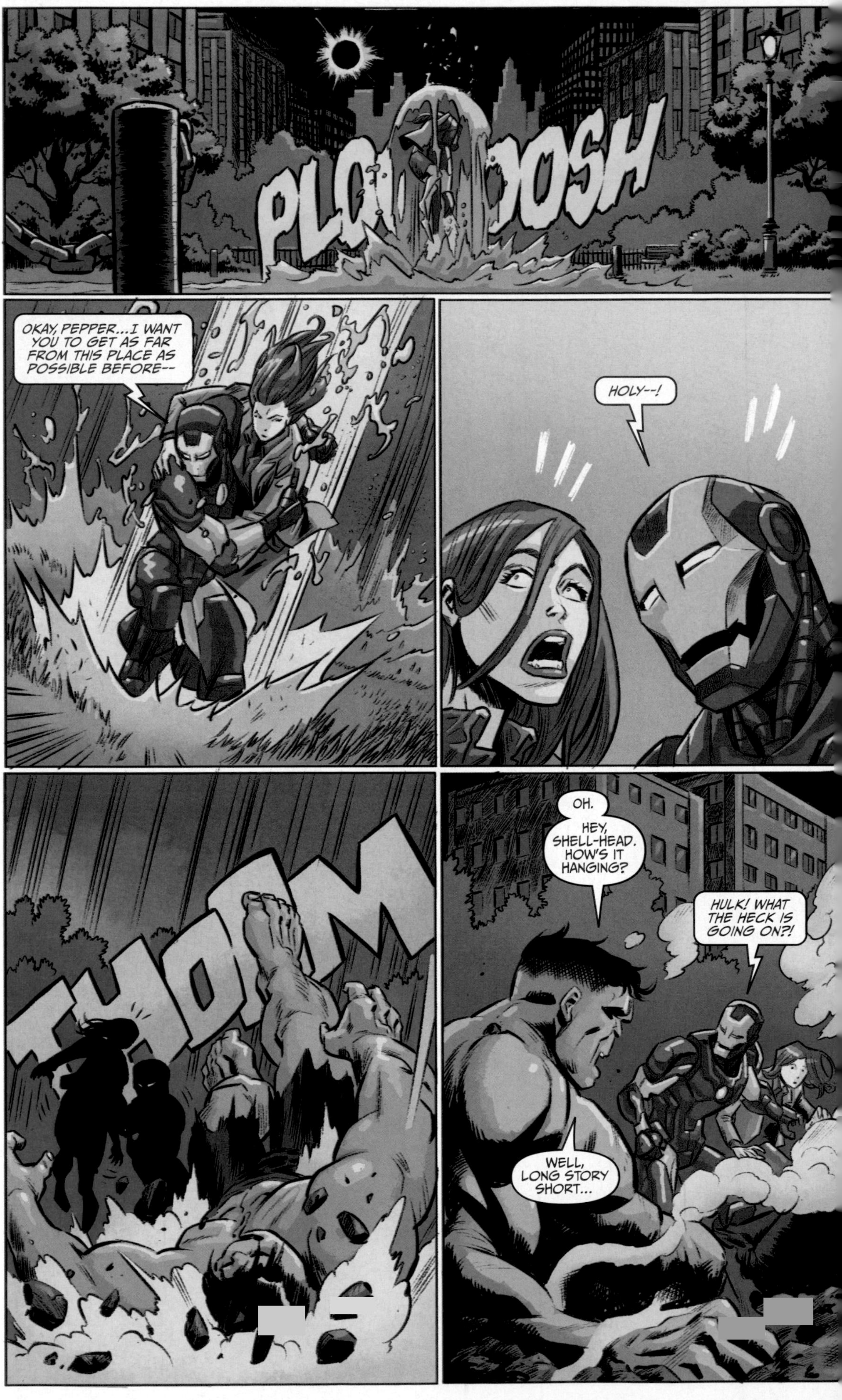

OKAY, PEPPER...I WANT YOU TO GET AS FAR FROM THIS PLACE AS POSSIBLE BEFORE--
HOLY--!
OH.
HEY, SHELL-HEAD. HOW'S IT HANGING?
HULK! WHAT THE HECK IS GOING ON?!
WELL, LONG STORY SHORT...

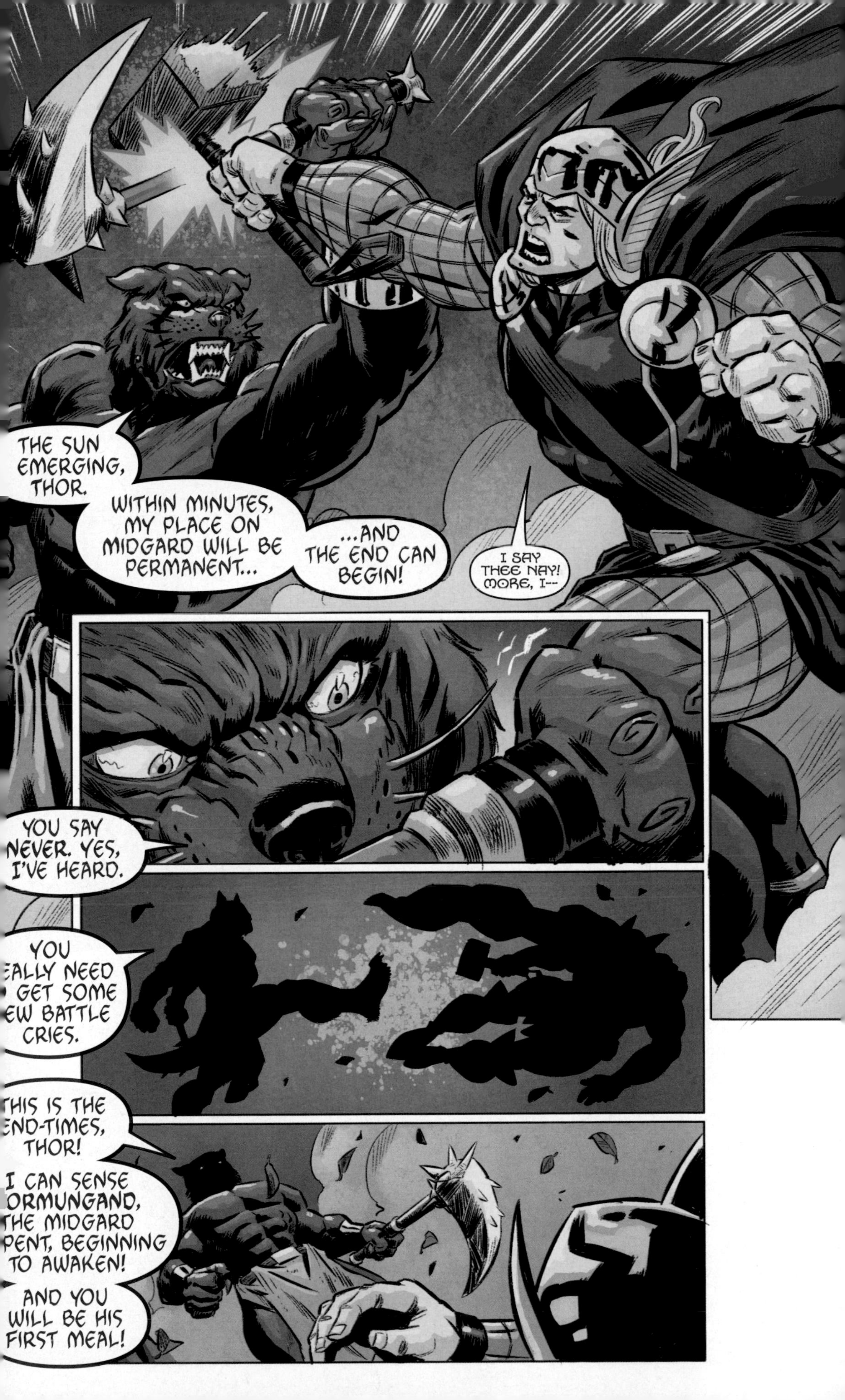
THE SUN EMERGING, THOR.
WITHIN MINUTES, MY PLACE ON MIDGARD WILL BE PERMANENT...
...AND THE END CAN BEGIN!
I SAY THEE NAY! MORE, I--
YOU SAY NEVER. YES, I'VE HEARD.
YOU EALLY NEED GET SOME EW BATTLE CRIES.
THIS IS THE ND-TIMES, THOR!
I CAN SENSE ORMUNGAND, THE MIDGARD PENT, BEGINNING TO AWAKEN!
AND YOU WILL BE HIS FIRST MEAL!

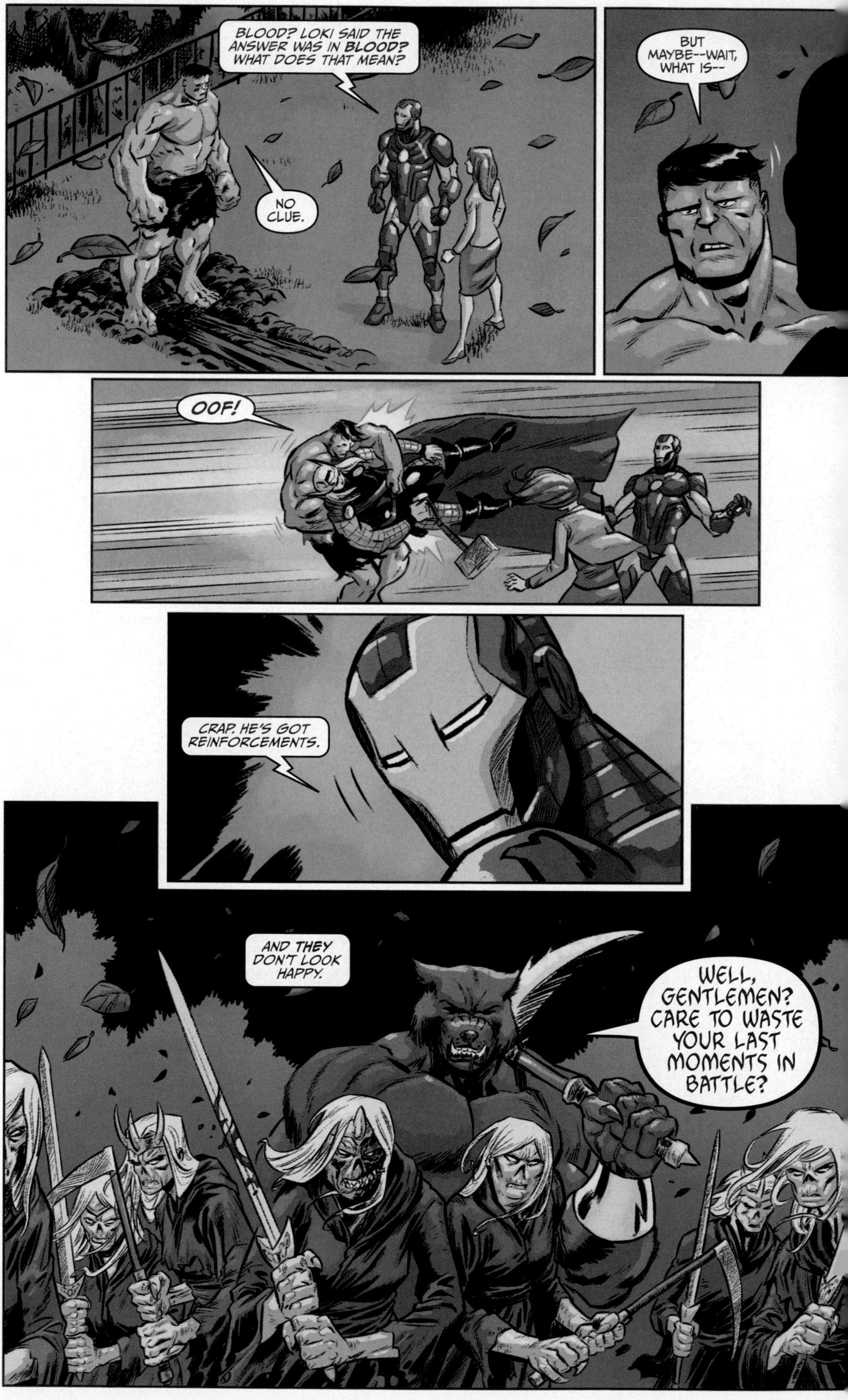
BLOOD? LOKI SAID THE ANSWER WAS IN BLOOD? WHAT DOES THAT MEAN?
NO CLUE.
BUT MAYBE--WAIT, WHAT IS--
OOF!
CRAP. HE'S GOT REINFORCEMENTS.
AND THEY DON'T LOOK HAPPY.
WELL, GENTLEMEN? CARE TO WASTE YOUR LAST MOMENTS IN BATTLE?

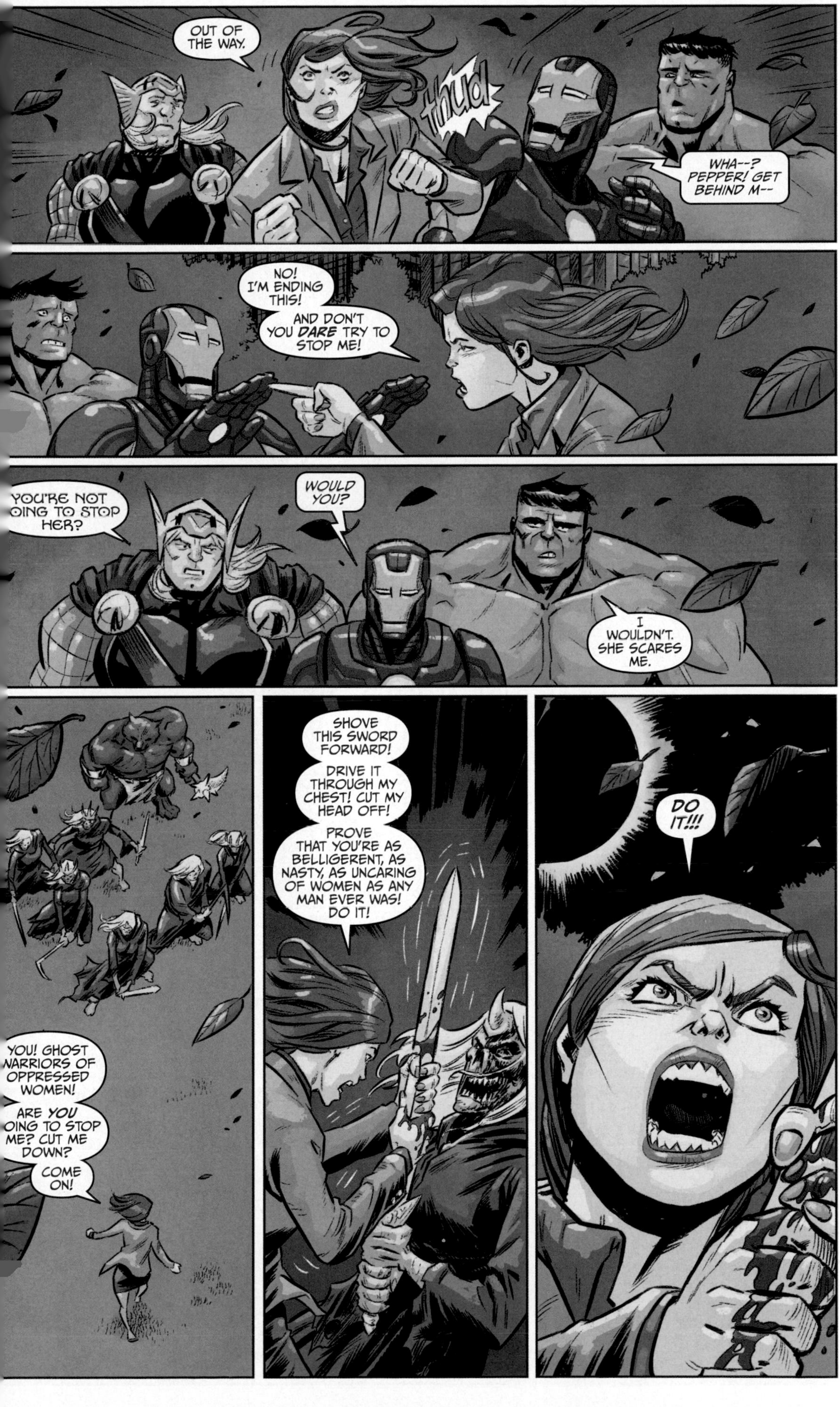
OUT OF THE WAY.
thud
WHA--? PEPPER! GET BEHIND M--
NO! I'M ENDING THIS!
AND DON'T YOU DARE TRY TO STOP ME!
YOU'RE NOT OING TO STOP HER?
WOULD YOU?
I WOULDN'T. SHE SCARES ME.
YOU! GHOST WARRIORS OF OPPRESSED WOMEN!
ARE YOU OING TO STOP ME? CUT ME DOWN?
COME ON!
SHOVE THIS SWORD FORWARD!
DRIVE IT THROUGH MY CHEST! CUT MY HEAD OFF!
PROVE THAT YOU'RE AS BELLIGERENT, AS NASTY, AS UNCARING OF WOMEN AS ANY MAN EVER WAS! DO IT!
DO IT!!!

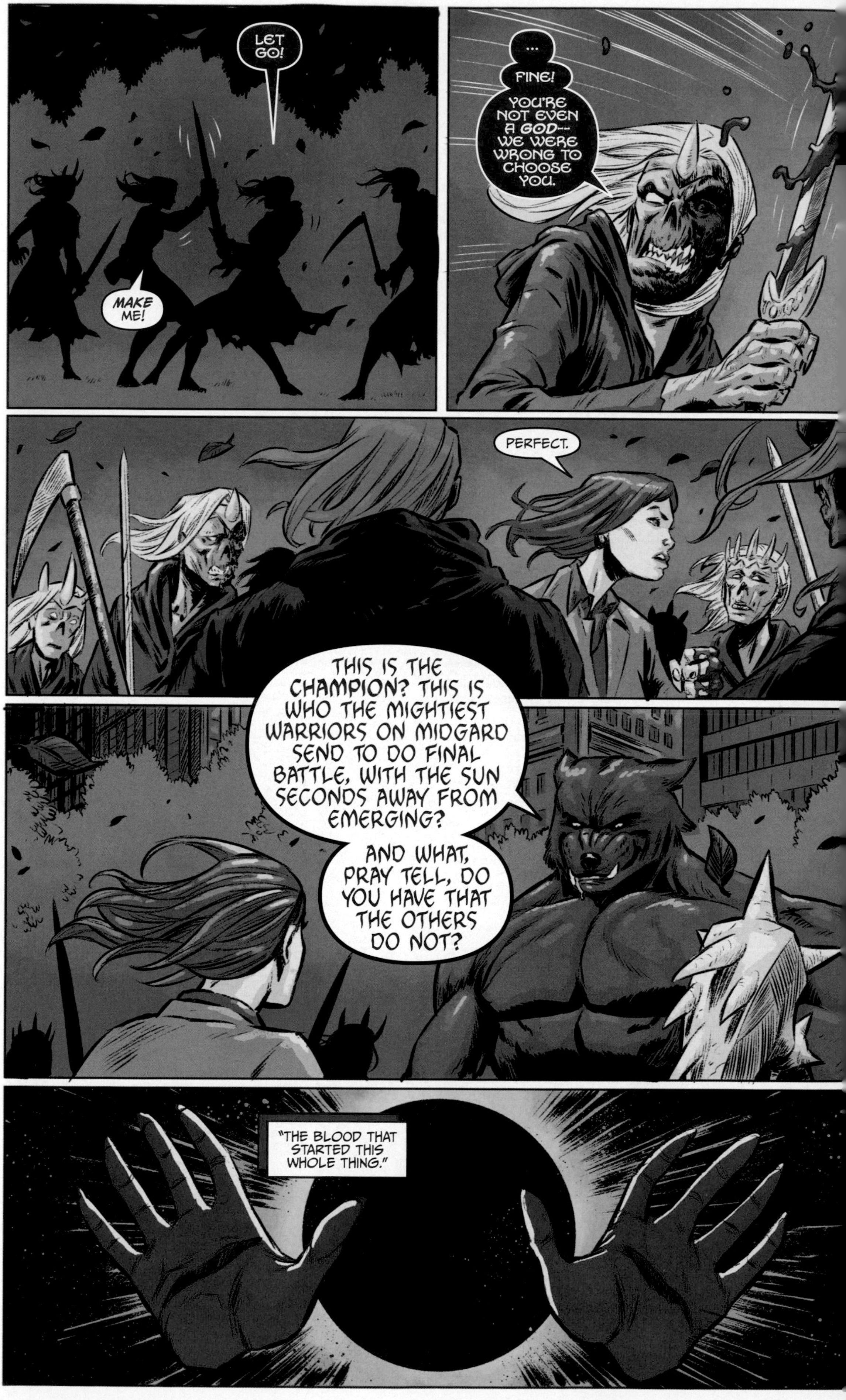
LET GO!
MAKE ME!
...
FINE!
YOU'RE NOT EVEN A GOD-- WE WERE WRONG TO CHOOSE YOU.
PERFECT.
THIS IS THE CHAMPION? THIS IS WHO THE MIGHTIEST WARRIORS ON MIDGARD SEND TO DO FINAL BATTLE, WITH THE SUN SECONDS AWAY FROM EMERGING?
AND WHAT, PRAY TELL, DO YOU HAVE THAT THE OTHERS DO NOT?
"THE BLOOD THAT STARTED THIS WHOLE THING."

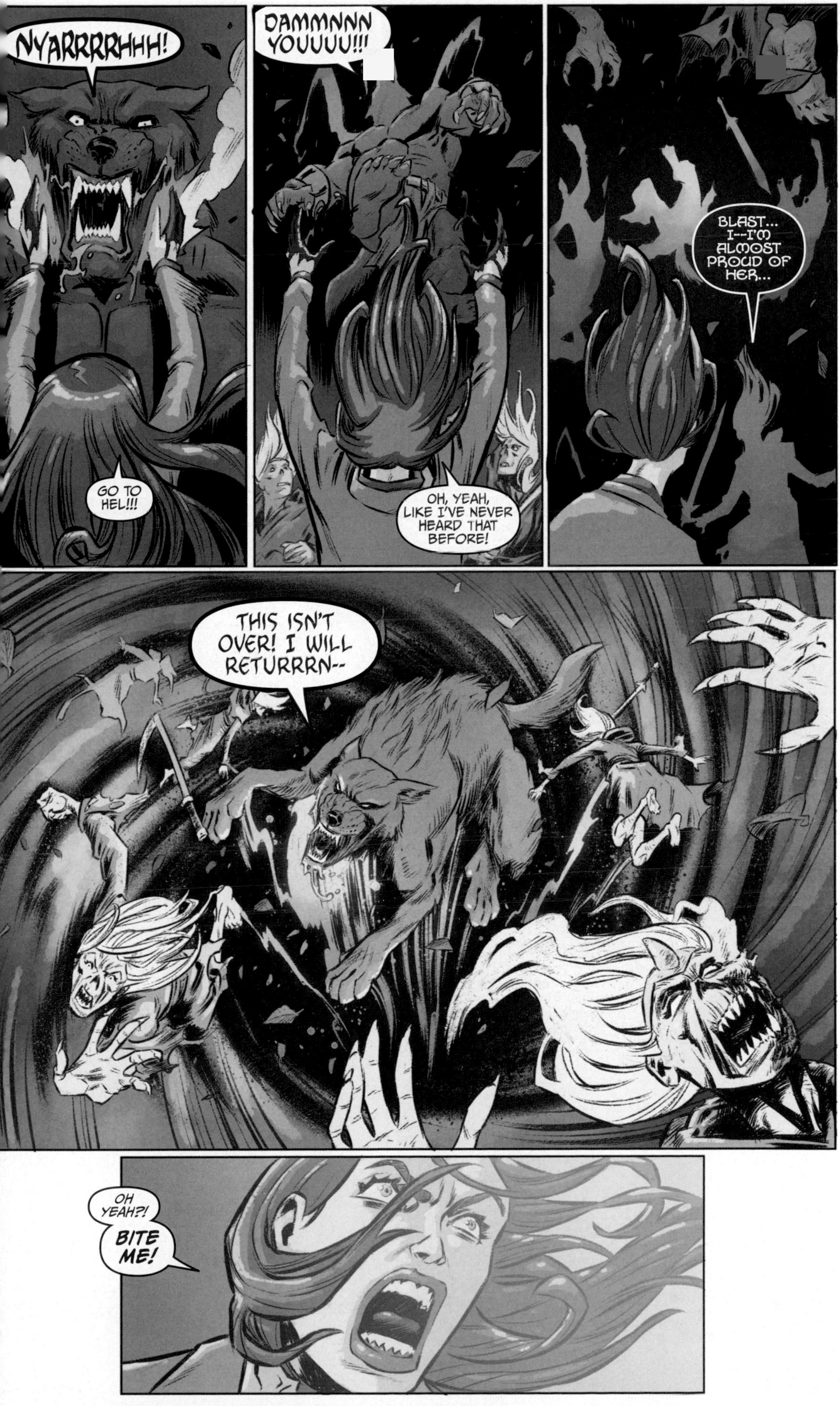
NYARRRRHHH!
GO TO HEL!!!
DAMMNNN YOUUUU!!!
OH, YEAH, LIKE I'VE NEVER HEARD THAT BEFORE!
BLAST... I--I'M ALMOST PROUD OF HER...
THIS ISN'T OVER! I WILL RETURRRN--
OH YEAH?!
BITE ME!

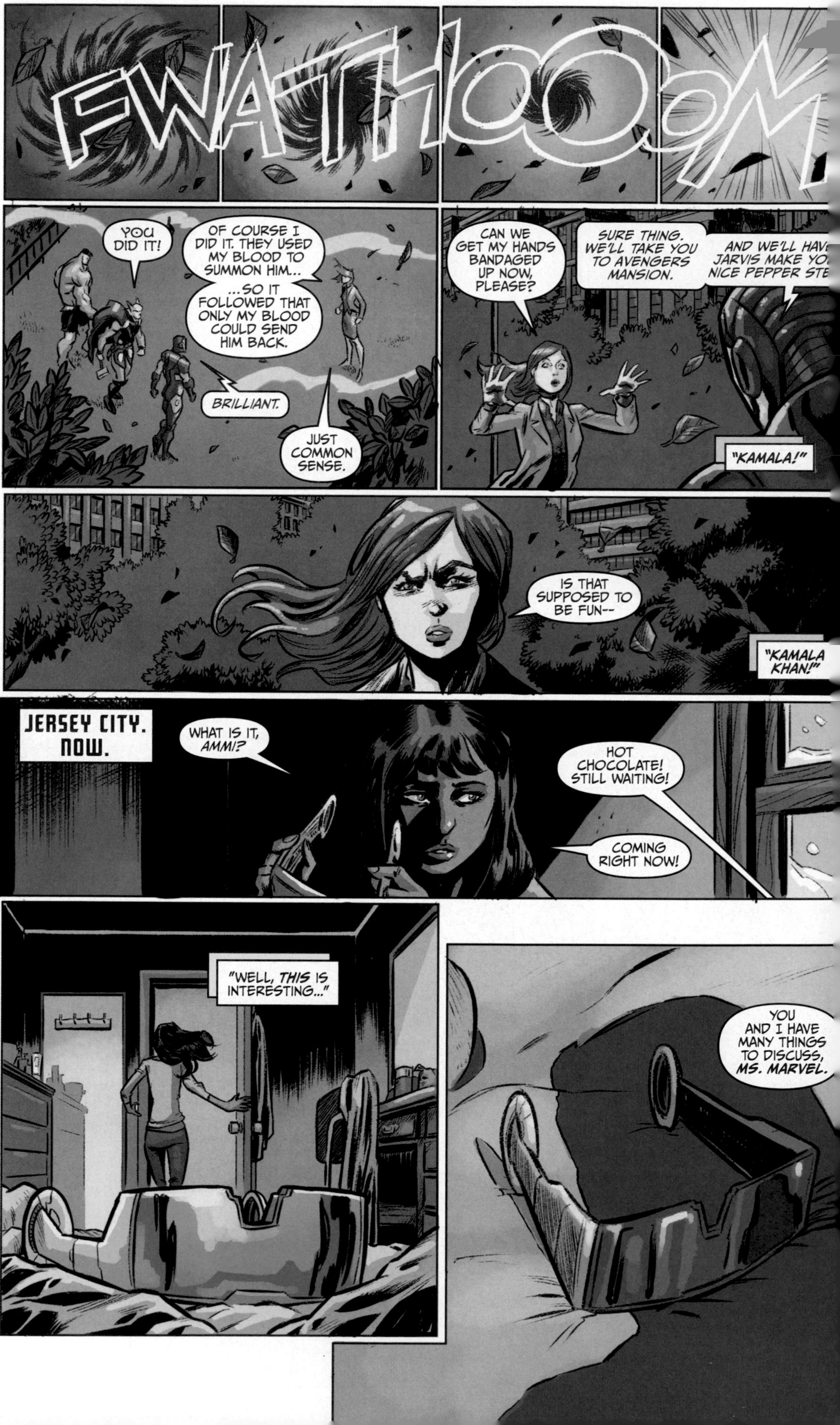

FWATHOOOM
YOU DID IT!
OF COURSE I DID IT. THEY USED MY BLOOD TO SUMMON HIM...
...SO IT FOLLOWED THAT ONLY MY BLOOD COULD SEND HIM BACK.
BRILLIANT.
JUST COMMON SENSE.
CAN WE GET MY HANDS BANDAGED UP NOW, PLEASE?
SURE THING. WE'LL TAKE YOU TO AVENGERS MANSION.
AND WE'LL HAV
JARVIS MAKE YO
NICE PEPPER STE
"KAMALA!"
IS THAT SUPPOSED TO BE FUN--
"KAMALA KHAN!"
JERSEY CITY. NOW.
WHAT IS IT, AMMI?
HOT CHOCOLATE! STILL WAITING!
COMING RIGHT NOW!
"WELL, THIS IS INTERESTING..."
YOU AND I HAVE MANY THINGS TO DISCUSS, MS. MARVEL.

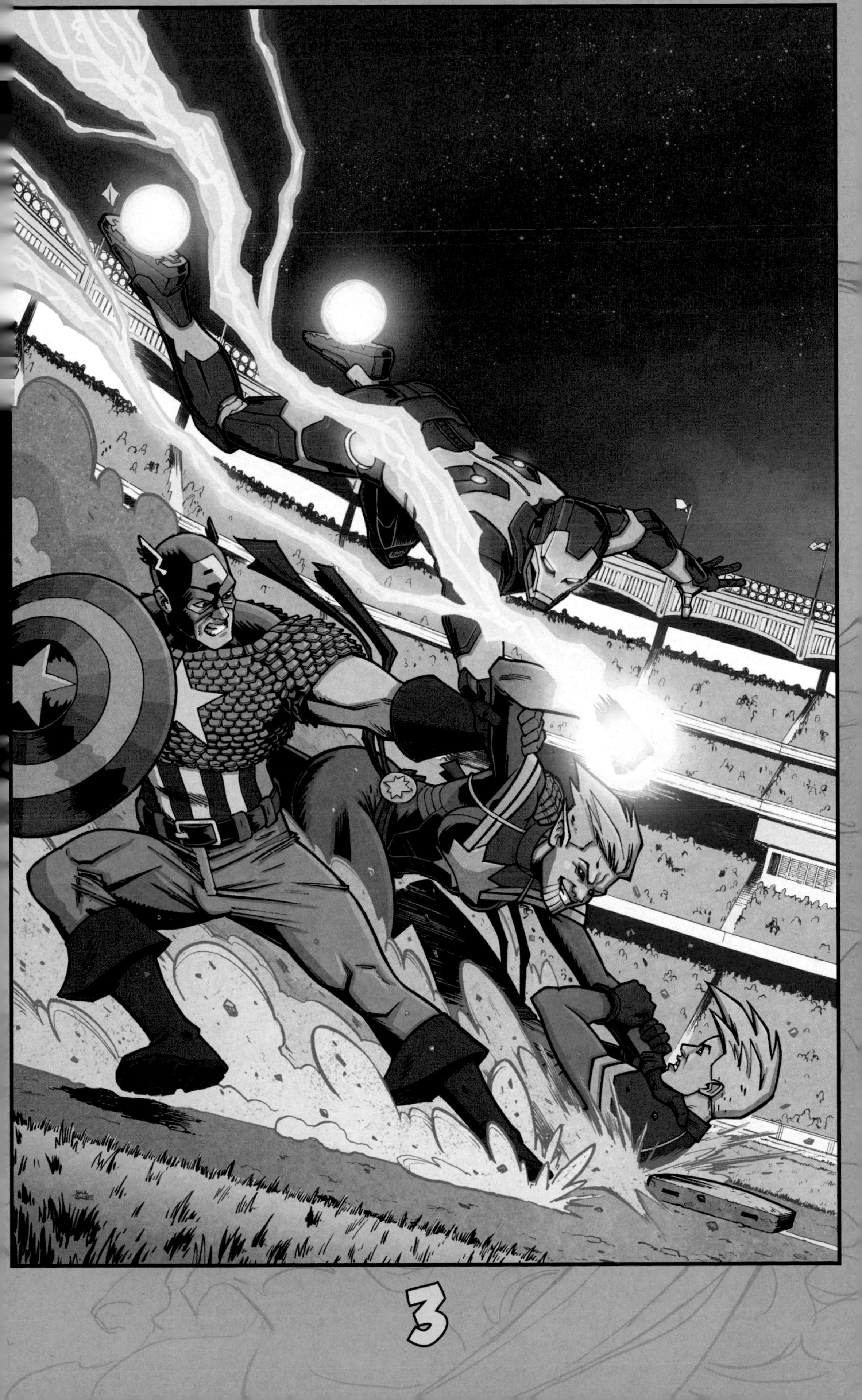

3

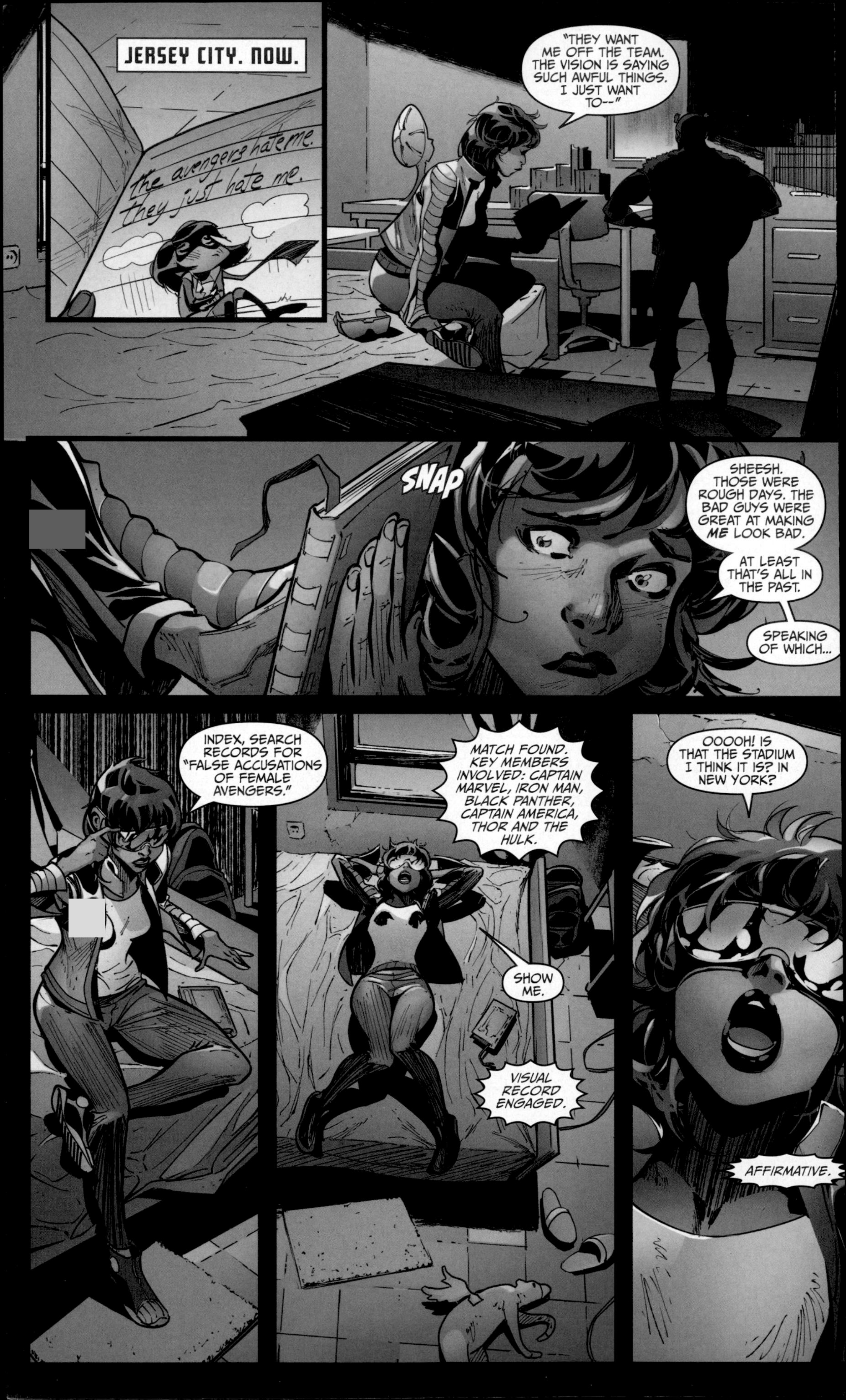

JERSEY CITY. NOW.
the avengers hate me.
they just hate me.
"THEY WANT ME OFF THE TEAM. THE VISION IS SAYING SUCH AWFUL THINGS. I JUST WANT TO--"
SNAP
SHEESH. THOSE WERE ROUGH DAYS. THE BAD GUYS WERE GREAT AT MAKING ME LOOK BAD.
AT LEAST THAT'S ALL IN THE PAST.
SPEAKING OF WHICH...
INDEX, SEARCH RECORDS FOR "FALSE ACCUSATIONS OF FEMALE AVENGERS."
MATCH FOUND. KEY MEMBERS INVOLVED: CAPTAIN MARVEL, IRON MAN, BLACK PANTHER, CAPTAIN AMERICA, THOR AND THE HULK.
SHOW ME.
VISUAL RECORD ENGAGED.
OOOOH! IS THAT THE STADIUM I THINK IT IS? IN NEW YORK?
AFFIRMATIVE.

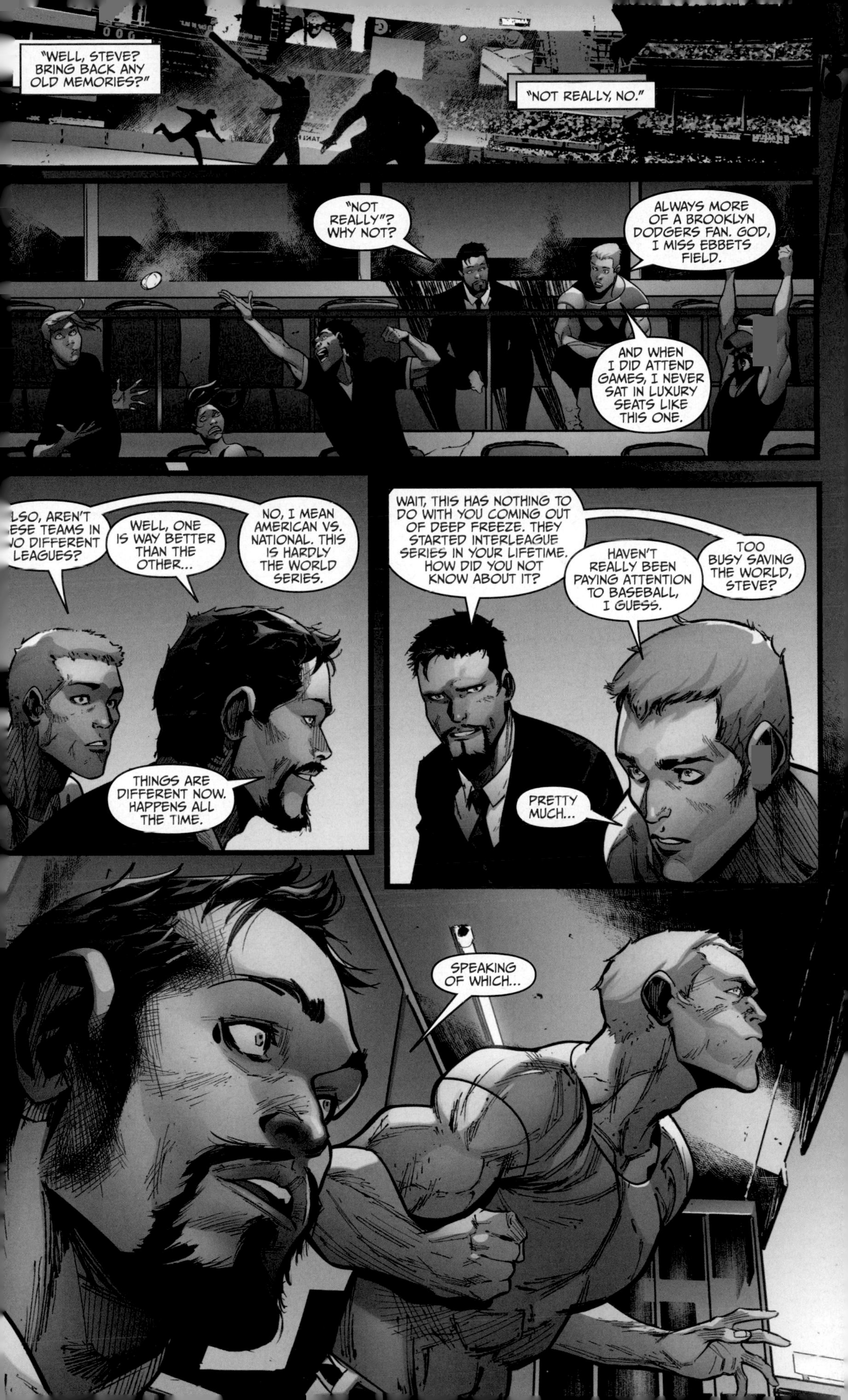
"WELL, STEVE? BRING BACK ANY OLD MEMORIES?"
"NOT REALLY, NO."
"NOT REALLY"? WHY NOT?
ALWAYS MORE OF A BROOKLYN DODGERS FAN. GOD, I MISS EBBETS FIELD.
AND WHEN I DID ATTEND GAMES, I NEVER SAT IN LUXURY SEATS LIKE THIS ONE.
LSO, AREN'T ESE TEAMS IN O DIFFERENT LEAGUES?
WELL, ONE IS WAY BETTER THAN THE OTHER...
NO, I MEAN AMERICAN VS. NATIONAL. THIS IS HARDLY THE WORLD SERIES.
THINGS ARE DIFFERENT NOW. HAPPENS ALL THE TIME.
WAIT, THIS HAS NOTHING TO DO WITH YOU COMING OUT OF DEEP FREEZE. THEY STARTED INTERLEAGUE SERIES IN YOUR LIFETIME. HOW DID YOU NOT KNOW ABOUT IT?
HAVEN'T REALLY BEEN PAYING ATTENTION TO BASEBALL, I GUESS.
TOO BUSY SAVING THE WORLD, STEVE?
PRETTY MUCH...
SPEAKING OF WHICH...

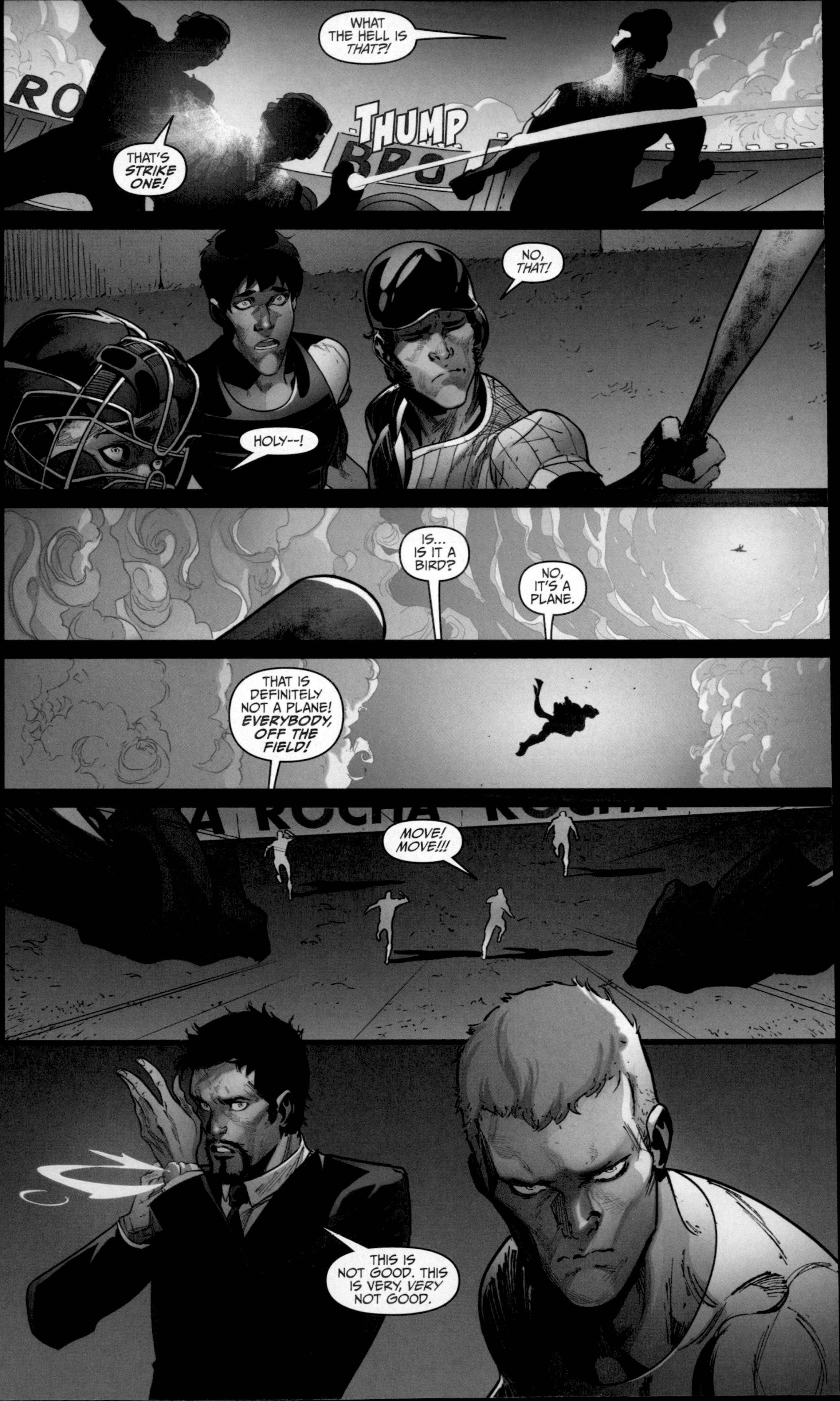

WHAT THE HELL IS THAT?!
THUMP
THAT'S STRIKE ONE!
NO, THAT!
HOLY--!
IS... IS IT A BIRD?
NO, IT'S A PLANE.
THAT IS DEFINITELY NOT A PLANE! EVERYBODY, OFF THE FIELD!
MOVE! MOVE!!!
THIS IS NOT GOOD. THIS IS VERY, VERY NOT GOOD.

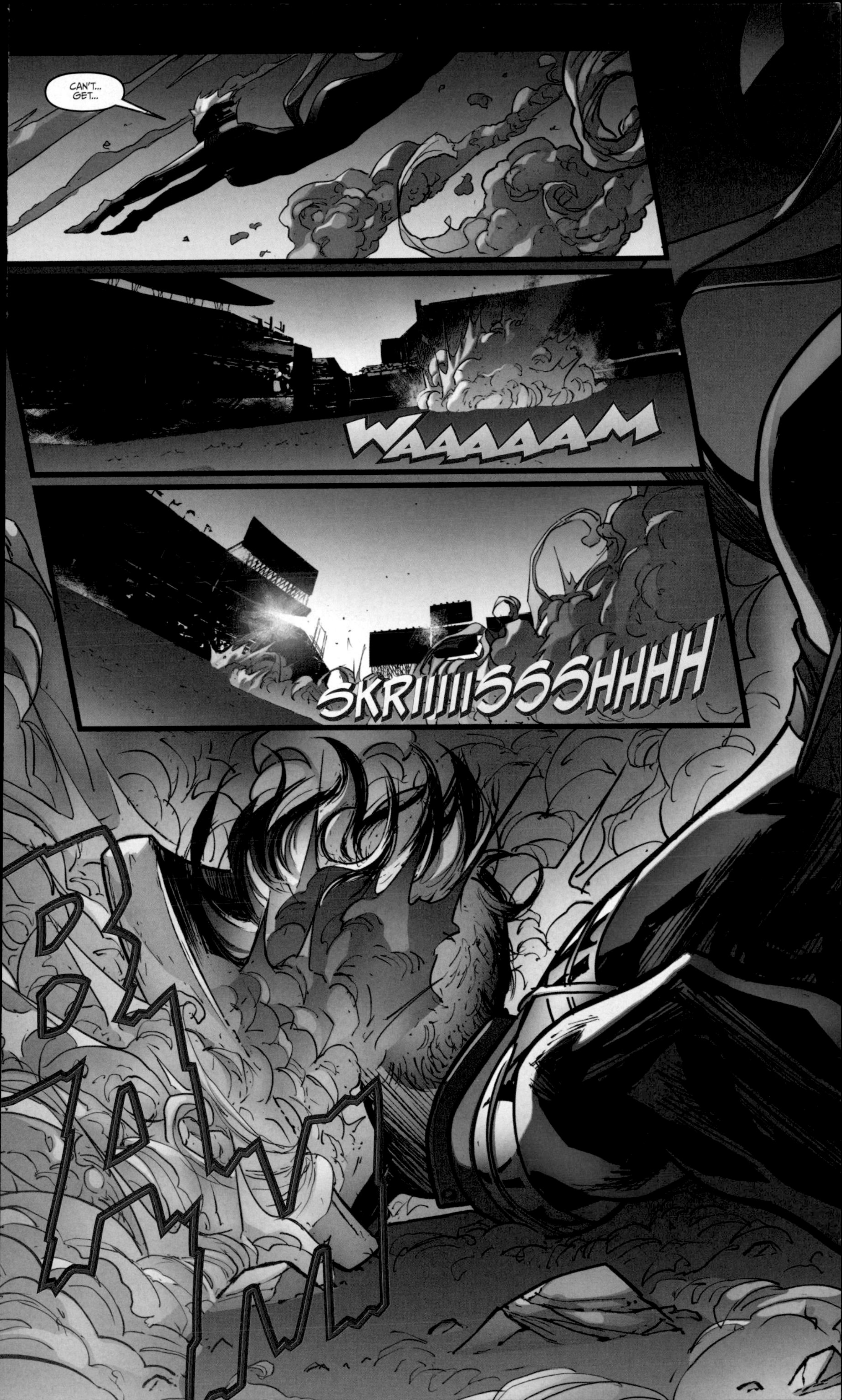
CAN'T... GET...
WAAAAAM
SKRIIIIISSSHHHH
BAM

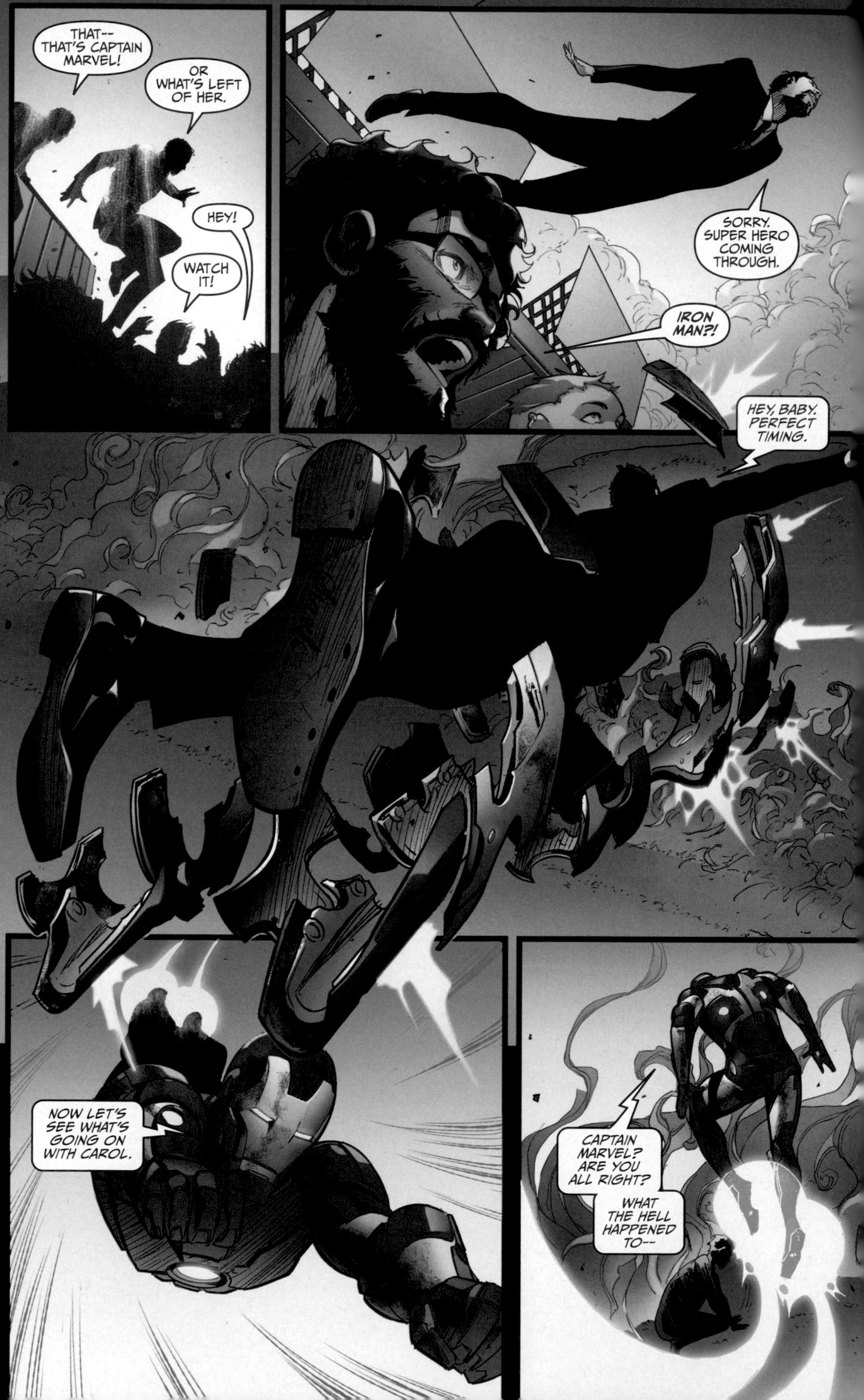
THAT-- THAT'S CAPTAIN MARVEL!
OR WHAT'S LEFT OF HER.
HEY!
WATCH IT!
SORRY. SUPER HERO COMING THROUGH.
IRON MAN?!
HEY, BABY. PERFECT TIMING.
NOW LET'S SEE WHAT'S GOING ON WITH CAROL.
CAPTAIN MARVEL? ARE YOU ALL RIGHT?
WHAT THE HELL HAPPENED TO--

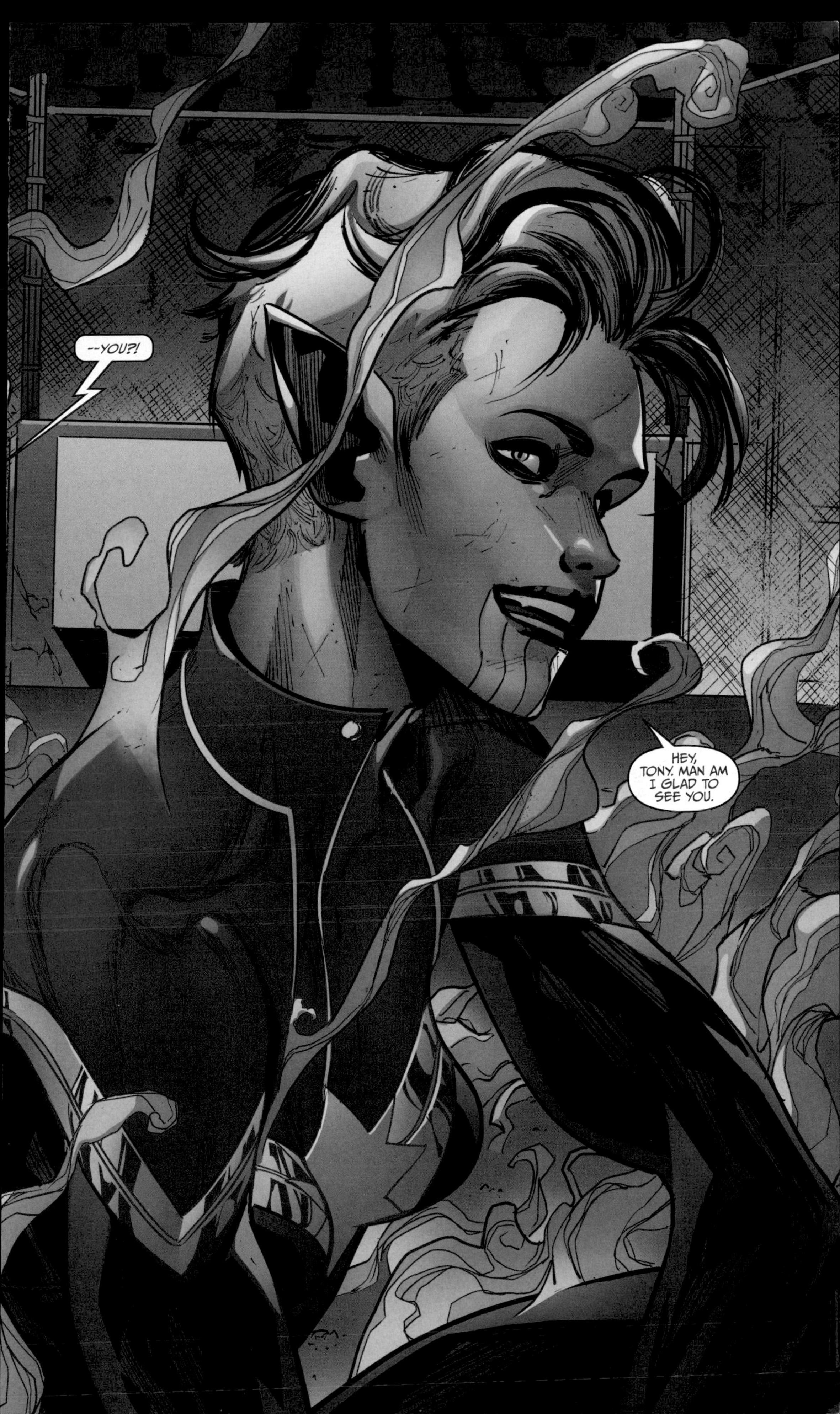
--YOU?!
HEY, TONY. MAN AM I GLAD TO SEE YOU.

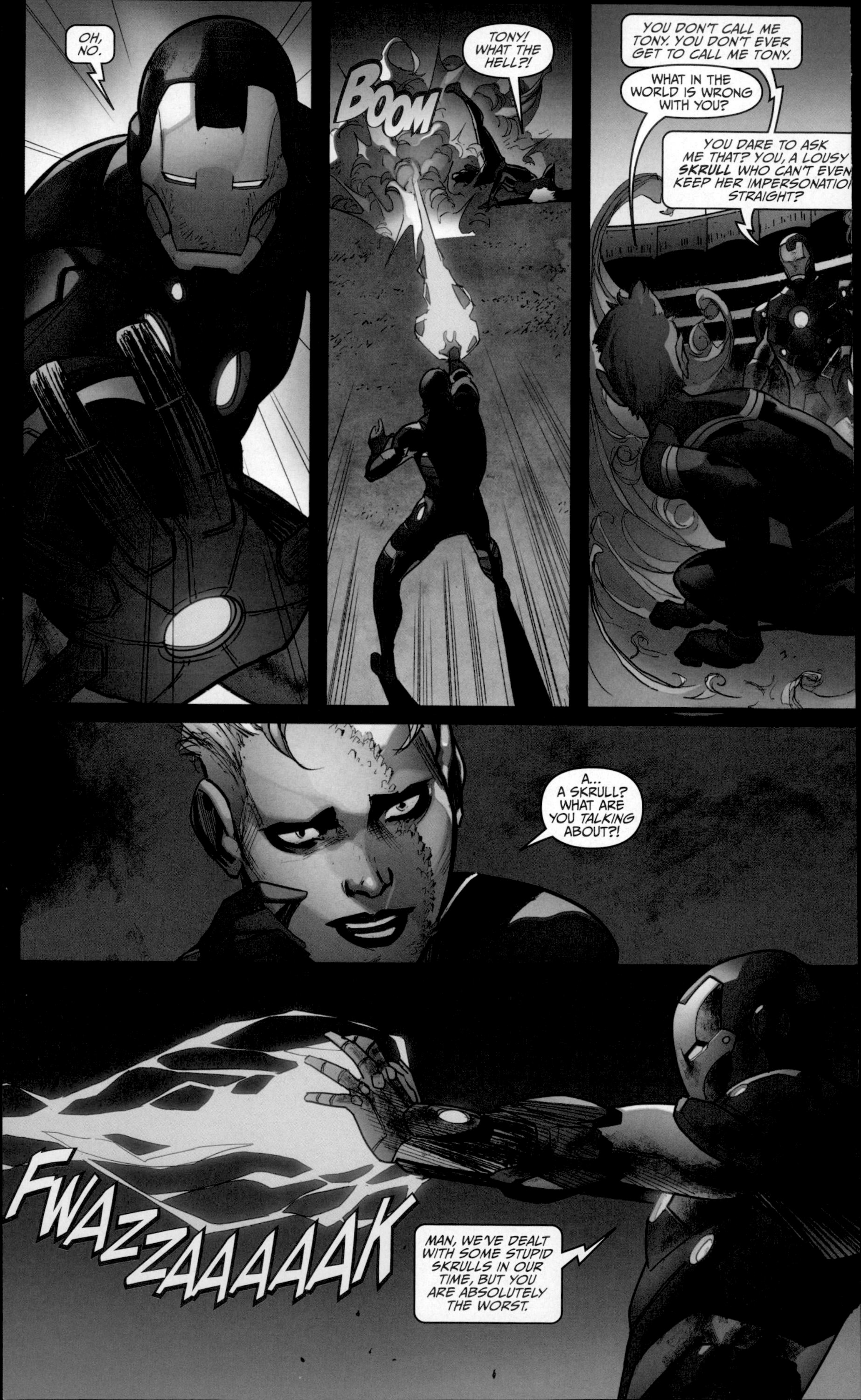
OH, NO.
TONY! WHAT THE HELL?!
BOOM
YOU DON'T CALL ME TONY. YOU DON'T EVER GET TO CALL ME TONY.
WHAT IN THE WORLD IS WRONG WITH YOU?
YOU DARE TO ASK ME THAT? YOU, A LOUSY **SKRULL** WHO CAN'T EVEN KEEP HER IMPERSONATION STRAIGHT?
A... A SKRULL? WHAT ARE YOU *TALKING* ABOUT?!
FWAZZAAAAAAK
MAN, WE'VE DEALT WITH SOME STUPID SKRULLS IN OUR TIME, BUT YOU ARE ABSOLUTELY THE WORST.

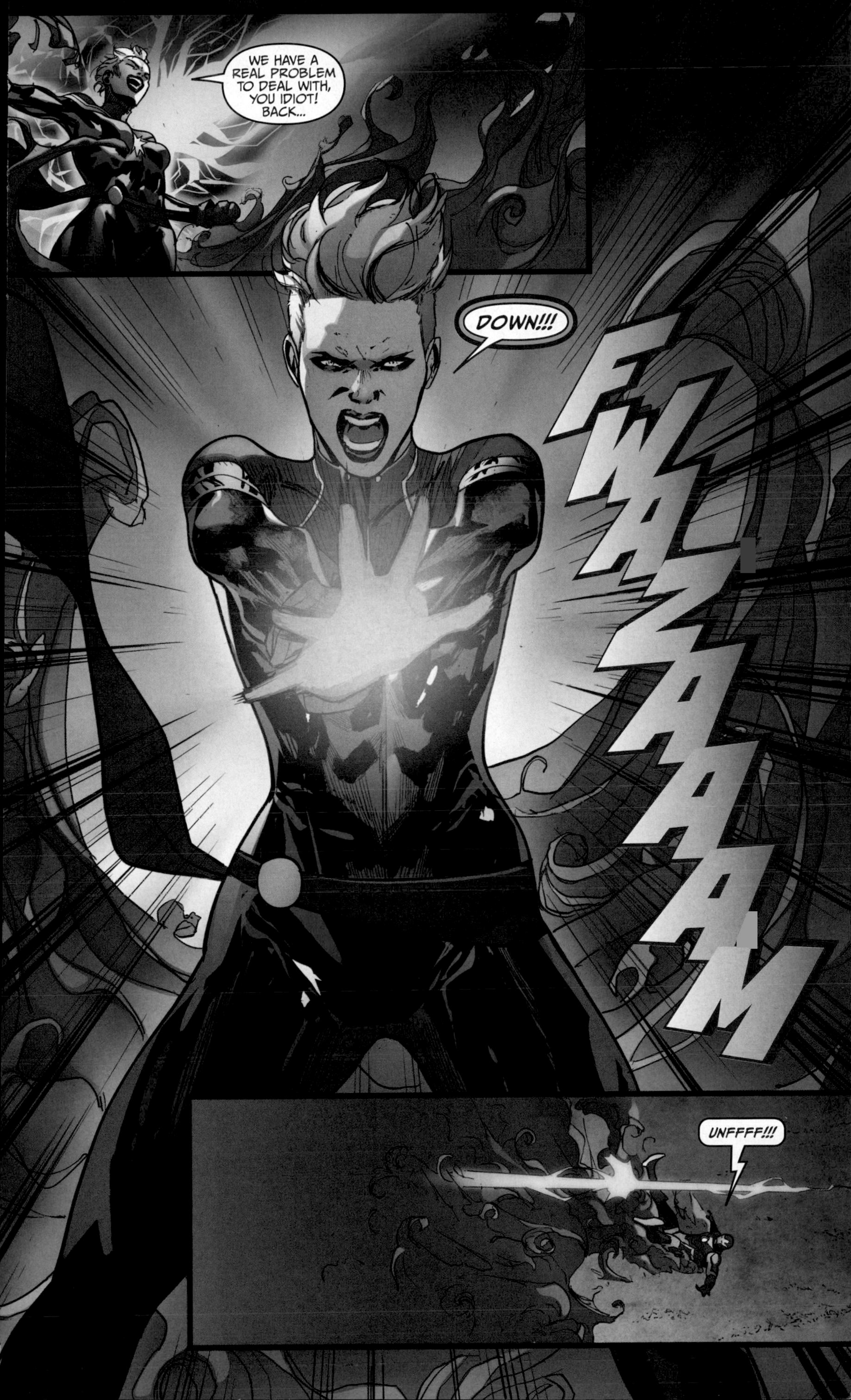
WE HAVE A REAL PROBLEM TO DEAL WITH, YOU IDIOT! BACK...
DOWN!!!
FWAZAAAM
UNFFFF!!!

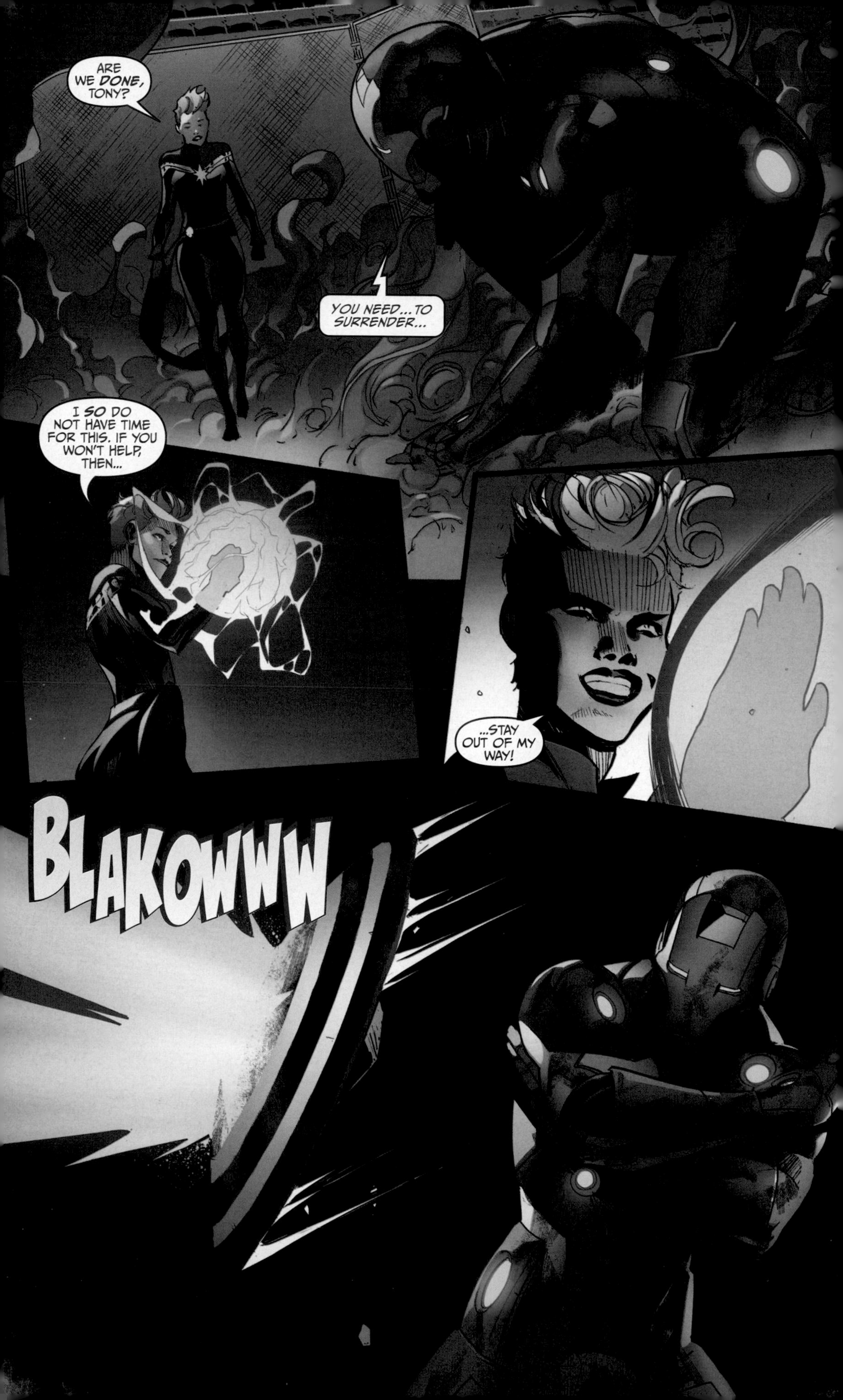
ARE WE DONE, TONY?
YOU NEED...TO SURRENDER...
I SO DO NOT HAVE TIME FOR THIS. IF YOU WON'T HELP, THEN...
...STAY OUT OF MY WAY!
BLAKOWWW

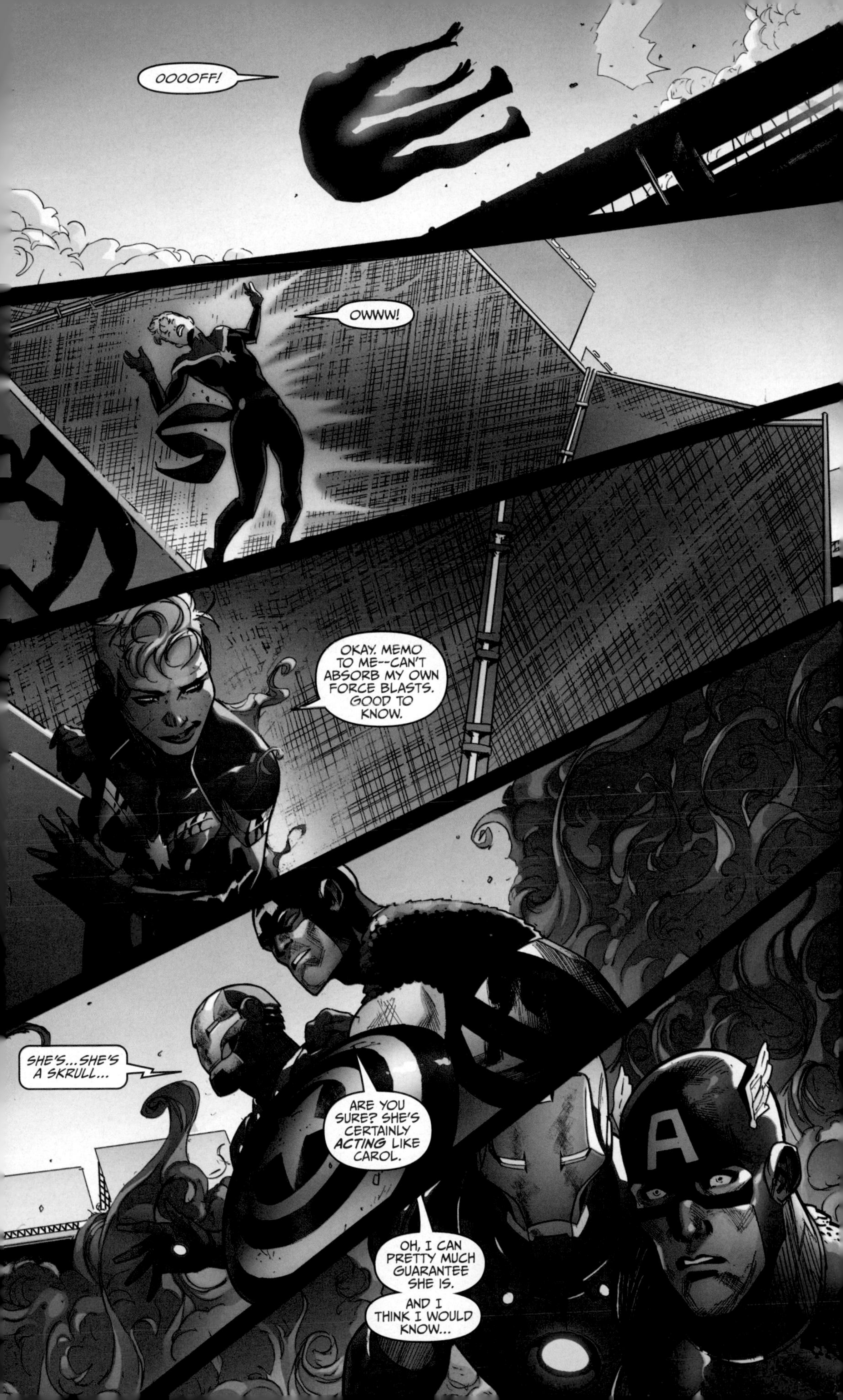
OOOOFF!
OWWW!
OKAY. MEMO TO ME--CAN'T ABSORB MY OWN FORCE BLASTS. GOOD TO KNOW.
SHE'S...SHE'S A SKRULL...
ARE YOU SURE? SHE'S CERTAINLY ACTING LIKE CAROL.
OH, I CAN PRETTY MUCH GUARANTEE SHE IS.
AND I THINK I WOULD KNOW...

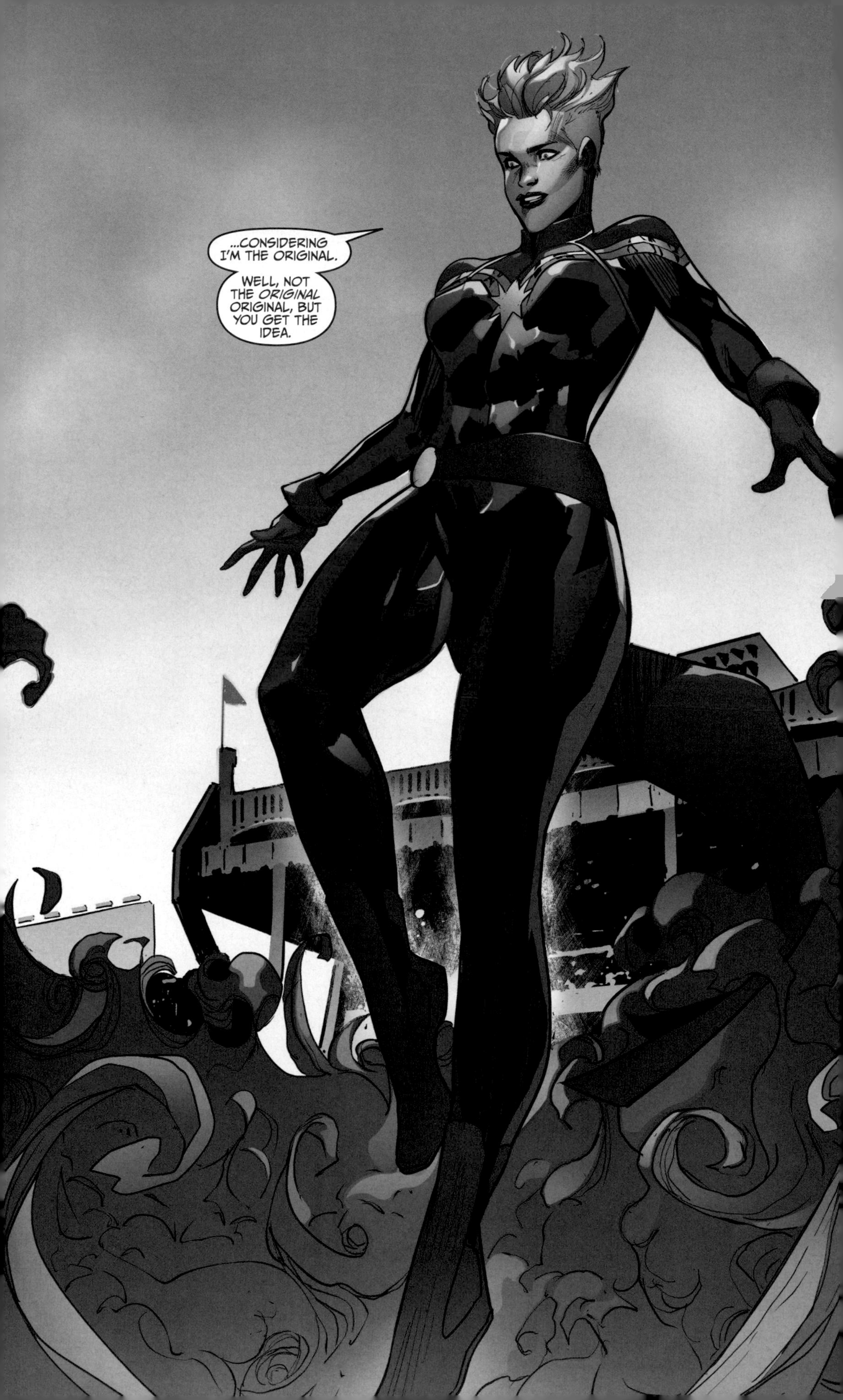
...CONSIDERING I'M THE ORIGINAL.
WELL, NOT THE *ORIGINAL* ORIGINAL, BUT YOU GET THE IDEA.

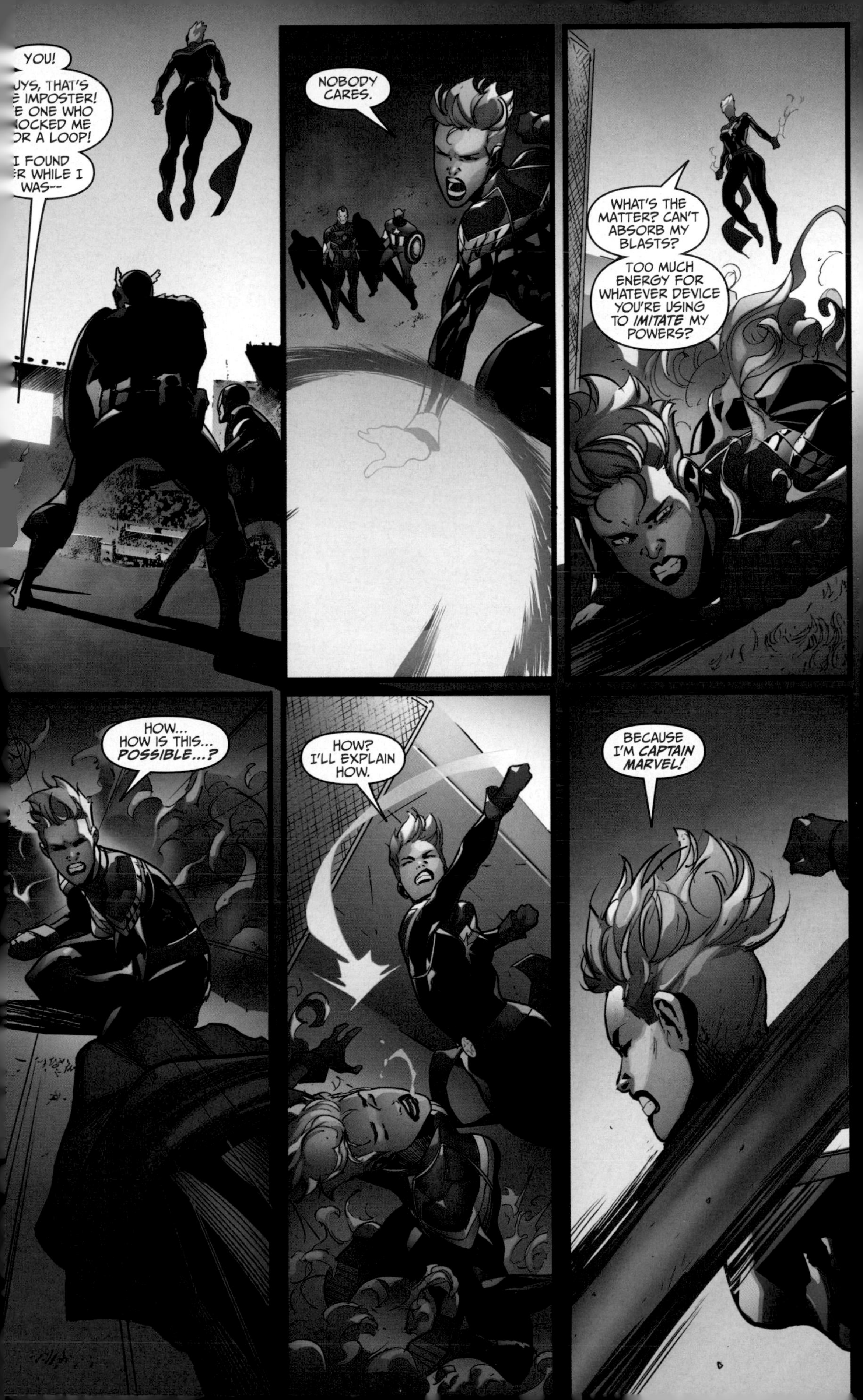
YOU!
UYS, THAT'S
E IMPOSTER!
E ONE WHO
NOCKED ME
OR A LOOP!
I FOUND
ER WHILE I
WAS--
NOBODY CARES.
WHAT'S THE MATTER? CAN'T ABSORB MY BLASTS?
TOO MUCH ENERGY FOR WHATEVER DEVICE YOU'RE USING TO IMITATE MY POWERS?
HOW... HOW IS THIS... POSSIBLE...?
HOW? I'LL EXPLAIN HOW.
BECAUSE I'M CAPTAIN MARVEL!

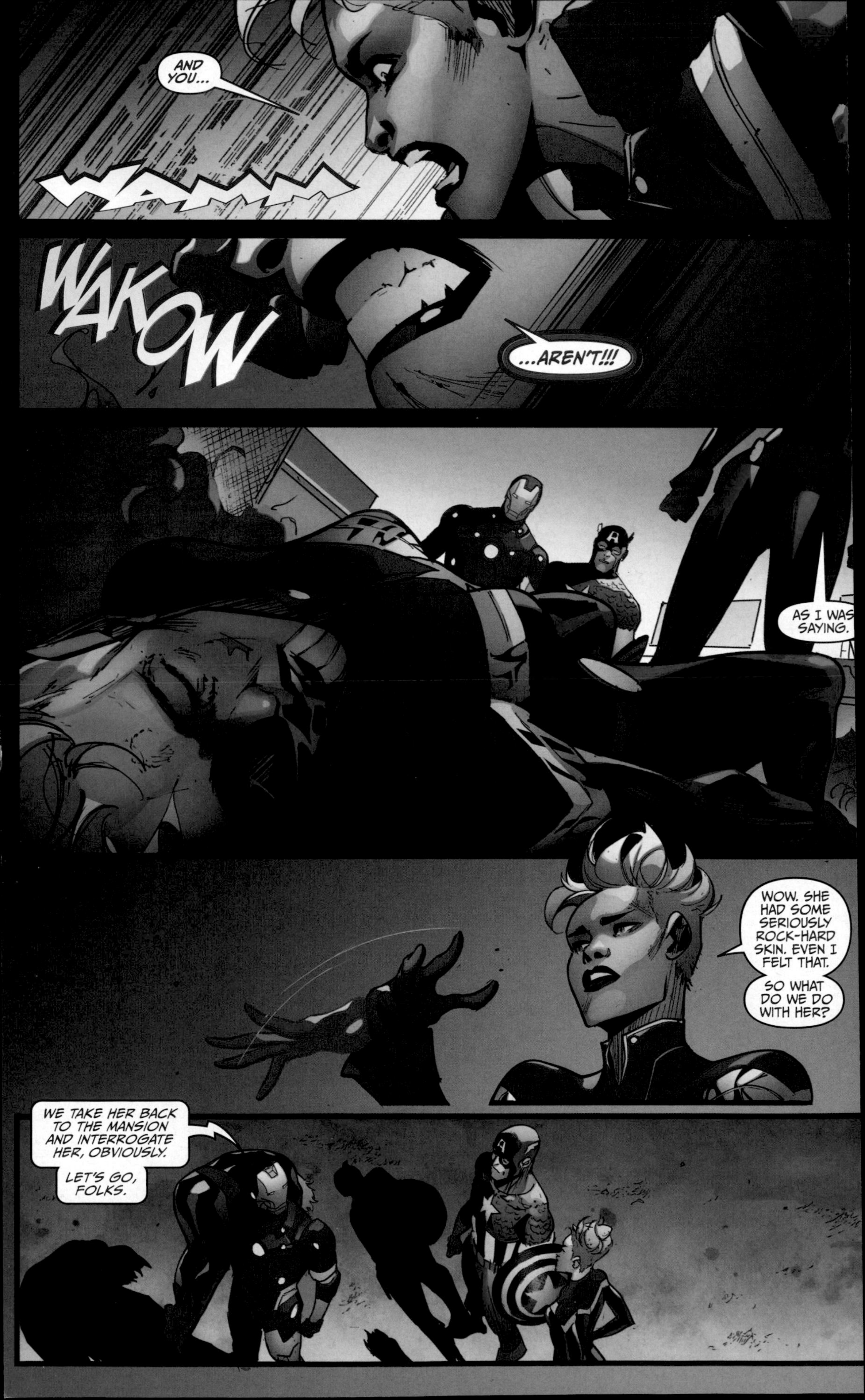
AND YOU...
WAMM
WAKOW
...AREN'T!!!
AS I WAS SAYING.
WOW. SHE HAD SOME SERIOUSLY ROCK-HARD SKIN. EVEN I FELT THAT.
SO WHAT DO WE DO WITH HER?
WE TAKE HER BACK TO THE MANSION AND INTERROGATE HER, OBVIOUSLY.
LET'S GO, FOLKS.

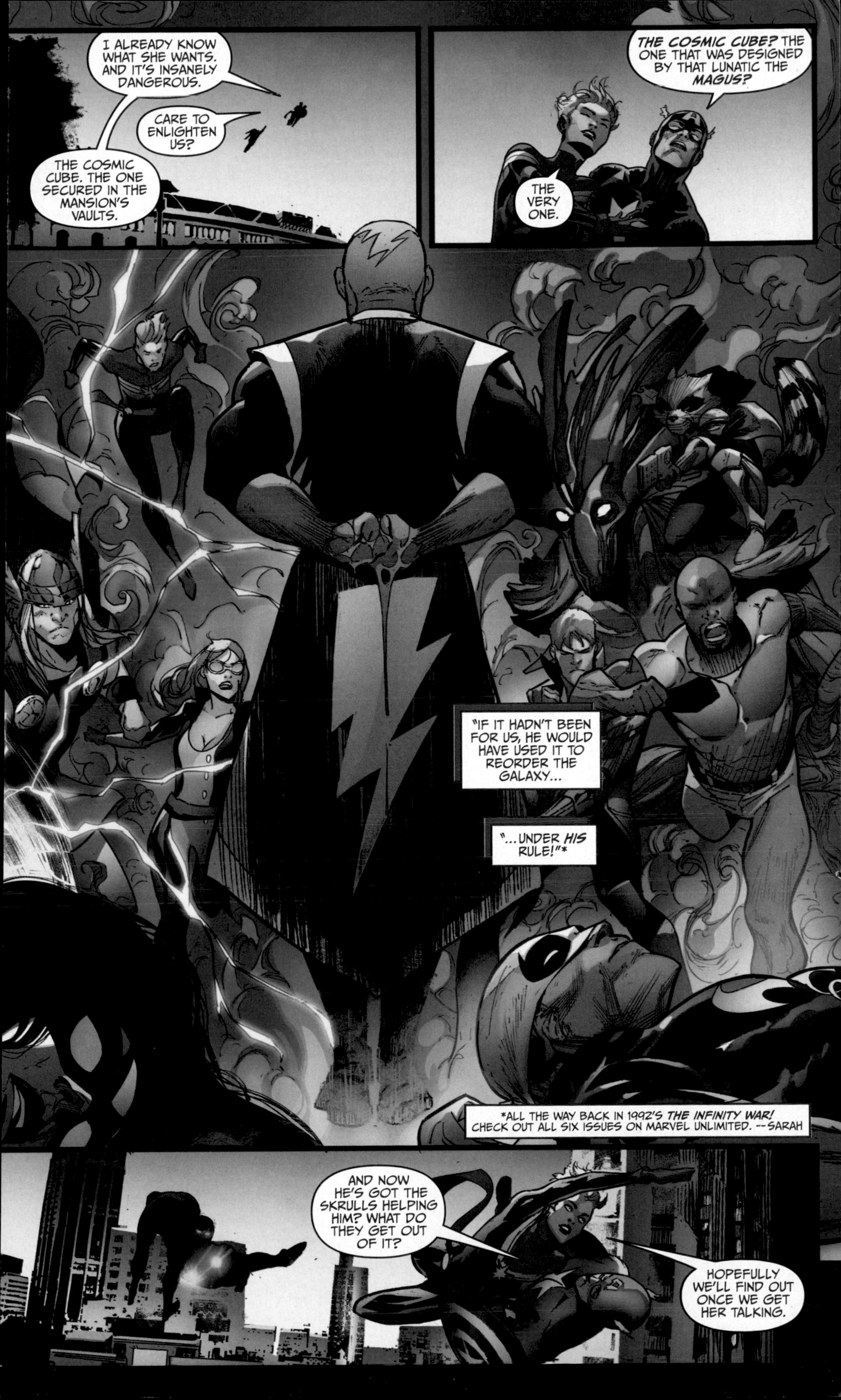

I ALREADY KNOW WHAT SHE WANTS. AND IT'S INSANELY DANGEROUS.
CARE TO ENLIGHTEN US?
THE COSMIC CUBE. THE ONE SECURED IN THE MANSION'S VAULTS.
THE COSMIC CUBE? THE ONE THAT WAS DESIGNED BY THAT LUNATIC THE MAGUS?
THE VERY ONE.
"IF IT HADN'T BEEN FOR US, HE WOULD HAVE USED IT TO REORDER THE GALAXY...
"...UNDER HIS RULE!"*
*ALL THE WAY BACK IN 1992'S THE INFINITY WAR! CHECK OUT ALL SIX ISSUES ON MARVEL UNLIMITED. --SARAH
AND NOW HE'S GOT THE SKRULLS HELPING HIM? WHAT DO THEY GET OUT OF IT?
HOPEFULLY WE'LL FIND OUT ONCE WE GET HER TALKING.

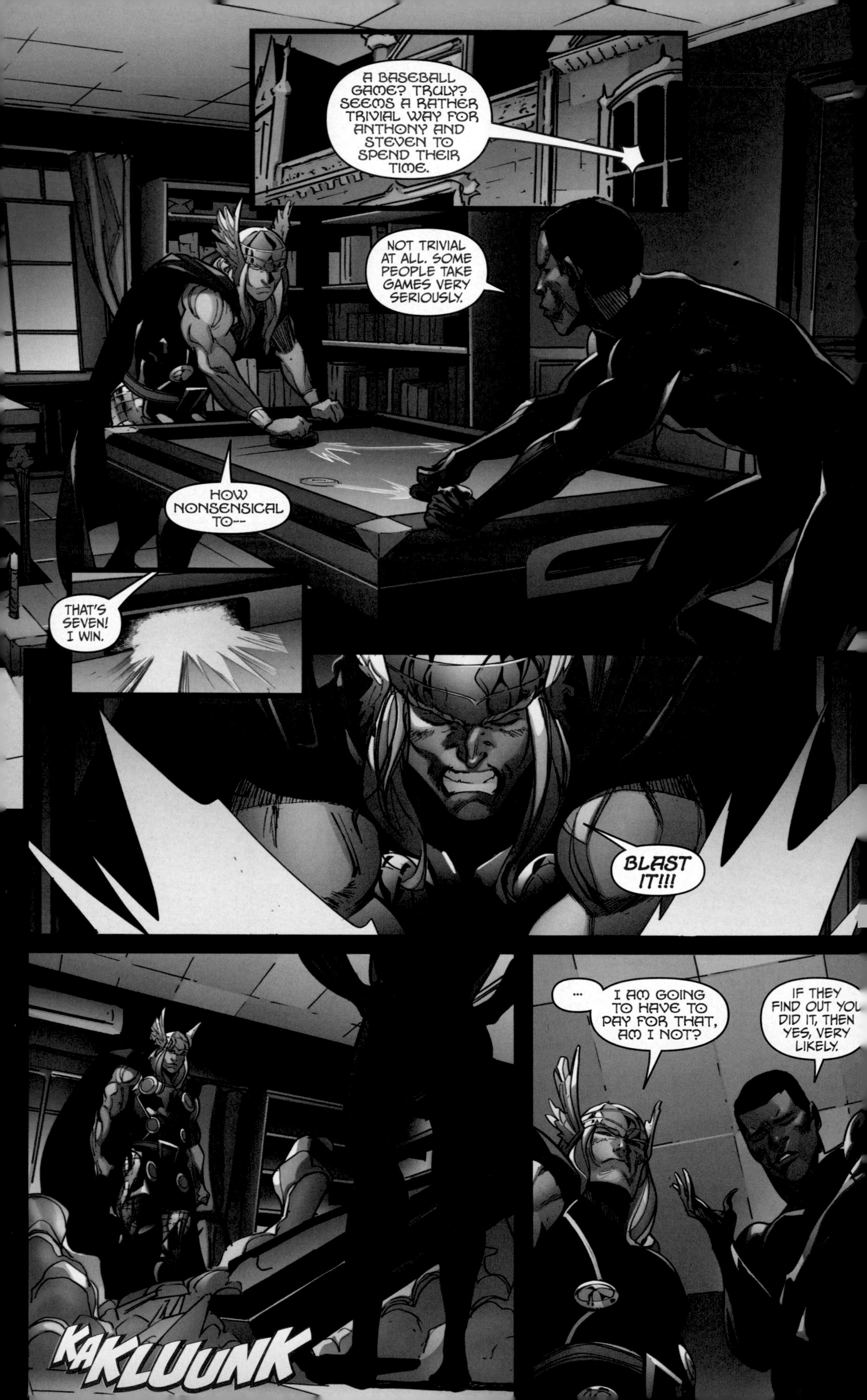
A BASEBALL GAME? TRULY? SEEMS A RATHER TRIVIAL WAY FOR ANTHONY AND STEVEN TO SPEND THEIR TIME.
NOT TRIVIAL AT ALL. SOME PEOPLE TAKE GAMES VERY SERIOUSLY.
HOW NONSENSICAL TO--
THAT'S SEVEN! I WIN.
BLAST IT!!!
KAKLUUNK
...
I AM GOING TO HAVE TO PAY FOR THAT, AM I NOT?
IF THEY FIND OUT YOU DID IT, THEN YES, VERY LIKELY.

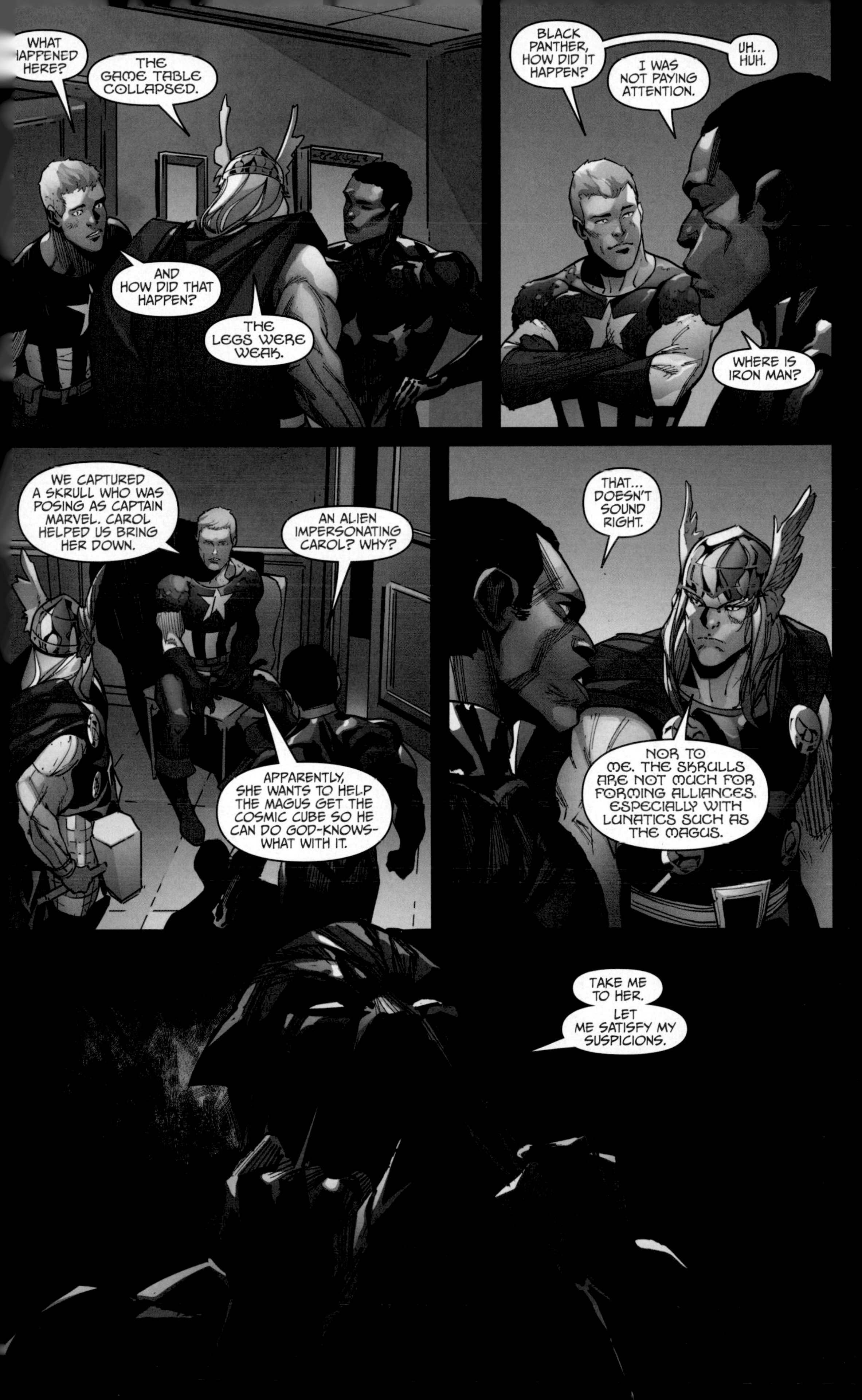
WHAT HAPPENED HERE?
THE GAME TABLE COLLAPSED.
AND HOW DID THAT HAPPEN?
THE LEGS WERE WEAK.
BLACK PANTHER, HOW DID IT HAPPEN?
I WAS NOT PAYING ATTENTION.
UH... HUH.
WHERE IS IRON MAN?
WE CAPTURED A SKRULL WHO WAS POSING AS CAPTAIN MARVEL. CAROL HELPED US BRING HER DOWN.
AN ALIEN IMPERSONATING CAROL? WHY?
APPARENTLY, SHE WANTS TO HELP THE MAGUS GET THE COSMIC CUBE SO HE CAN DO GOD-KNOWS-WHAT WITH IT.
THAT... DOESN'T SOUND RIGHT.
NOR TO ME. THE SKRULLS ARE NOT MUCH FOR FORMING ALLIANCES. ESPECIALLY WITH LUNATICS SUCH AS THE MAGUS.
TAKE ME TO HER.
LET ME SATISFY MY SUSPICIONS.

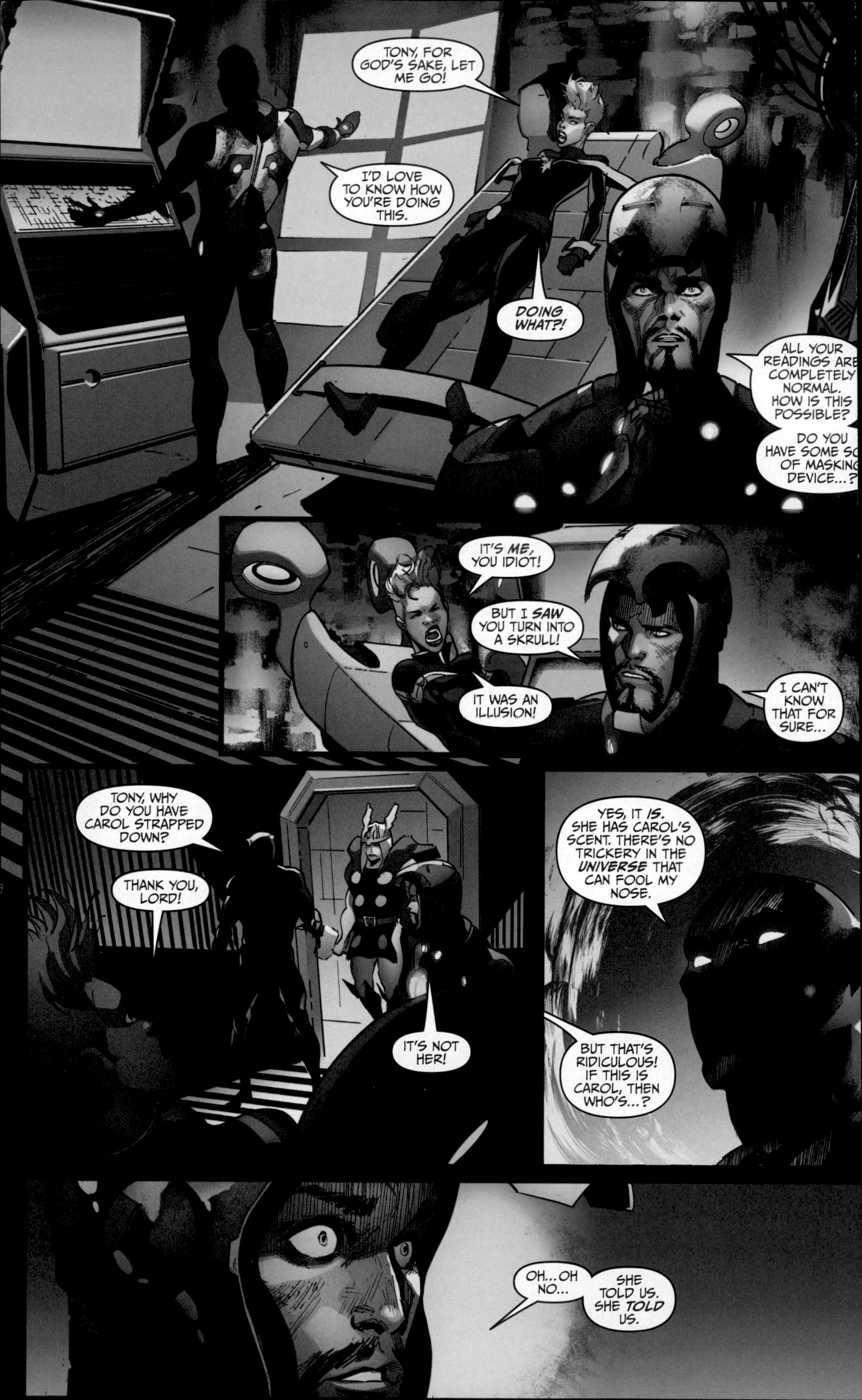
TONY, FOR GOD'S SAKE, LET ME GO!
I'D LOVE TO KNOW HOW YOU'RE DOING THIS.
DOING WHAT?!
ALL YOUR READINGS ARE COMPLETELY NORMAL. HOW IS THIS POSSIBLE?
DO YOU HAVE SOME SO OF MASKING DEVICE...?
IT'S *ME*, YOU IDIOT!
BUT I *SAW* YOU TURN INTO A SKRULL!
IT WAS AN ILLUSION!
I CAN'T KNOW THAT FOR SURE...
TONY, WHY DO YOU HAVE CAROL STRAPPED DOWN?
THANK YOU, LORD!
IT'S NOT HER!
YES, IT *IS.* SHE HAS CAROL'S SCENT. THERE'S NO TRICKERY IN THE ***UNIVERSE*** THAT CAN FOOL MY NOSE.
BUT THAT'S RIDICULOUS! IF THIS IS CAROL, THEN WHO'S...?
OH...OH NO...
SHE TOLD US. SHE *TOLD* US.

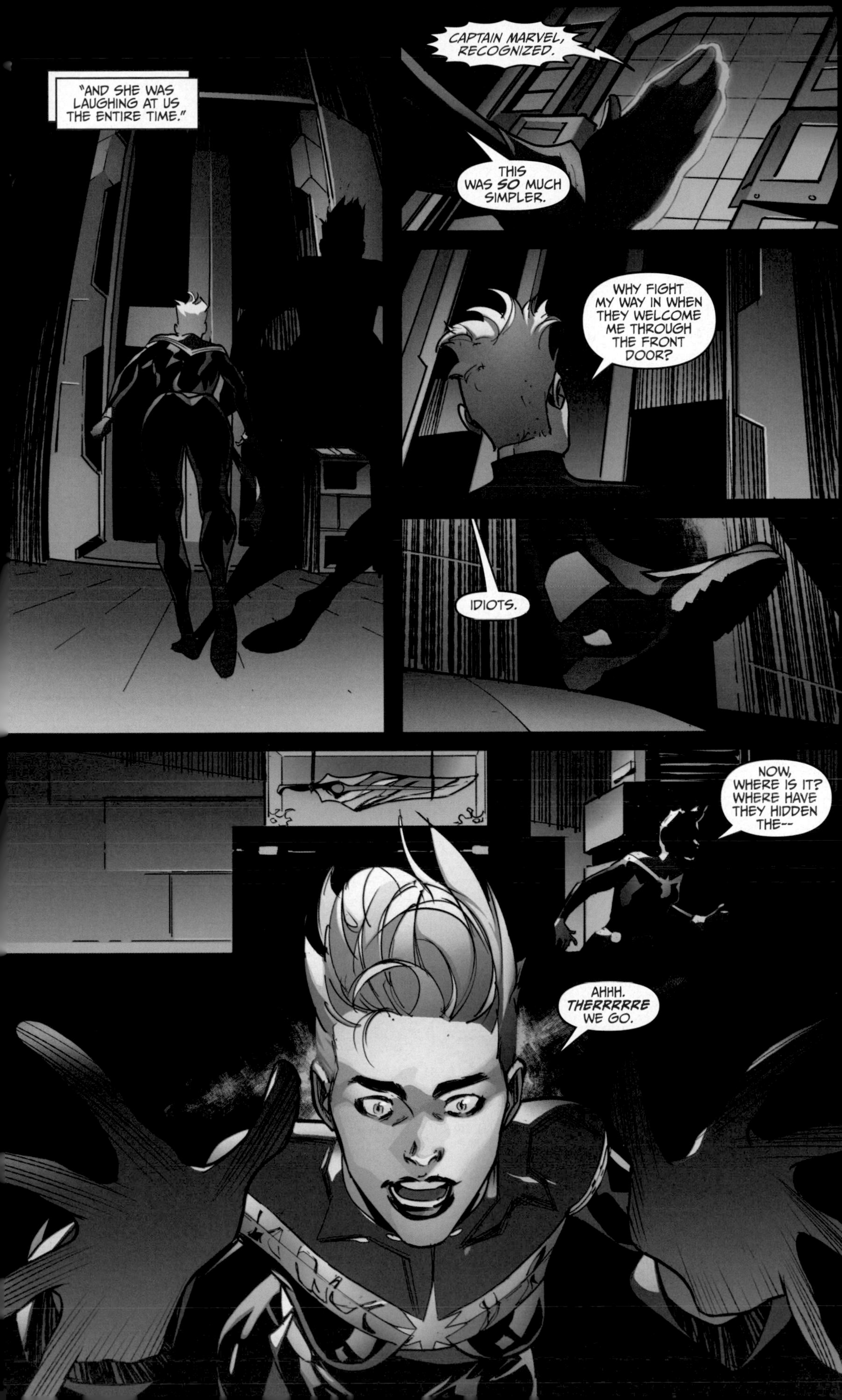

"AND SHE WAS LAUGHING AT US THE ENTIRE TIME."
CAPTAIN MARVEL, RECOGNIZED.
THIS WAS SO MUCH SIMPLER.
WHY FIGHT MY WAY IN WHEN THEY WELCOME ME THROUGH THE FRONT DOOR?
IDIOTS.
NOW, WHERE IS IT? WHERE HAVE THEY HIDDEN THE--
AHHH. THERRRRRE WE GO.

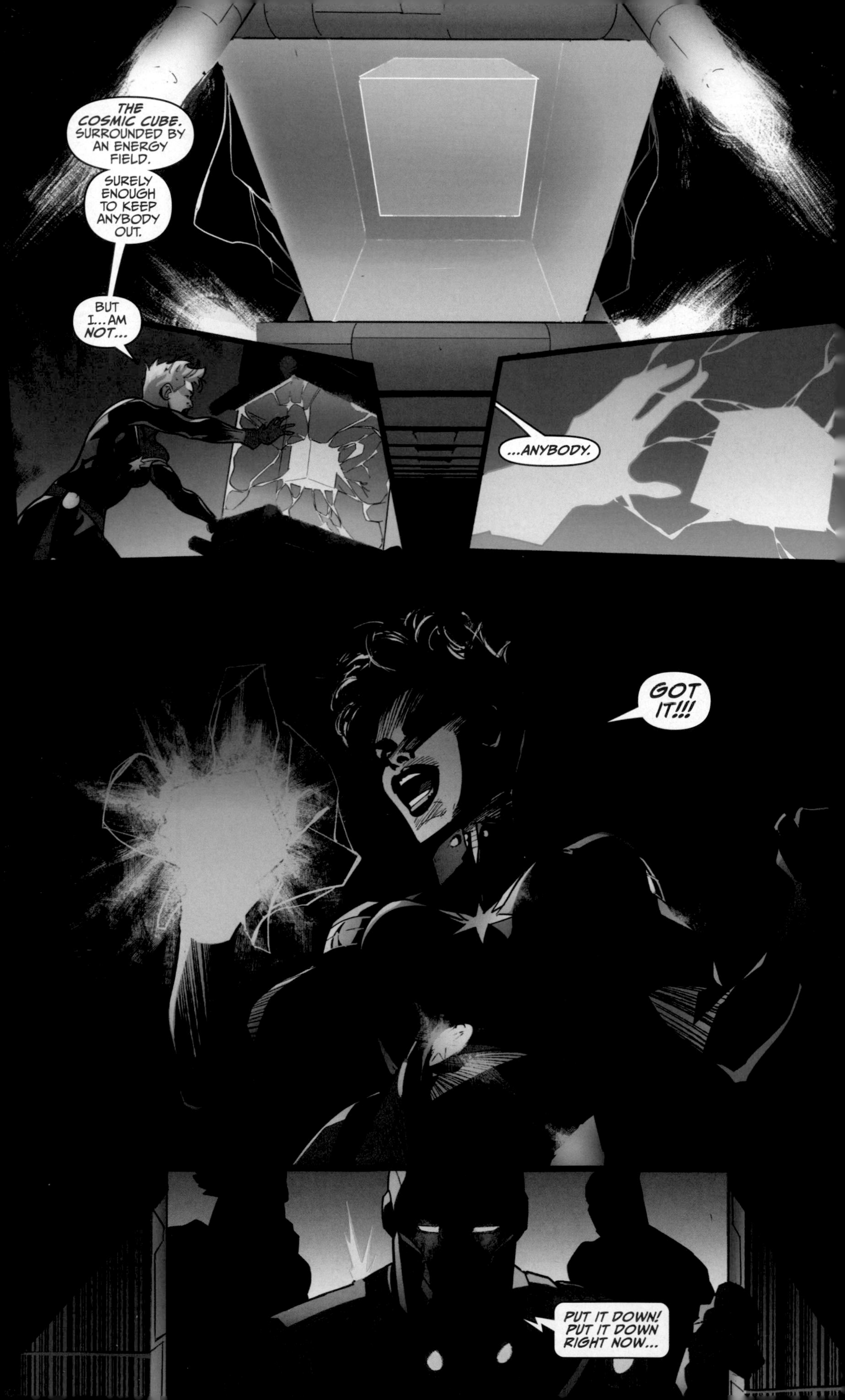
THE COSMIC CUBE. SURROUNDED BY AN ENERGY FIELD.
SURELY ENOUGH TO KEEP ANYBODY OUT.
BUT I...AM NOT...
...ANYBODY.
GOT IT!!!
PUT IT DOWN! PUT IT DOWN RIGHT NOW...

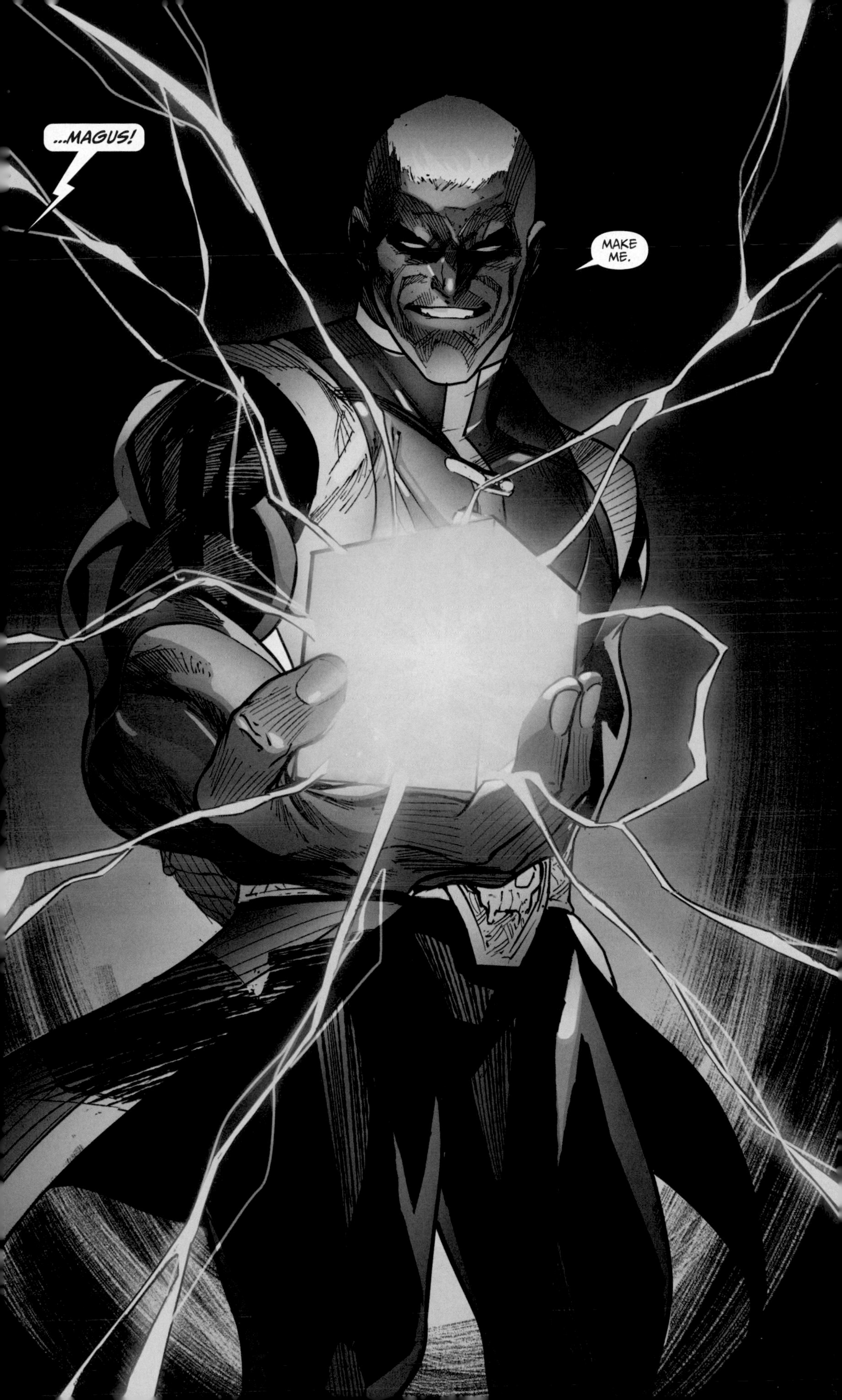
...MAGUS!
MAKE ME.

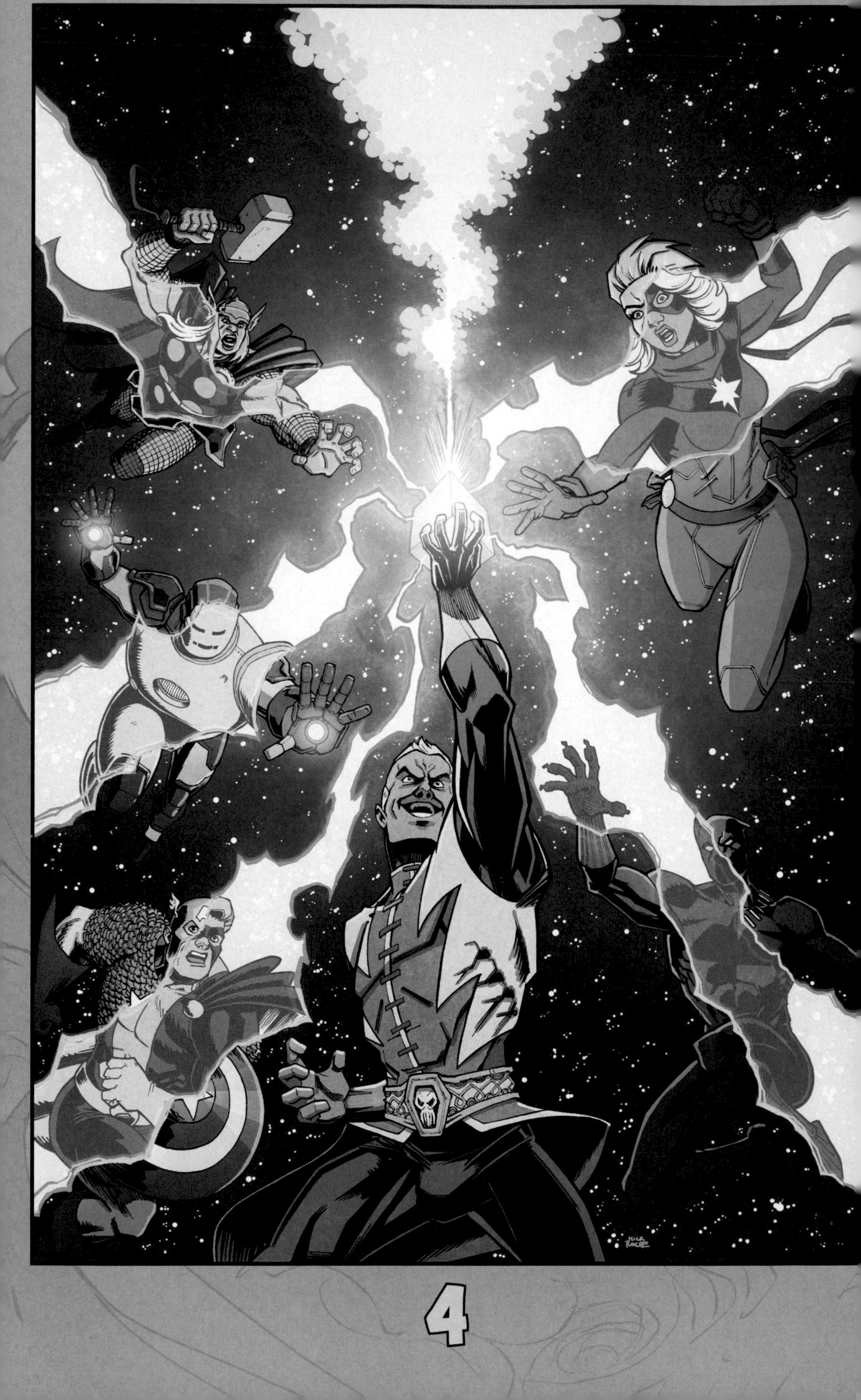

4

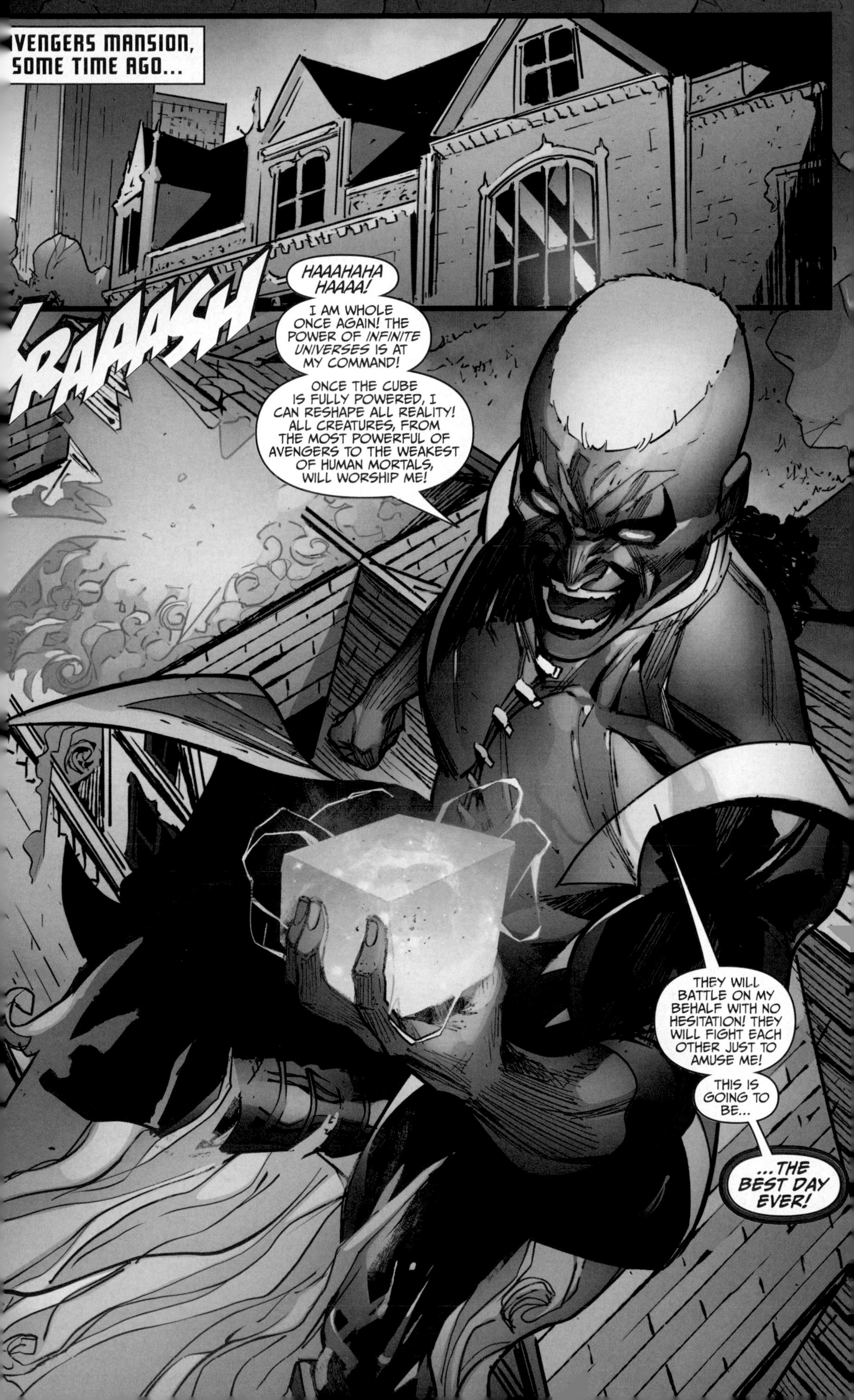

AVENGERS MANSION, SOME TIME AGO...
KRAAASH
HAAAHAHA HAAAA!
I AM WHOLE ONCE AGAIN! THE POWER OF INFINITE UNIVERSES IS AT MY COMMAND!
ONCE THE CUBE IS FULLY POWERED, I CAN RESHAPE ALL REALITY! ALL CREATURES, FROM THE MOST POWERFUL OF AVENGERS TO THE WEAKEST OF HUMAN MORTALS, WILL WORSHIP ME!
THEY WILL BATTLE ON MY BEHALF WITH NO HESITATION! THEY WILL FIGHT EACH OTHER JUST TO AMUSE ME!
THIS IS GOING TO BE...
...THE BEST DAY EVER!

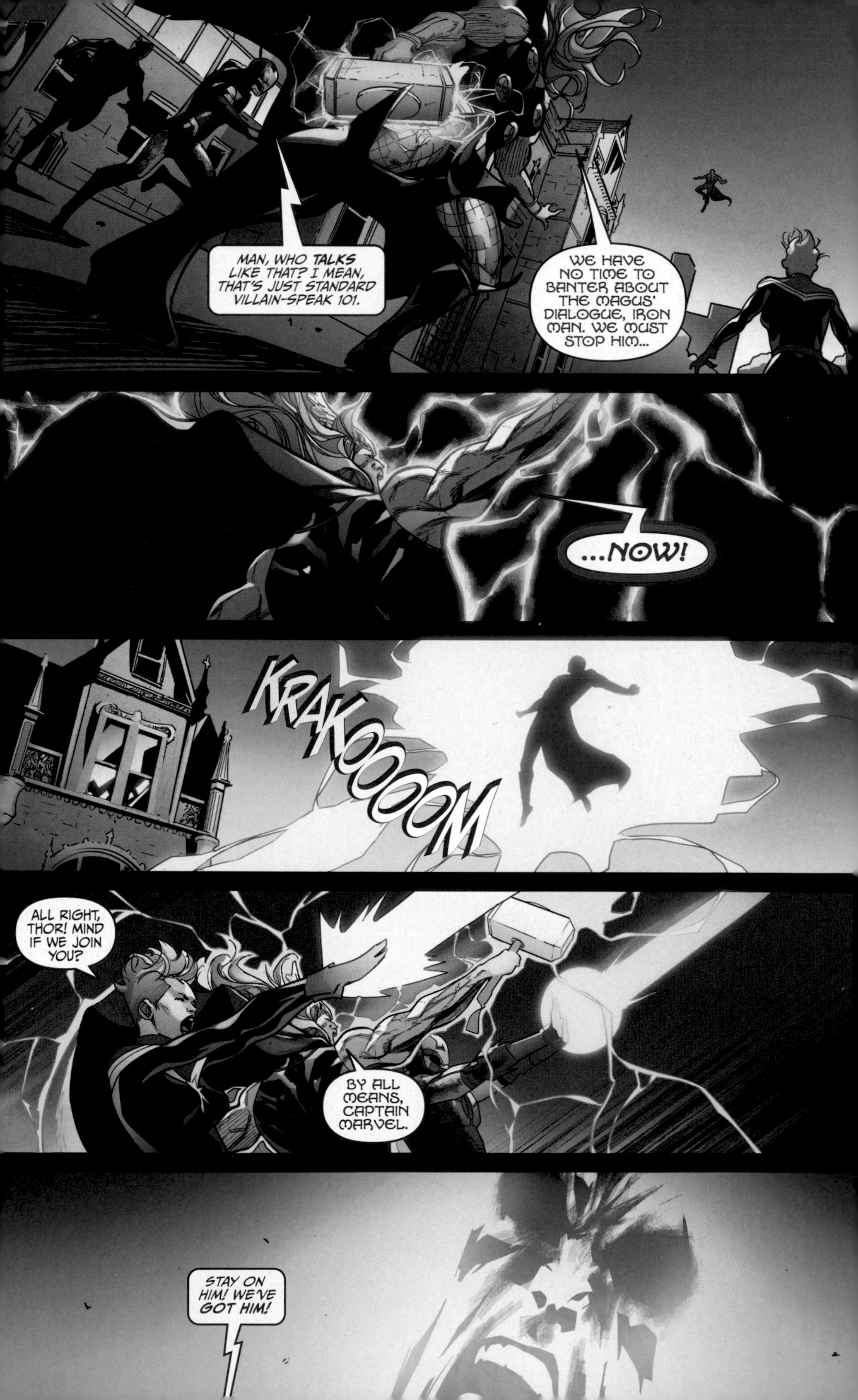
MAN, WHO TALKS LIKE THAT? I MEAN, THAT'S JUST STANDARD VILLAIN-SPEAK 101.
WE HAVE NO TIME TO BANTER ABOUT THE MAGUS' DIALOGUE, IRON MAN. WE MUST STOP HIM...
...NOW!
KRAKOOOOM
ALL RIGHT, THOR! MIND IF WE JOIN YOU?
BY ALL MEANS, CAPTAIN MARVEL.
STAY ON HIM! WE'VE GOT HIM!

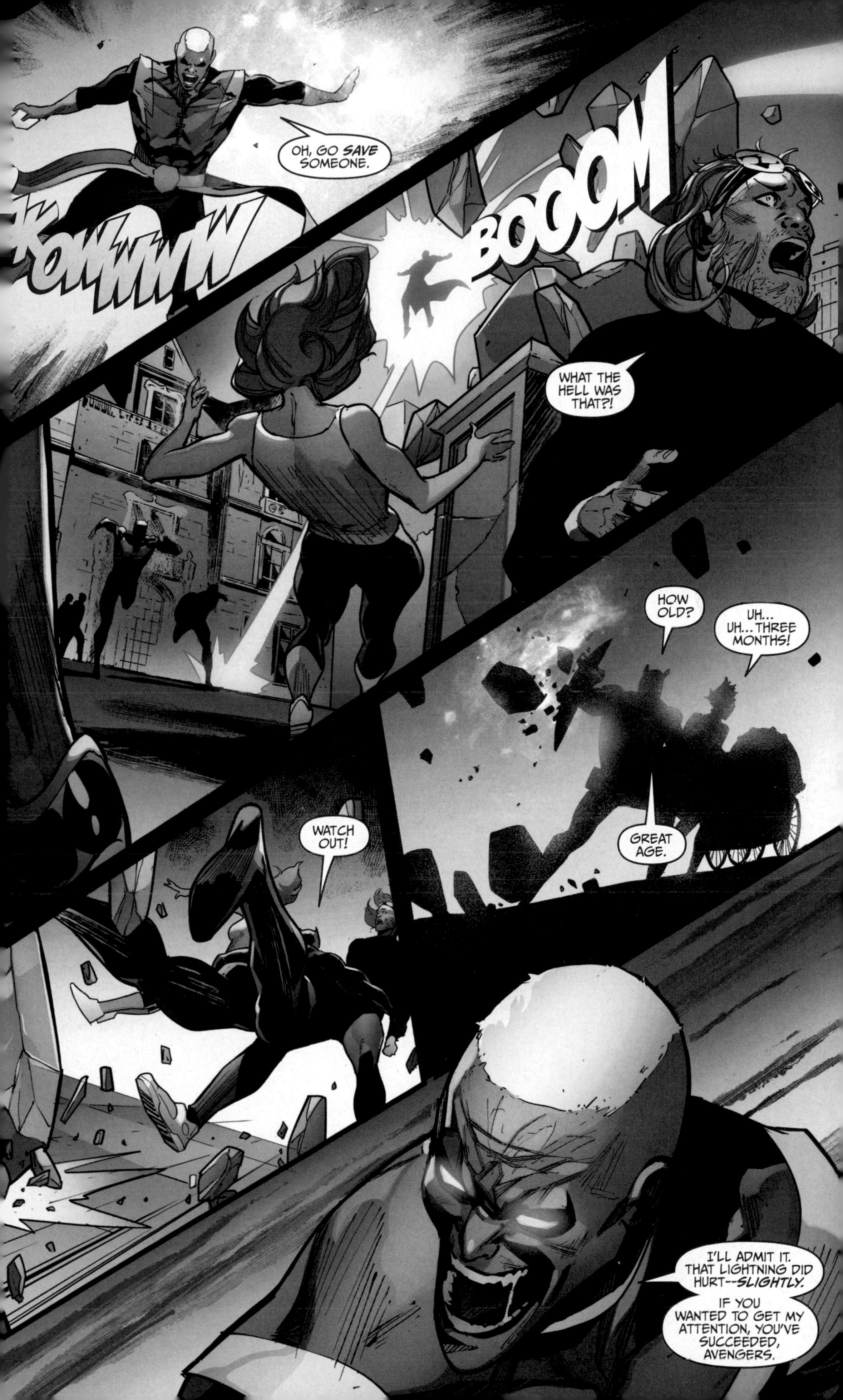
OH, GO SAVE SOMEONE.
KOWWW
BOOOM
WHAT THE HELL WAS THAT?!
HOW OLD?
UH... UH... THREE MONTHS!
GREAT AGE.
WATCH OUT!
I'LL ADMIT IT. THAT LIGHTNING DID HURT--SLIGHTLY.
IF YOU WANTED TO GET MY ATTENTION, YOU'VE SUCCEEDED, AVENGERS.

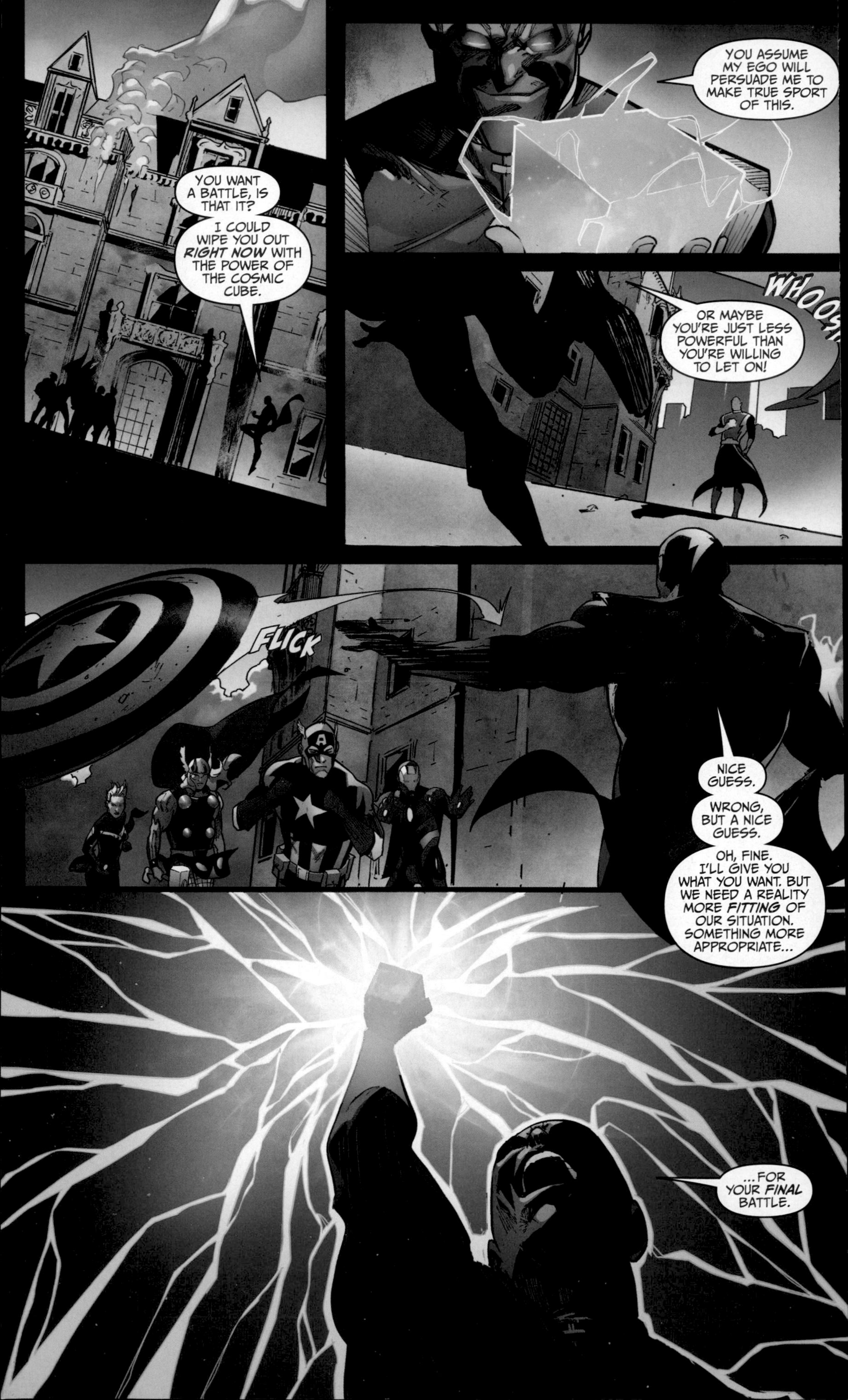

YOU WANT A BATTLE, IS THAT IT?
I COULD WIPE YOU OUT *RIGHT NOW* WITH THE POWER OF THE COSMIC CUBE.
YOU ASSUME MY EGO WILL PERSUADE ME TO MAKE TRUE SPORT OF THIS.
WHOOSH
OR MAYBE YOU'RE JUST LESS POWERFUL THAN YOU'RE WILLING TO LET ON!
FLICK
NICE GUESS.
WRONG, BUT A NICE GUESS.
OH, FINE. I'LL GIVE YOU WHAT YOU WANT. BUT WE NEED A REALITY MORE *FITTING* OF OUR SITUATION. SOMETHING MORE APPROPRIATE...
...FOR YOUR *FINAL* BATTLE.

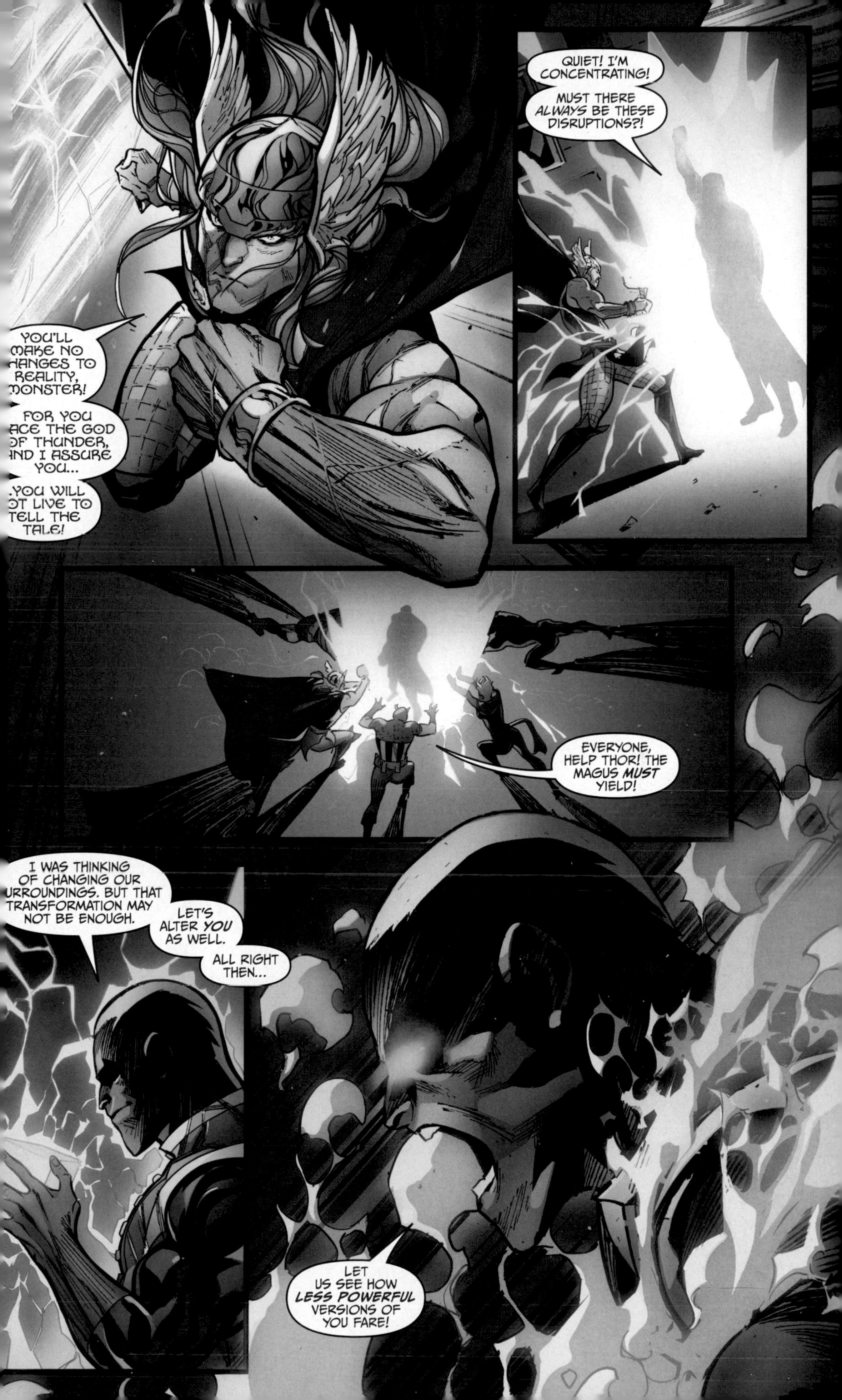
YOU'LL MAKE NO HANGES TO REALITY, MONSTER!
FOR YOU ACE THE GOD OF THUNDER, ND I ASSURE YOU...
.YOU WILL OT LIVE TO TELL THE TALE!
QUIET! I'M CONCENTRATING!
MUST THERE ALWAYS BE THESE DISRUPTIONS?!
EVERYONE, HELP THOR! THE MAGUS MUST YIELD!
I WAS THINKING OF CHANGING OUR URROUNDINGS. BUT THAT TRANSFORMATION MAY NOT BE ENOUGH.
LET'S ALTER YOU AS WELL.
ALL RIGHT THEN...
LET US SEE HOW LESS POWERFUL VERSIONS OF YOU FARE!

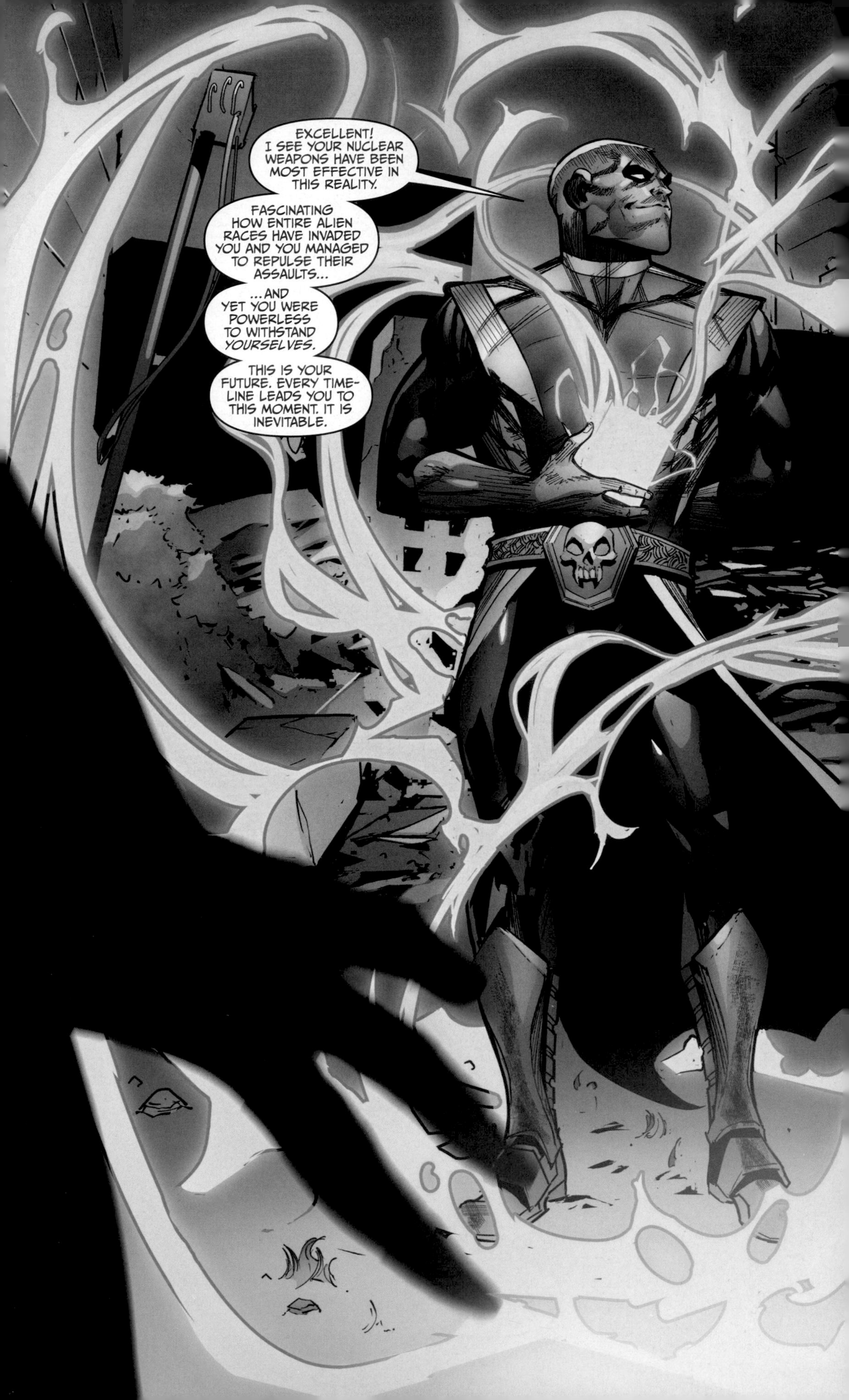

EXCELLENT! I SEE YOUR NUCLEAR WEAPONS HAVE BEEN MOST EFFECTIVE IN THIS REALITY.
FASCINATING HOW ENTIRE ALIEN RACES HAVE INVADED YOU AND YOU MANAGED TO REPULSE THEIR ASSAULTS...
...AND YET YOU WERE POWERLESS TO WITHSTAND *YOURSELVES*.
THIS IS YOUR FUTURE. EVERY TIME-LINE LEADS YOU TO THIS MOMENT. IT IS INEVITABLE.

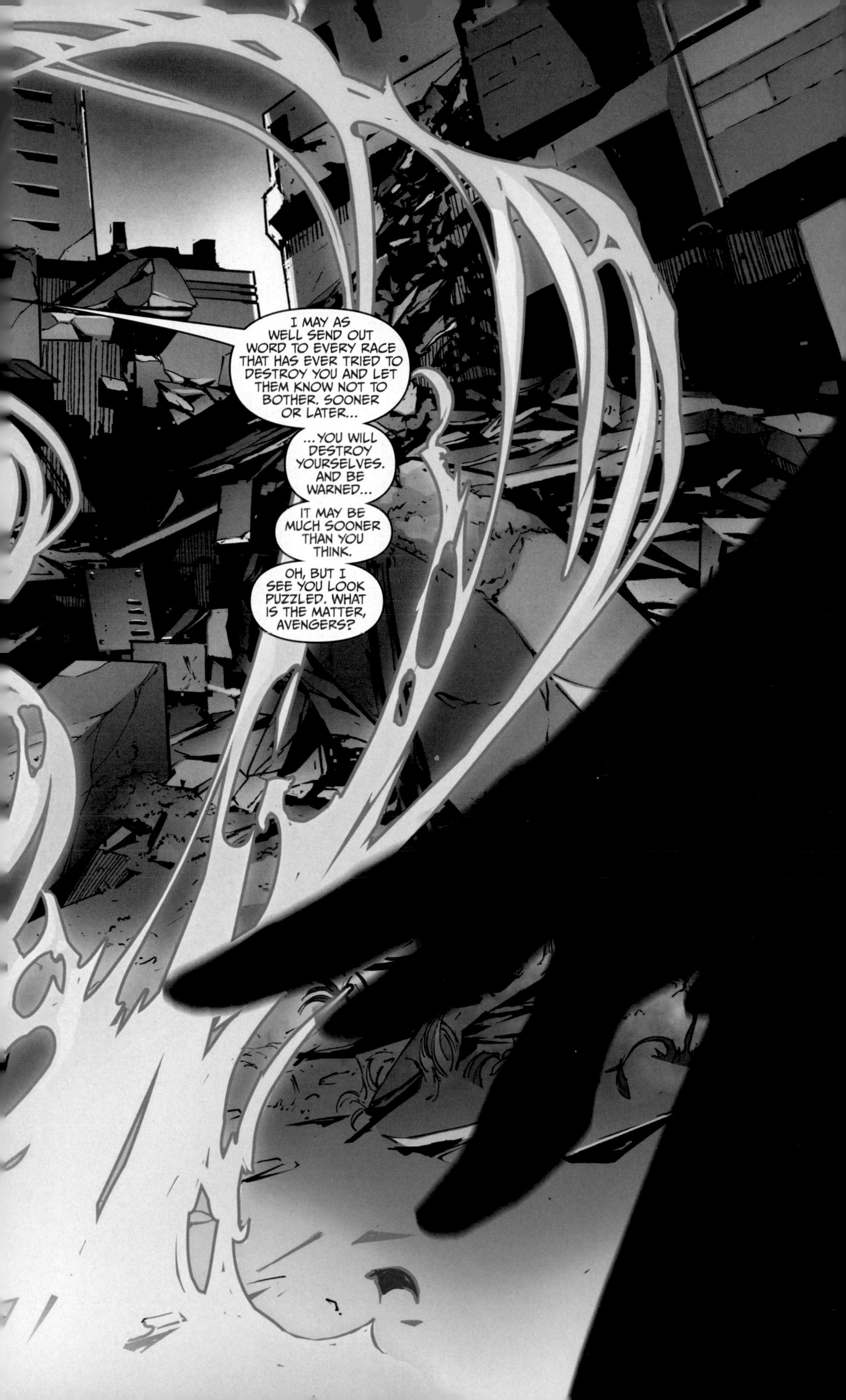
I MAY AS WELL SEND OUT WORD TO EVERY RACE THAT HAS EVER TRIED TO DESTROY YOU AND LET THEM KNOW NOT TO BOTHER. SOONER OR LATER...
...YOU WILL DESTROY YOURSELVES. AND BE WARNED...
IT MAY BE MUCH SOONER THAN YOU THINK.
OH, BUT I SEE YOU LOOK PUZZLED. WHAT IS THE MATTER, AVENGERS?

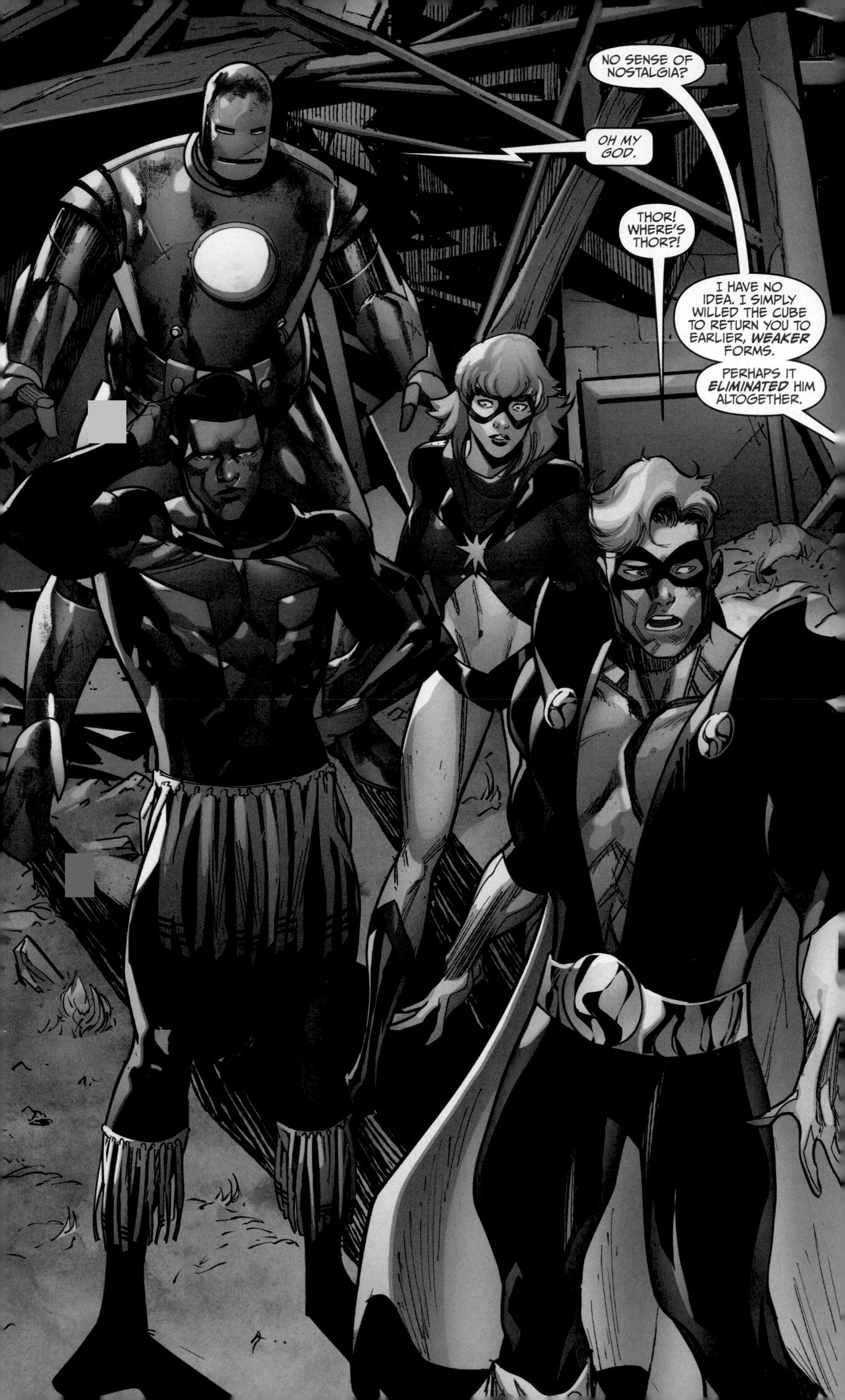
NO SENSE OF NOSTALGIA?
OH MY GOD.
THOR! WHERE'S THOR?!
I HAVE NO IDEA. I SIMPLY WILLED THE CUBE TO RETURN YOU TO EARLIER, WEAKER FORMS.
PERHAPS IT ELIMINATED HIM ALTOGETHER.

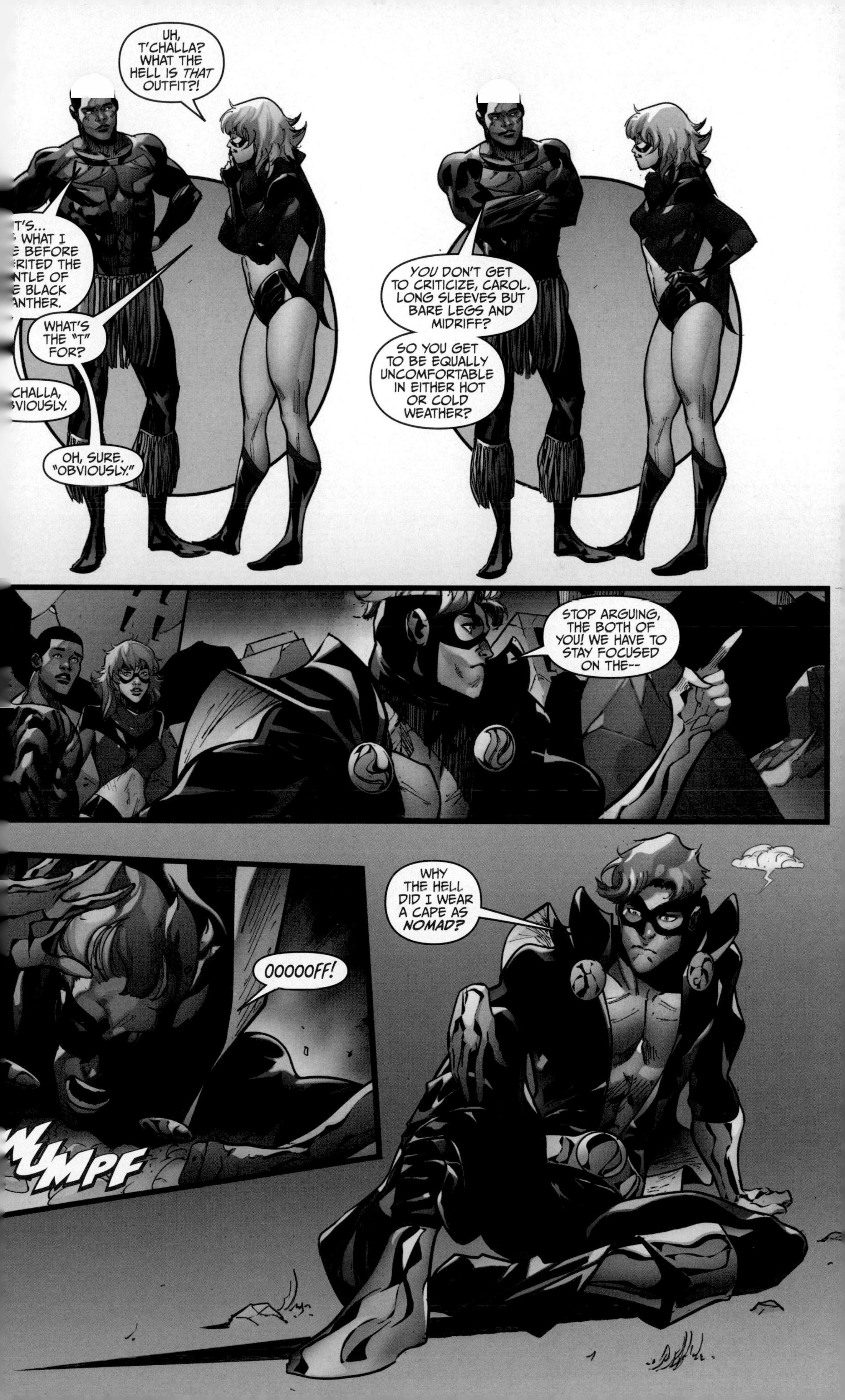
UH, T'CHALLA? WHAT THE HELL IS *THAT* OUTFIT?!
T'S... WHAT I E BEFORE RITED THE NTLE OF E BLACK ANTHER.
WHAT'S THE "T" FOR?
CHALLA, BVIOUSLY.
OH, SURE. "OBVIOUSLY."
YOU DON'T GET TO CRITICIZE, CAROL. LONG SLEEVES BUT BARE LEGS AND MIDRIFF?
SO YOU GET TO BE EQUALLY UNCOMFORTABLE IN EITHER HOT OR COLD WEATHER?
STOP ARGUING, THE BOTH OF YOU! WE HAVE TO STAY FOCUSED ON THE--
MUMPF
OOOOOFF!
WHY THE HELL DID I WEAR A CAPE AS *NOMAD?*

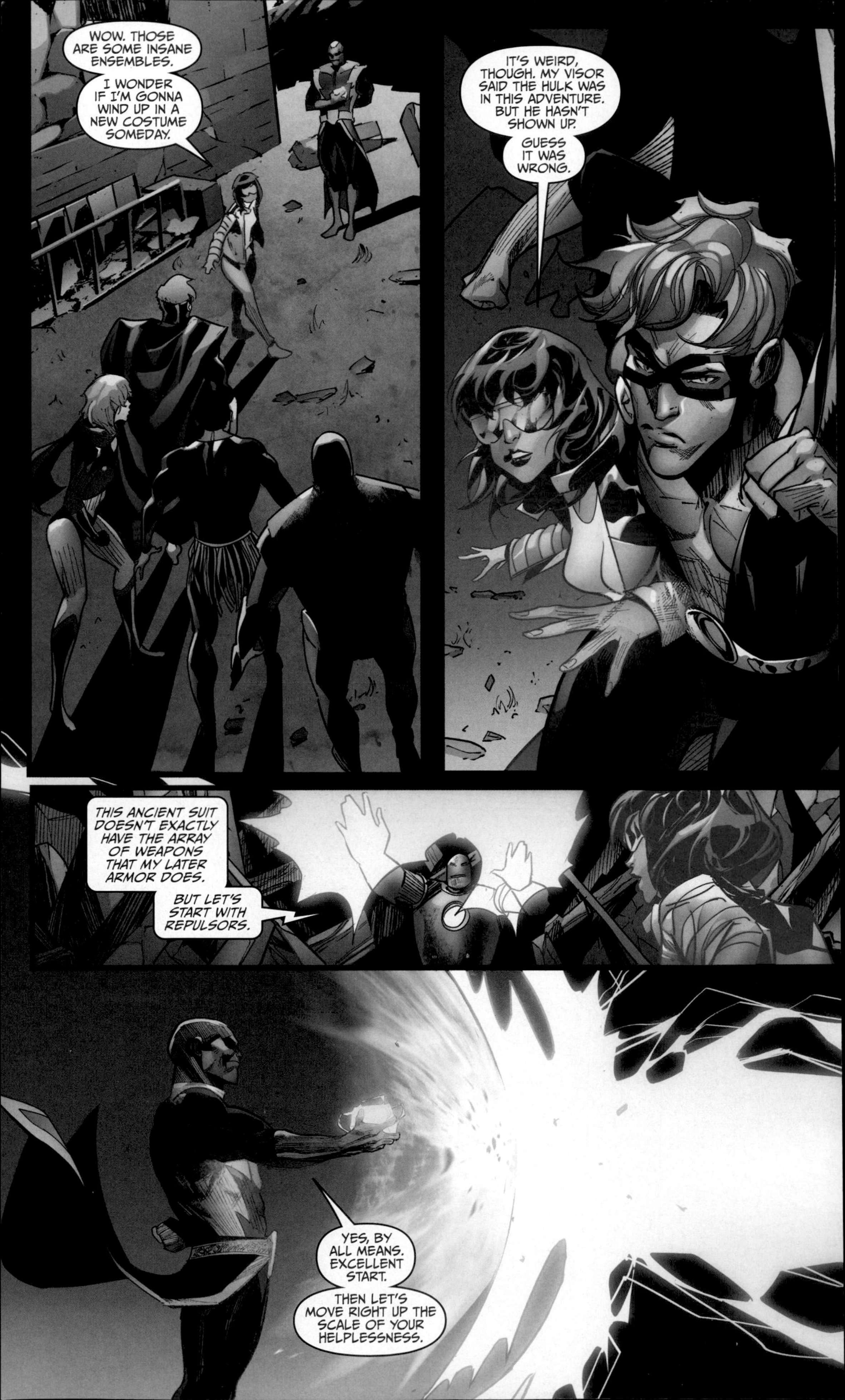
WOW. THOSE ARE SOME INSANE ENSEMBLES.
I WONDER IF I'M GONNA WIND UP IN A NEW COSTUME SOMEDAY.
IT'S WEIRD, THOUGH. MY VISOR SAID THE HULK WAS IN THIS ADVENTURE. BUT HE HASN'T SHOWN UP.
GUESS IT WAS WRONG.
THIS ANCIENT SUIT DOESN'T EXACTLY HAVE THE ARRAY OF WEAPONS THAT MY LATER ARMOR DOES.
BUT LET'S START WITH REPULSORS.
YES, BY ALL MEANS. EXCELLENT START.
THEN LET'S MOVE RIGHT UP THE SCALE OF YOUR HELPLESSNESS.

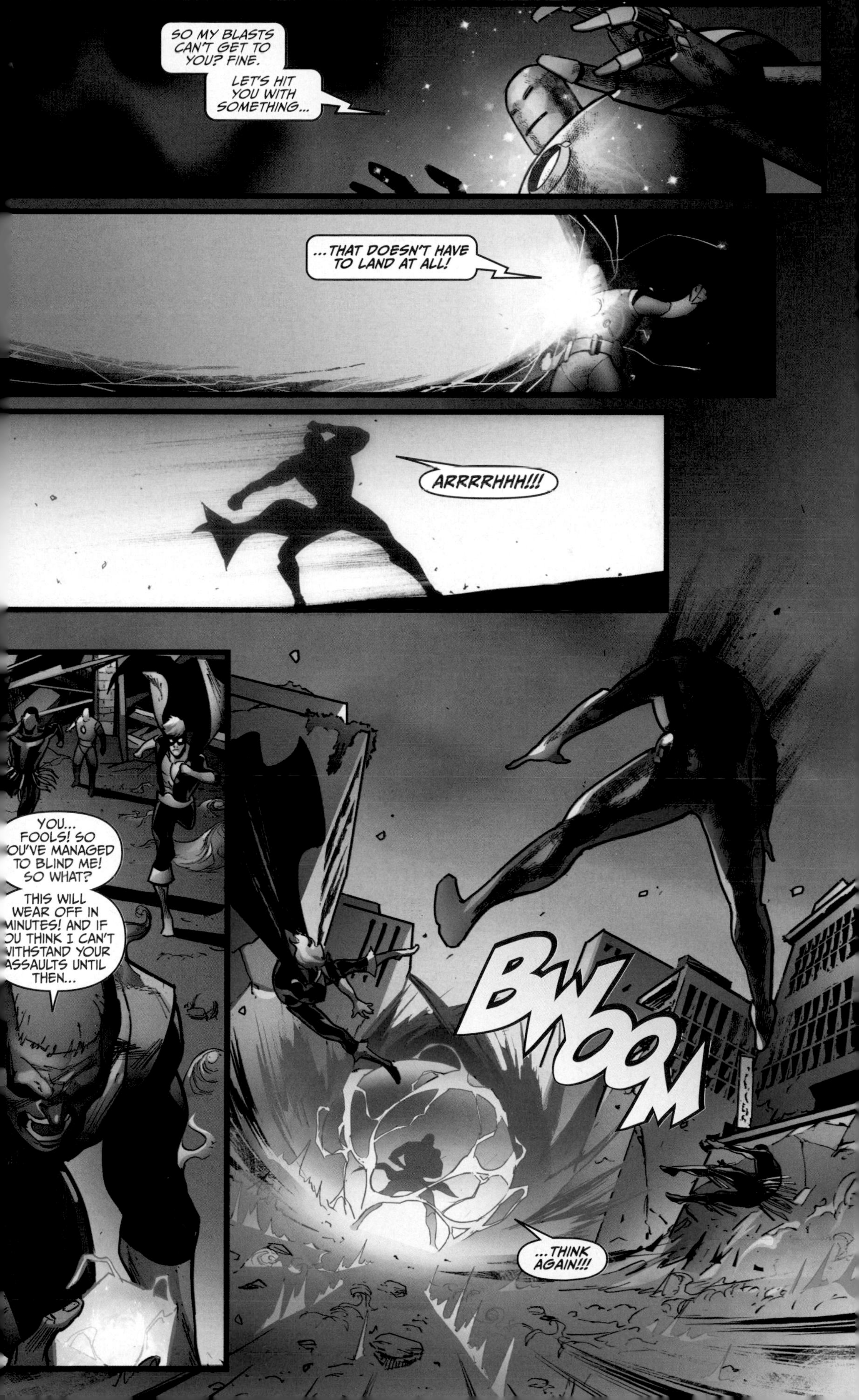

SO MY BLASTS CAN'T GET TO YOU? FINE.
LET'S HIT YOU WITH SOMETHING...
...THAT DOESN'T HAVE TO LAND AT ALL!
ARRRRHHH!!!
YOU... FOOLS! SO OU'VE MANAGED TO BLIND ME! SO WHAT?
THIS WILL WEAR OFF IN INUTES! AND IF OU THINK I CAN'T ITHSTAND YOUR SSAULTS UNTIL THEN...
BWOOOM
...THINK AGAIN!!!

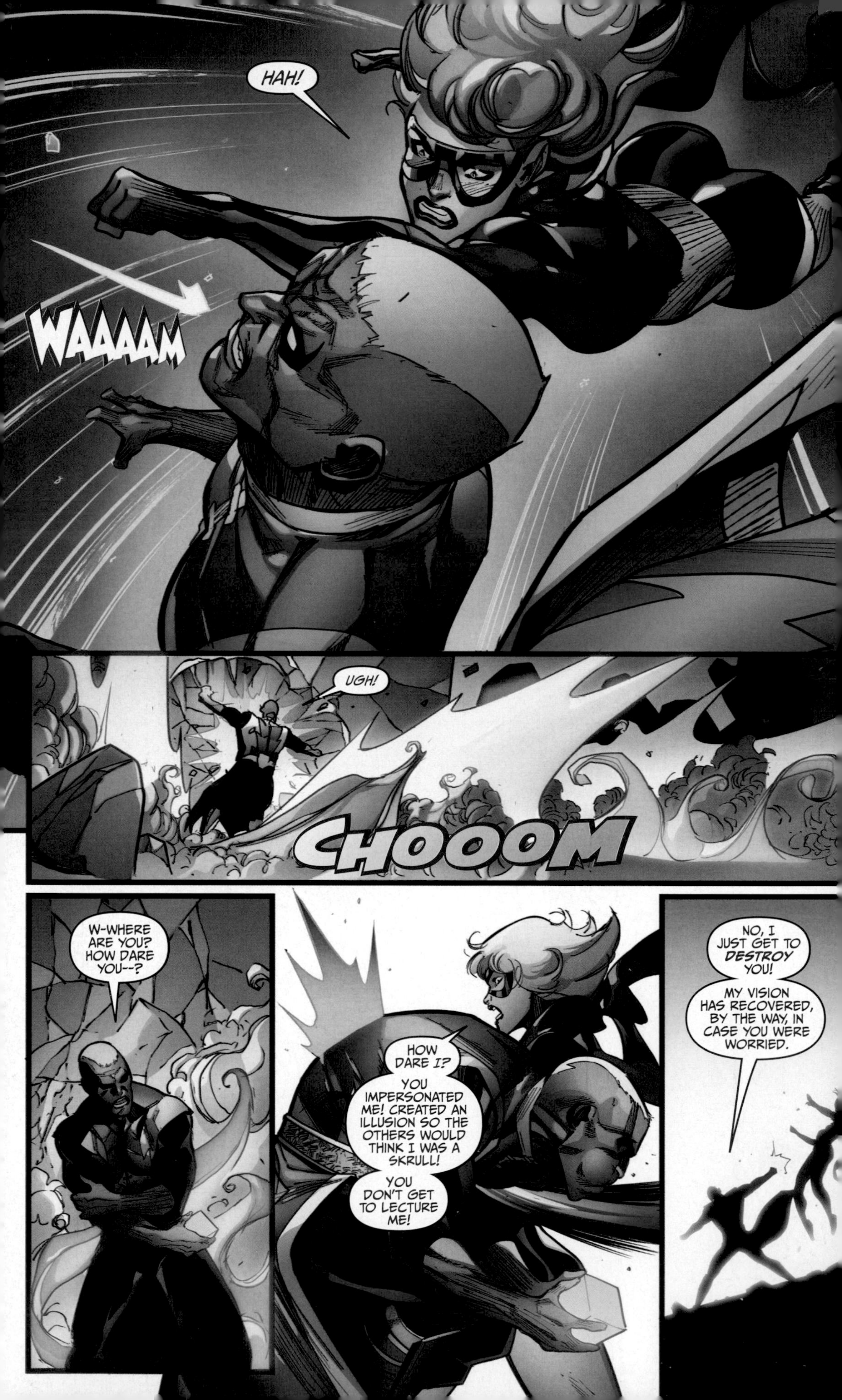

HAH!
WAAAAM
UGH!
CHOOOM
W-WHERE ARE YOU? HOW DARE YOU--?
HOW DARE I?
YOU IMPERSONATED ME! CREATED AN ILLUSION SO THE OTHERS WOULD THINK I WAS A SKRULL!
YOU DON'T GET TO LECTURE ME!
NO, I JUST GET TO *DESTROY* YOU!
MY VISION HAS RECOVERED, BY THE WAY, IN CASE YOU WERE WORRIED.

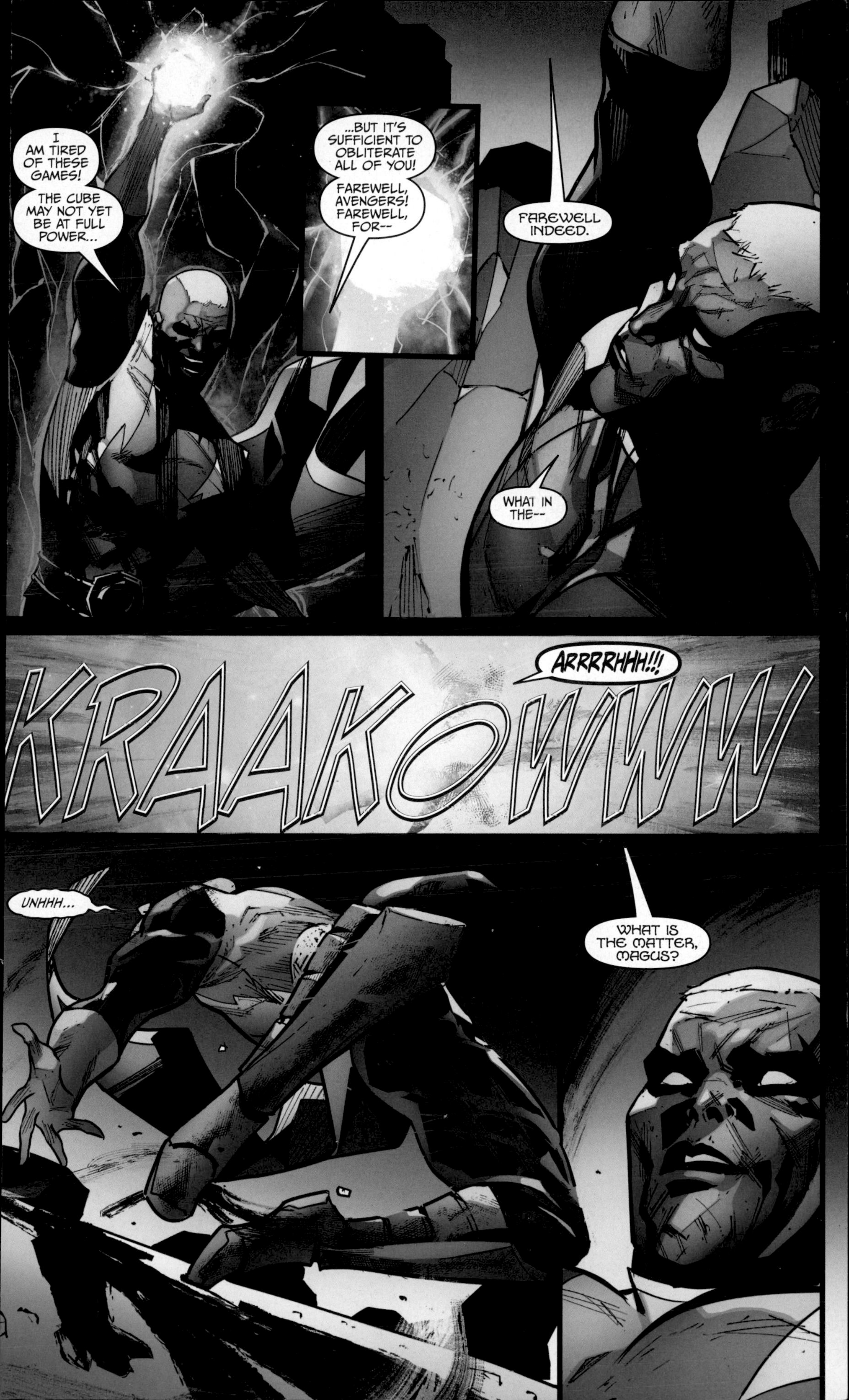
I AM TIRED OF THESE GAMES!
THE CUBE MAY NOT YET BE AT FULL POWER...
...BUT IT'S SUFFICIENT TO OBLITERATE ALL OF YOU!
FAREWELL, AVENGERS! FAREWELL, FOR--
FAREWELL INDEED.
WHAT IN THE--
KRAAKOWWW
ARRRRHHH!!!
UNHHH...
WHAT IS THE MATTER, MAGUS?

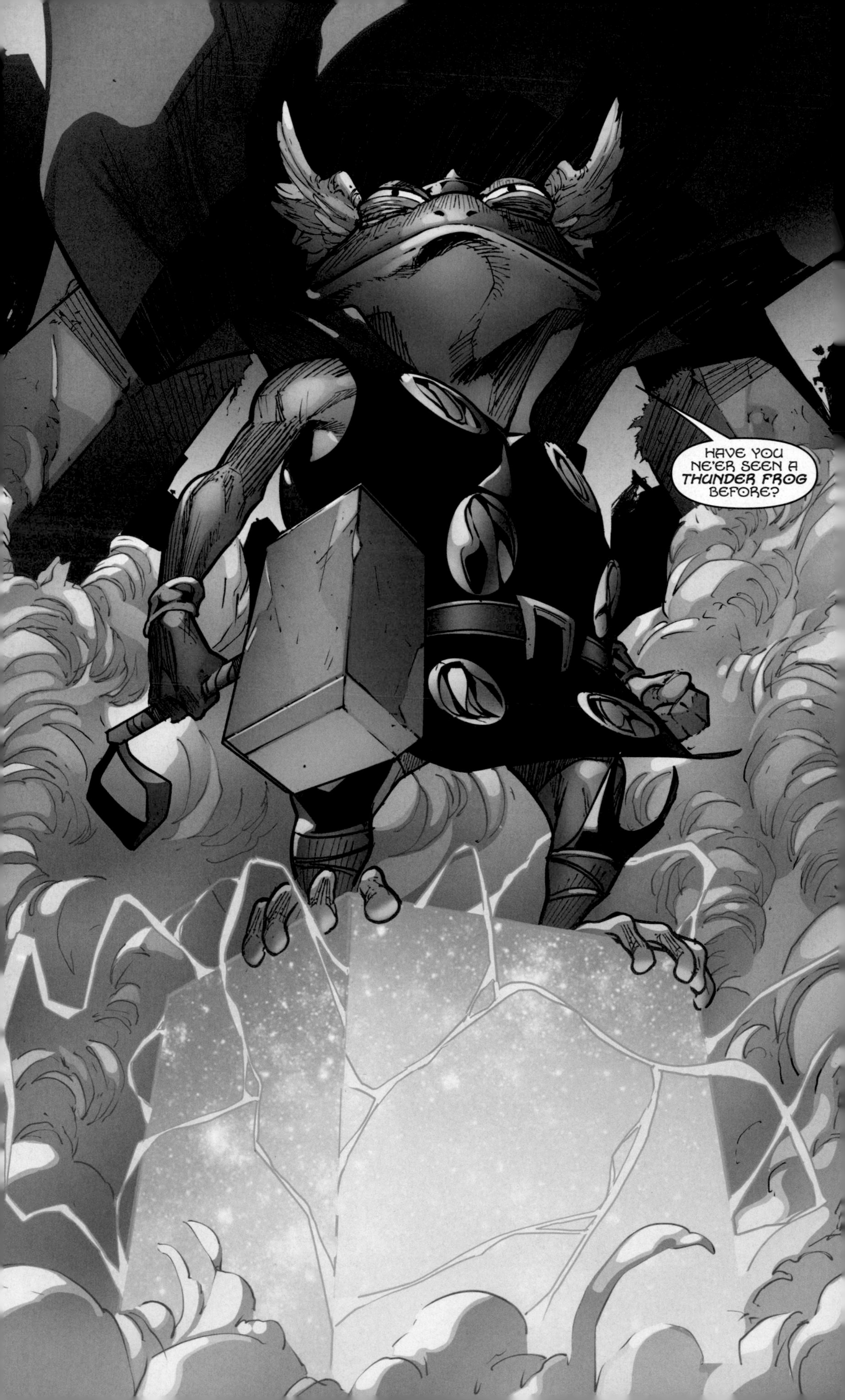
HAVE YOU NE'ER SEEN A *THUNDER FROG* BEFORE?

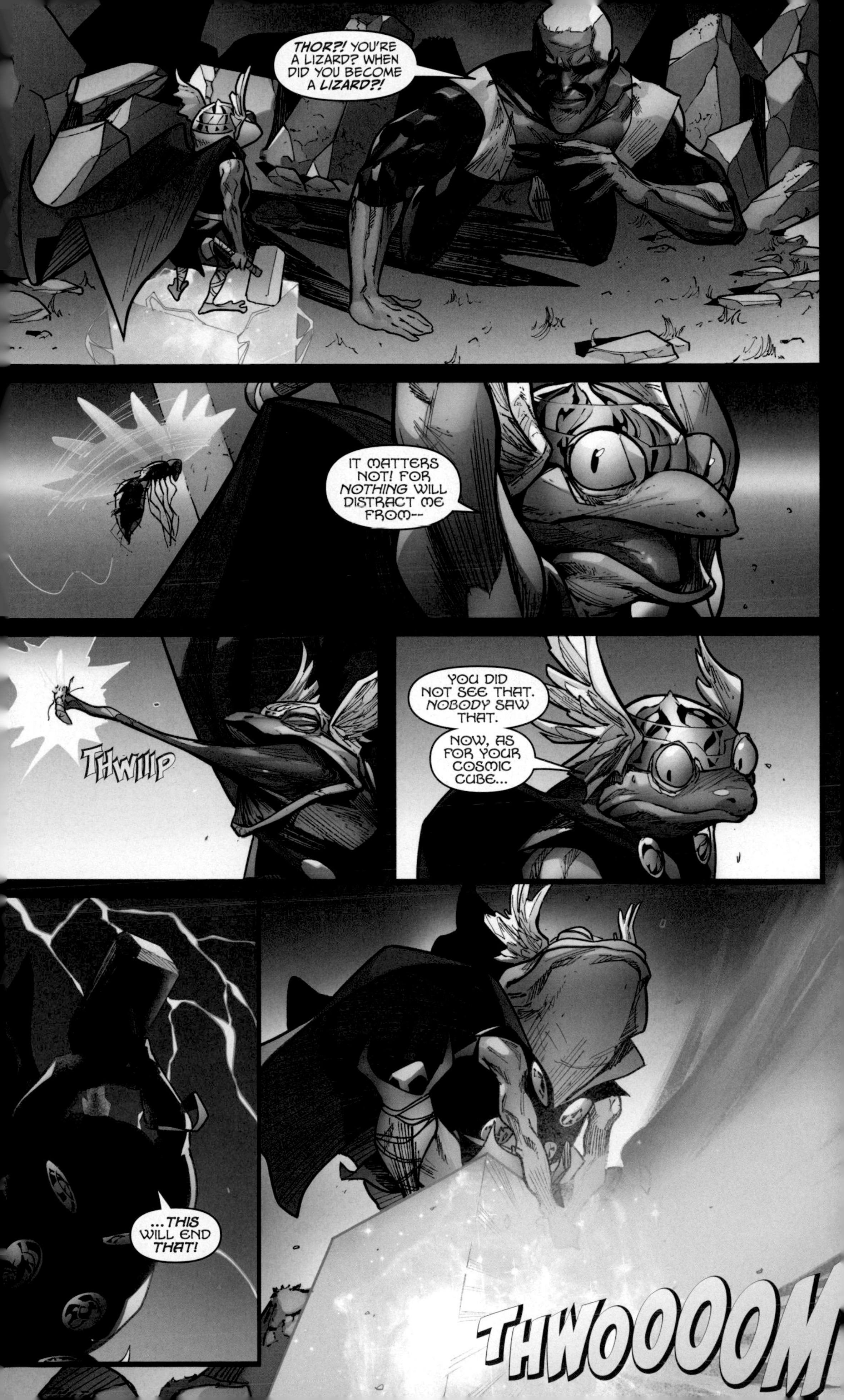
THOR?! YOU'RE A LIZARD? WHEN DID YOU BECOME A LIZARD?!
IT MATTERS NOT! FOR NOTHING WILL DISTRACT ME FROM--
THWIIIP
YOU DID NOT SEE THAT. NOBODY SAW THAT.
NOW, AS FOR YOUR COSMIC CUBE...
...THIS WILL END THAT!
THWOOOOM

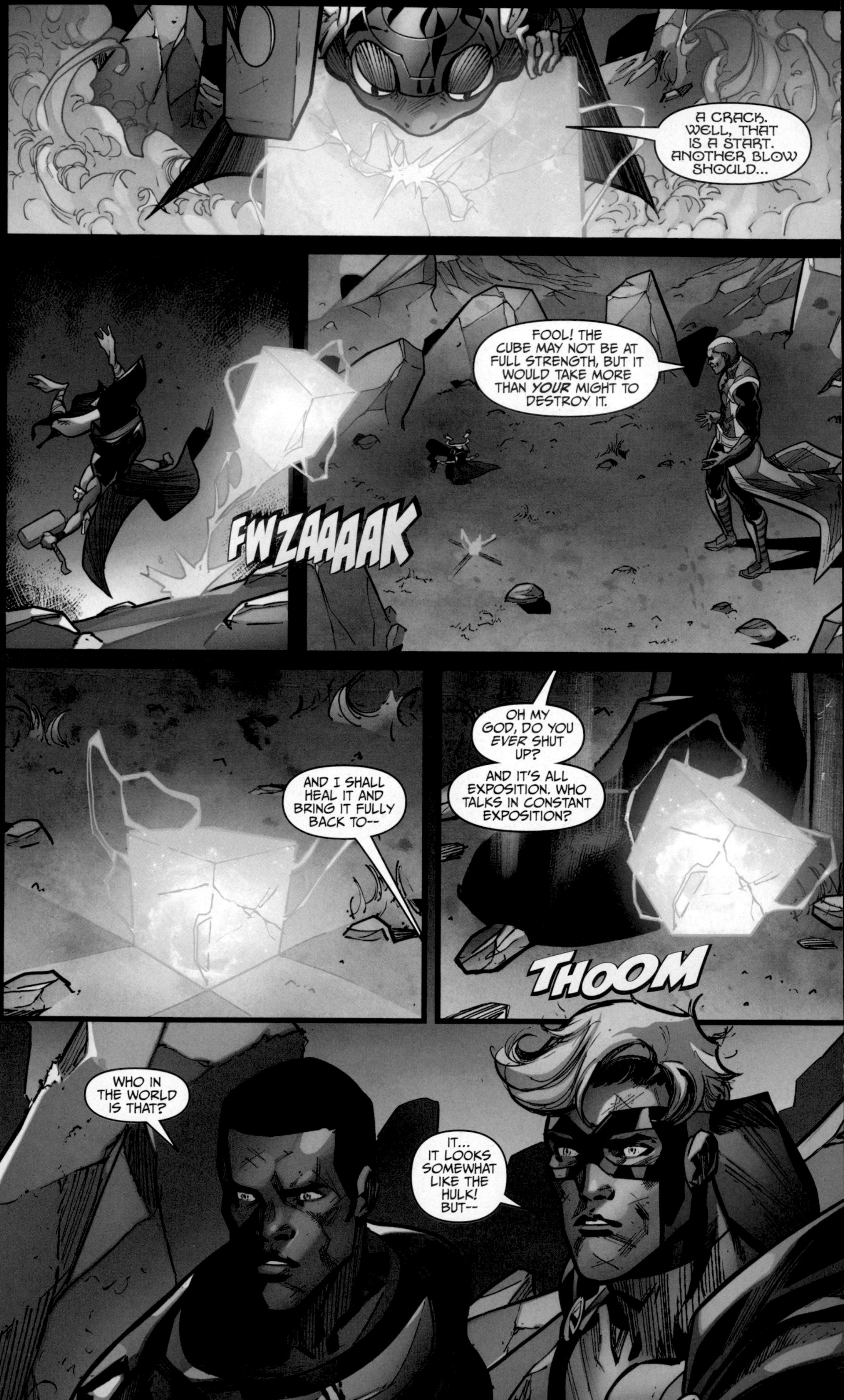
A CRACK. WELL, THAT IS A START. ANOTHER BLOW SHOULD...
FWZAAAAK
FOOL! THE CUBE MAY NOT BE AT FULL STRENGTH, BUT IT WOULD TAKE MORE THAN YOUR MIGHT TO DESTROY IT.
AND I SHALL HEAL IT AND BRING IT FULLY BACK TO--
OH MY GOD, DO YOU EVER SHUT UP?
AND IT'S ALL EXPOSITION. WHO TALKS IN CONSTANT EXPOSITION?
THOOM
WHO IN THE WORLD IS THAT?
IT... IT LOOKS SOMEWHAT LIKE THE HULK! BUT--

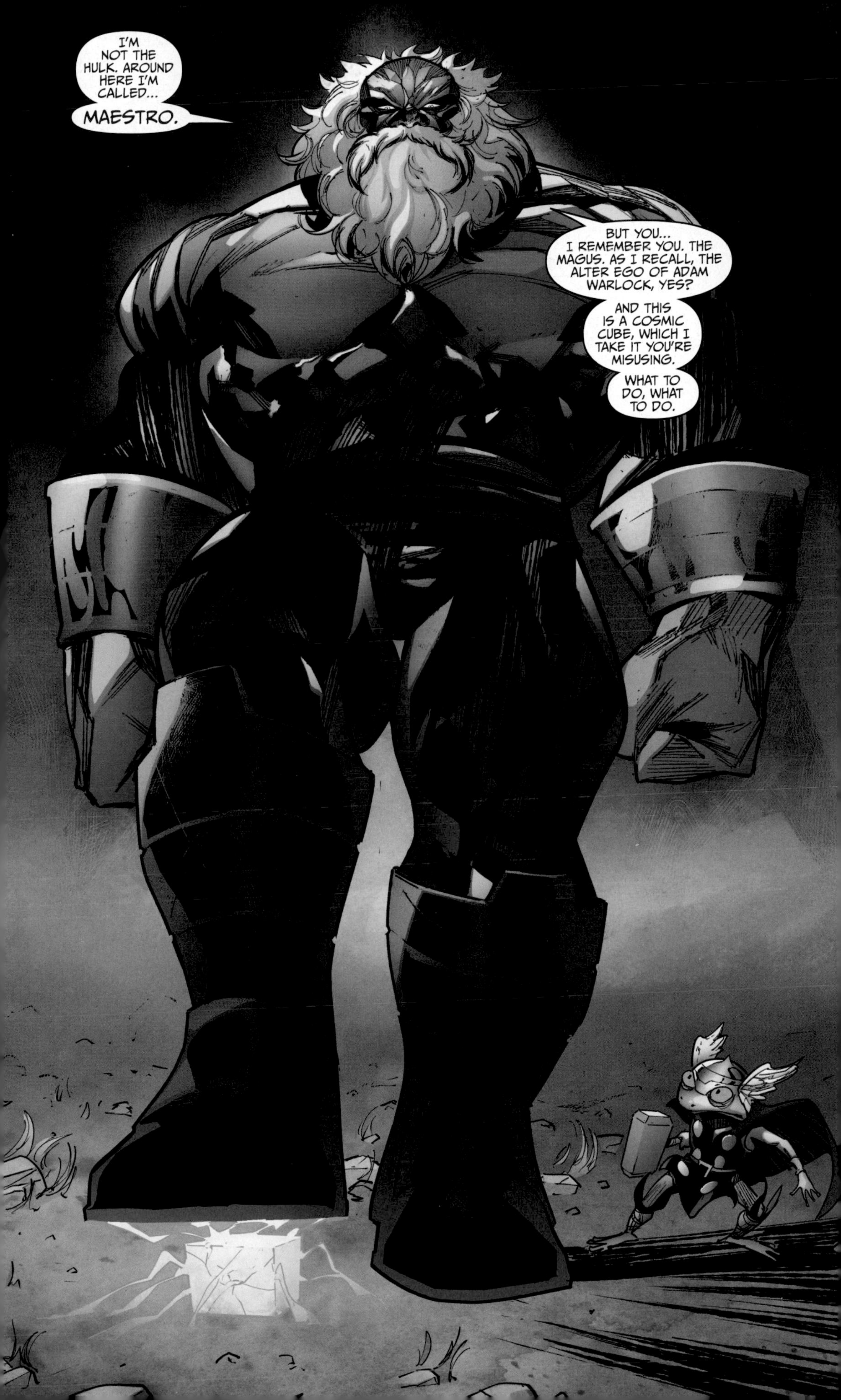
I'M NOT THE HULK. AROUND HERE I'M CALLED...
MAESTRO.
BUT YOU... I REMEMBER YOU. THE MAGUS. AS I RECALL, THE ALTER EGO OF ADAM WARLOCK, YES?
AND THIS IS A COSMIC CUBE, WHICH I TAKE IT YOU'RE MISUSING.
WHAT TO DO, WHAT TO DO.

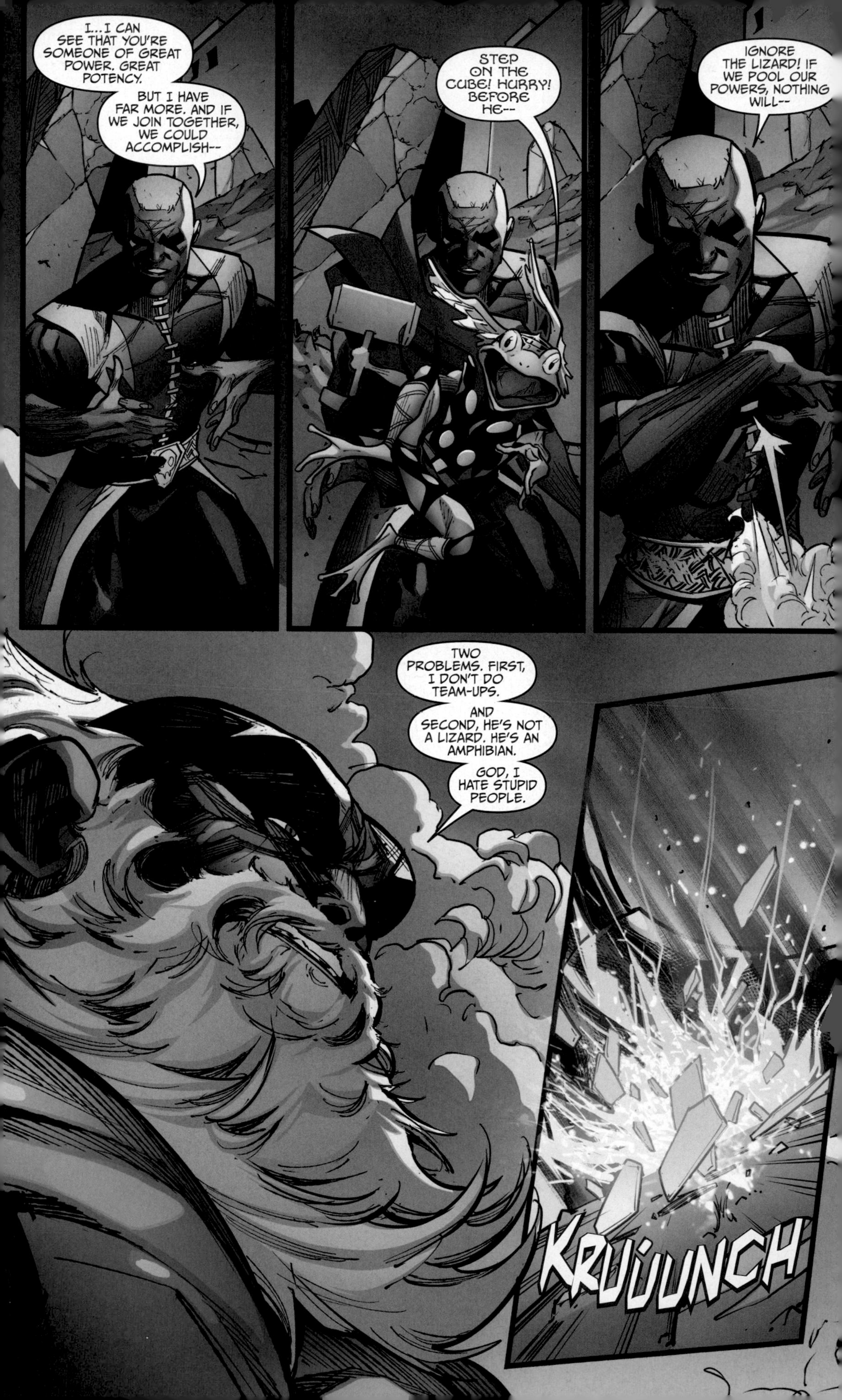
I...I CAN SEE THAT YOU'RE SOMEONE OF GREAT POWER. GREAT POTENCY.
BUT I HAVE FAR MORE. AND IF WE JOIN TOGETHER, WE COULD ACCOMPLISH--
STEP ON THE CUBE! HURRY! BEFORE HE--
IGNORE THE LIZARD! IF WE POOL OUR POWERS, NOTHING WILL--
TWO PROBLEMS. FIRST, I DON'T DO TEAM-UPS.
AND SECOND, HE'S NOT A LIZARD. HE'S AN AMPHIBIAN.
GOD, I HATE STUPID PEOPLE.
KRUUUNCH

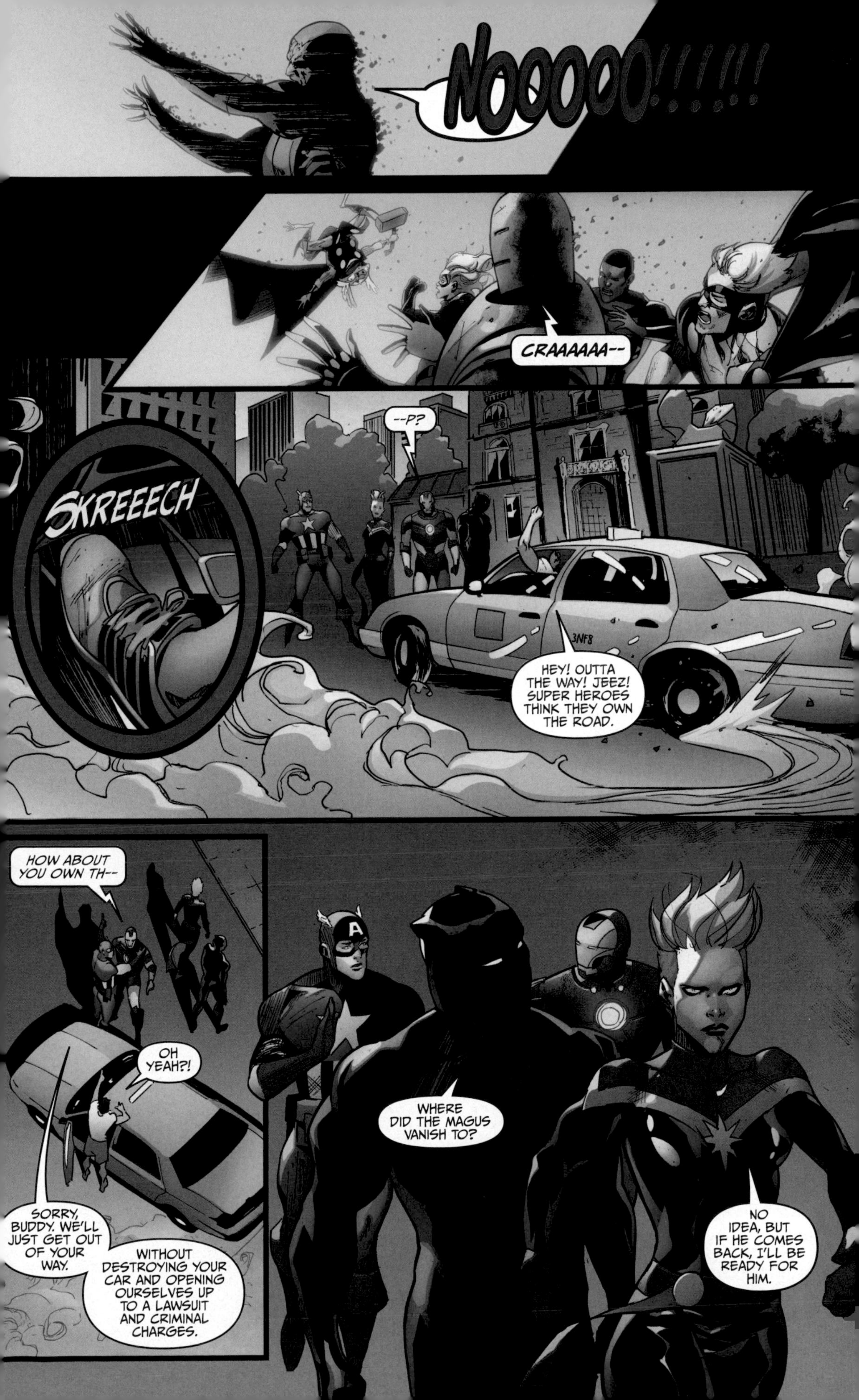
NOOOOO!!!!!!
CRAAAAAA--
SKREEECH
--P?
3NF8
HEY! OUTTA THE WAY! JEEZ! SUPER HEROES THINK THEY OWN THE ROAD.
HOW ABOUT YOU OWN TH--
OH YEAH?!
SORRY, BUDDY. WE'LL JUST GET OUT OF YOUR WAY.
WITHOUT DESTROYING YOUR CAR AND OPENING OURSELVES UP TO A LAWSUIT AND CRIMINAL CHARGES.
WHERE DID THE MAGUS VANISH TO?
NO IDEA, BUT IF HE COMES BACK, I'LL BE READY FOR HIM.

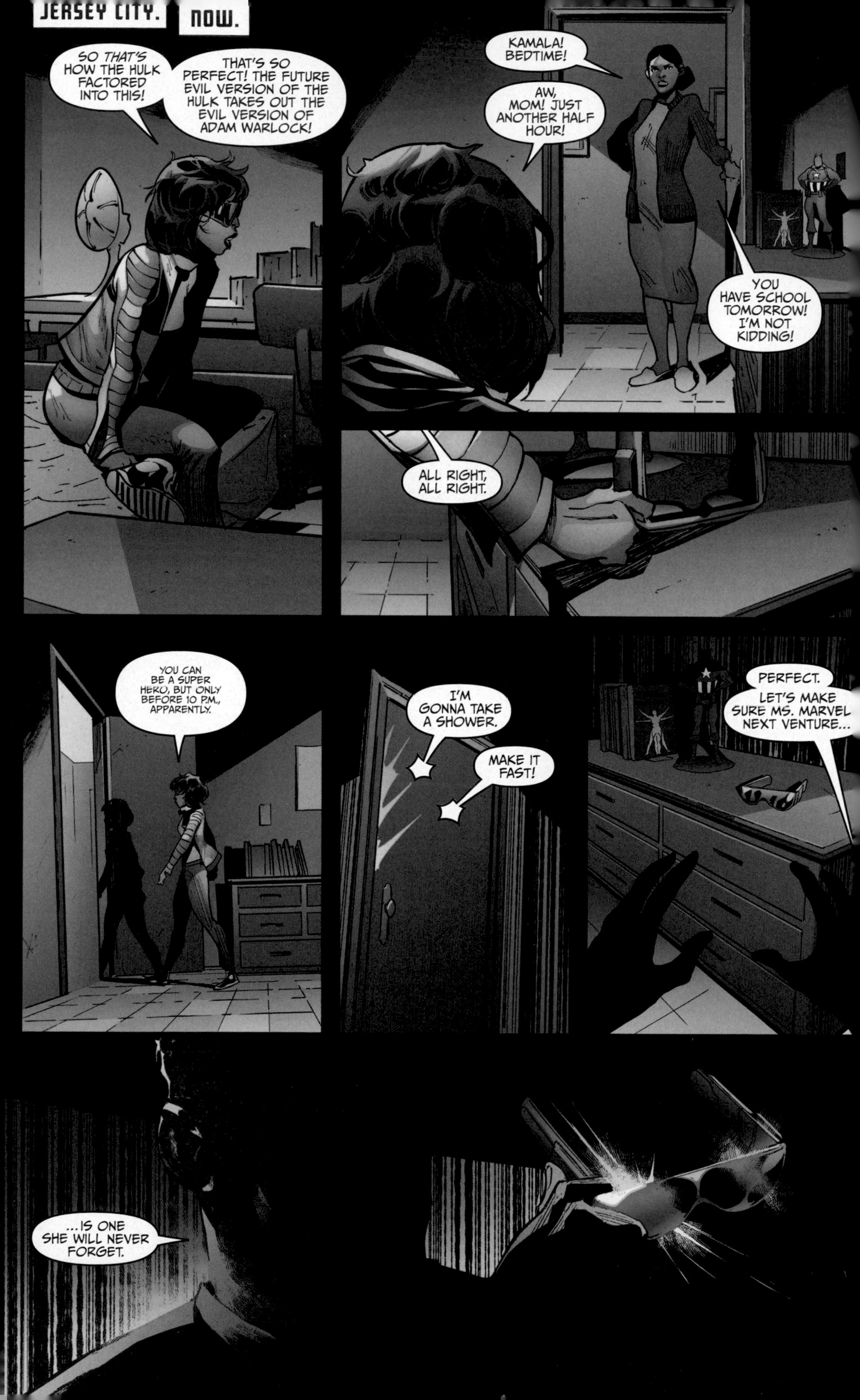
JERSEY CITY.
NOW.
SO THAT'S HOW THE HULK FACTORED INTO THIS!
THAT'S SO PERFECT! THE FUTURE EVIL VERSION OF THE HULK TAKES OUT THE EVIL VERSION OF ADAM WARLOCK!
KAMALA! BEDTIME!
AW, MOM! JUST ANOTHER HALF HOUR!
YOU HAVE SCHOOL TOMORROW! I'M NOT KIDDING!
ALL RIGHT, ALL RIGHT.
YOU CAN BE A SUPER HERO, BUT ONLY BEFORE 10 P.M., APPARENTLY.
I'M GONNA TAKE A SHOWER.
MAKE IT FAST!
PERFECT.
LET'S MAKE SURE MS. MARVEL NEXT VENTURE...
...IS ONE SHE WILL NEVER FORGET.

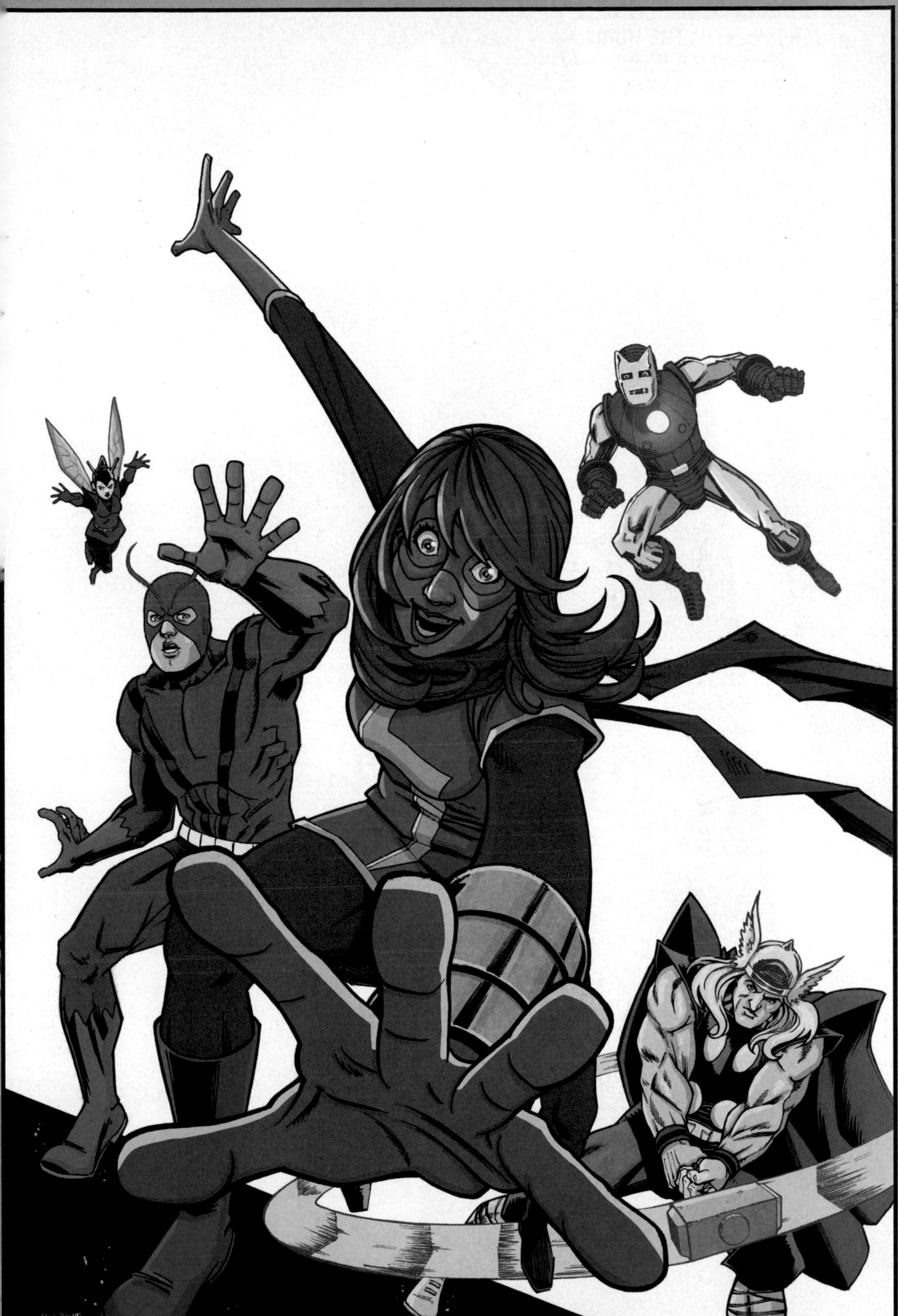
NICK ROCHE
(JACK KIRBY)

5

JERSEY CITY. THE HOME OF KAMALA KHAN, A.K.A. MS. MARVEL.

CRAP. BEEN LYING HERE FOR, LIKE, AN HOUR.

I NEED SOMETHING TO PUT MY BRAIN TO SLEEP.

SEEING THE MAESTRO SHOW UP IN MY LAST "ADVENTURE" MAKES ME WONDER...

...WHAT WAS THE HULK LIKE IN THE OLD DAYS? WHEN HE AND THE AVENGERS DIDN'T GET ALONG.

INDEX, SEARCH RECORDS FOR A REALLY EARLY ADVENTURE WHERE THE HULK FOUGHT THE AVENGERS.

MATCH FOUND. KEY MEMBERS INVOLVED: THOR, IRO... MAN, GIANT-MAN, THE WASP, THE HULK, SUB-MARINER.

WO... BEF... CAP... AME... EV...

PLAY IT.

OKAY...WE'R... ON GIBRALTA... HULK AND NAM... HAVE CHALLEN... THE AVENGE... TO A--

WHOA! NAMOR IS REALLY RIPPED.

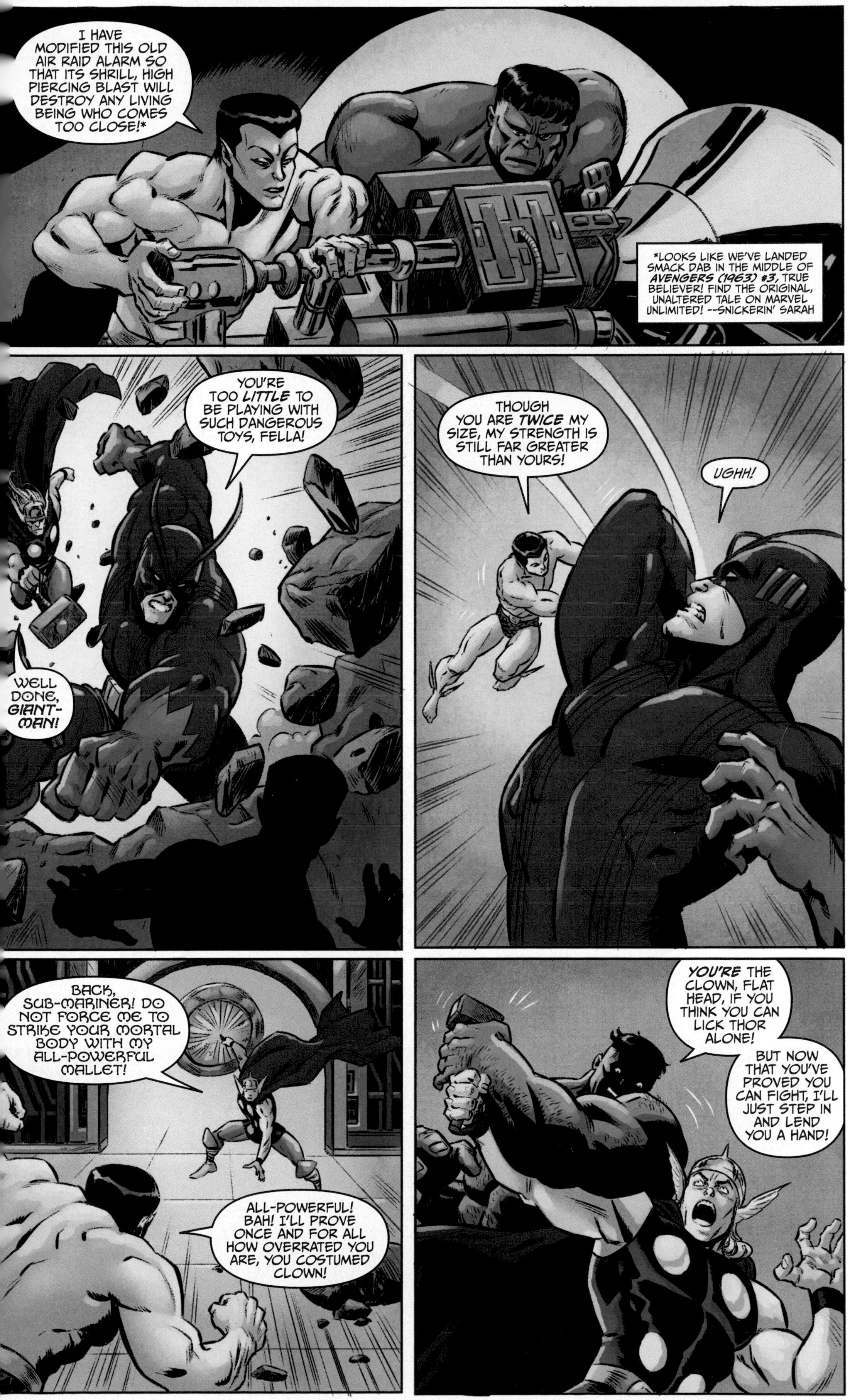
I HAVE MODIFIED THIS OLD AIR RAID ALARM SO THAT ITS SHRILL, HIGH PIERCING BLAST WILL DESTROY ANY LIVING BEING WHO COMES TOO CLOSE!*
*LOOKS LIKE WE'VE LANDED SMACK DAB IN THE MIDDLE OF AVENGERS (1963) #3, TRUE BELIEVER! FIND THE ORIGINAL, UNALTERED TALE ON MARVEL UNLIMITED! --SNICKERIN' SARAH
YOU'RE TOO LITTLE TO BE PLAYING WITH SUCH DANGEROUS TOYS, FELLA!
WELL DONE, GIANT-MAN!
THOUGH YOU ARE TWICE MY SIZE, MY STRENGTH IS STILL FAR GREATER THAN YOURS!
UGHH!
BACK, SUB-MARINER! DO NOT FORCE ME TO STRIKE YOUR MORTAL BODY WITH MY ALL-POWERFUL MALLET!
ALL-POWERFUL! BAH! I'LL PROVE ONCE AND FOR ALL HOW OVERRATED YOU ARE, YOU COSTUMED CLOWN!
YOU'RE THE CLOWN, FLAT HEAD, IF YOU THINK YOU CAN LICK THOR ALONE!
BUT NOW THAT YOU'VE PROVED YOU CAN FIGHT, I'LL JUST STEP IN AND LEND YOU A HAND!

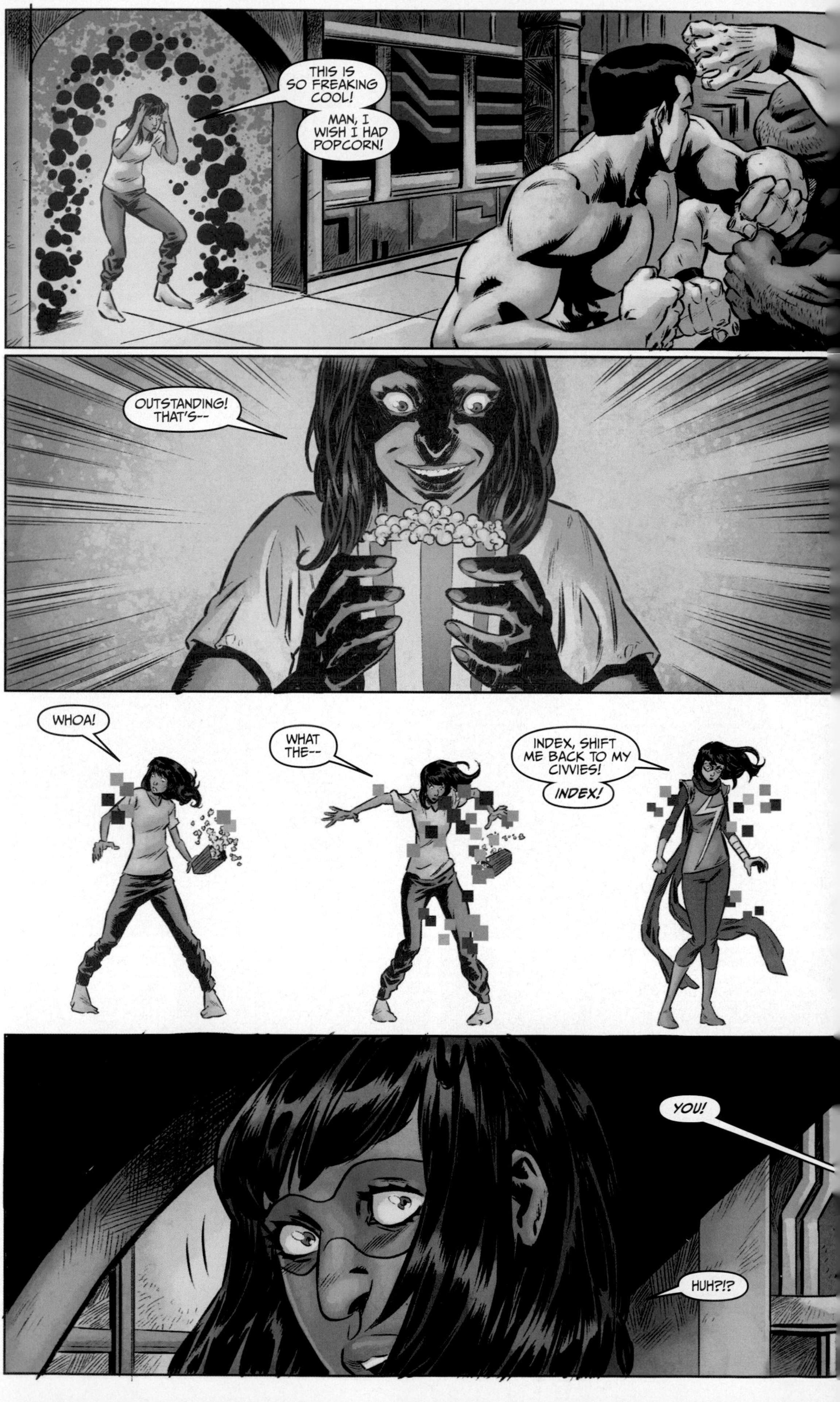
THIS IS SO FREAKING COOL!
MAN, I WISH I HAD POPCORN!
OUTSTANDING! THAT'S--
WHOA!
WHAT THE--
INDEX, SHIFT ME BACK TO MY CIVVIES!
INDEX!
YOU!
HUH?!?

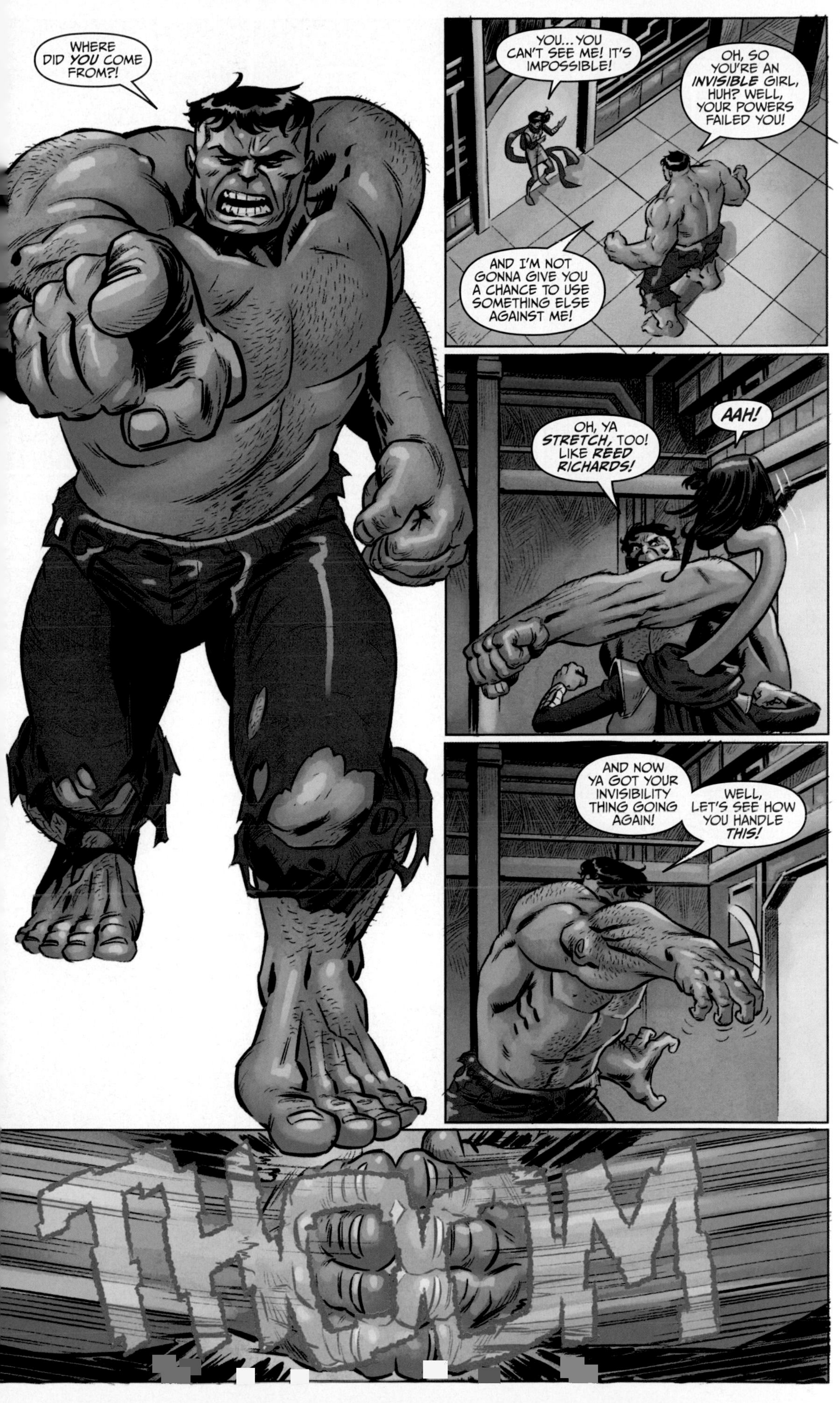
WHERE DID YOU COME FROM?!
YOU... YOU CAN'T SEE ME! IT'S IMPOSSIBLE!
OH, SO YOU'RE AN INVISIBLE GIRL, HUH? WELL, YOUR POWERS FAILED YOU!
AND I'M NOT GONNA GIVE YOU A CHANCE TO USE SOMETHING ELSE AGAINST ME!
OH, YA STRETCH, TOO! LIKE REED RICHARDS!
AAH!
AND NOW YA GOT YOUR INVISIBILITY THING GOING AGAIN!
WELL, LET'S SEE HOW YOU HANDLE THIS!
THOOM

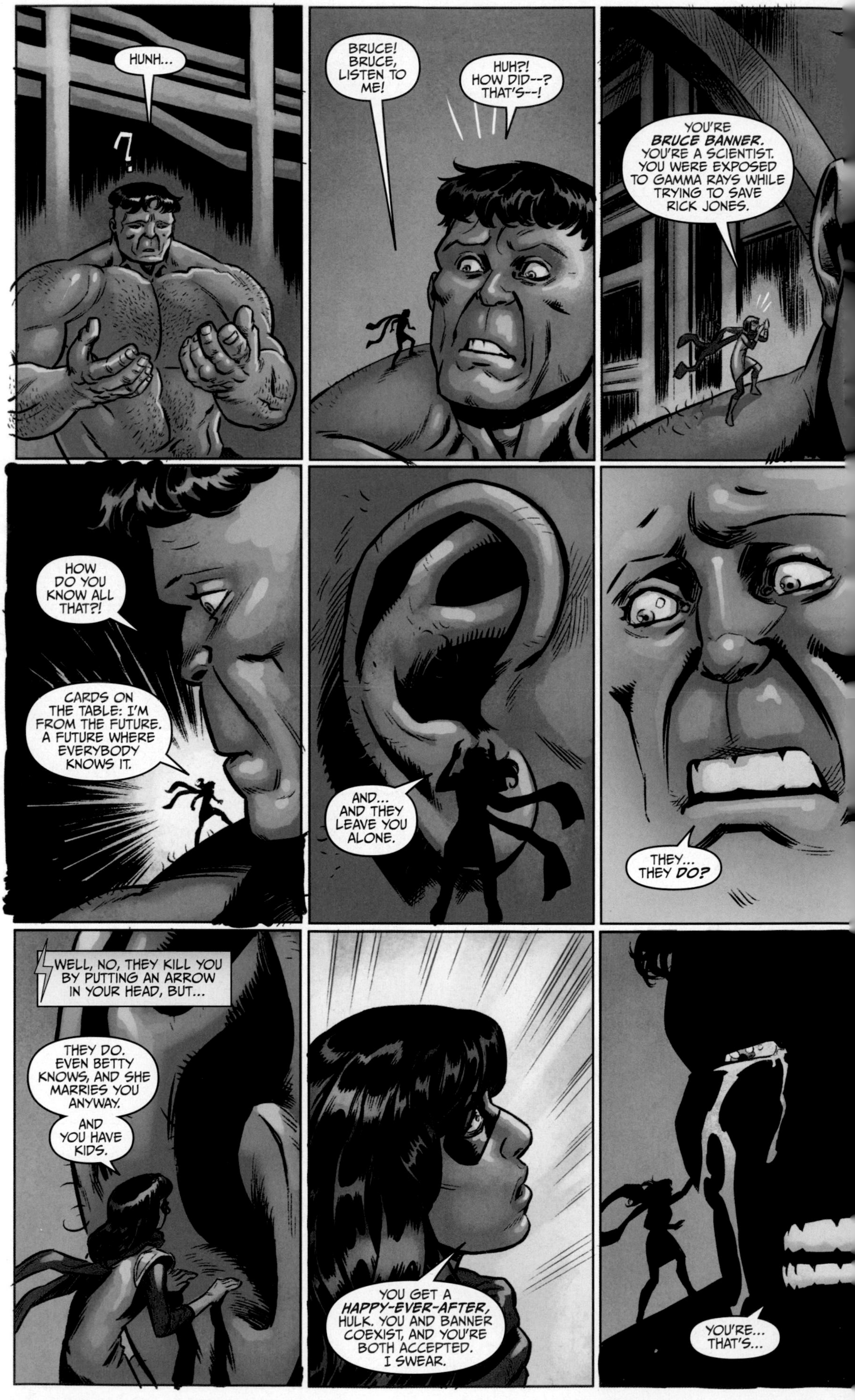
HUNH...
?
BRUCE! BRUCE, LISTEN TO ME!
HUH?! HOW DID--? THAT'S--!
YOU'RE BRUCE BANNER. YOU'RE A SCIENTIST. YOU WERE EXPOSED TO GAMMA RAYS WHILE TRYING TO SAVE RICK JONES.
HOW DO YOU KNOW ALL THAT?!
CARDS ON THE TABLE: I'M FROM THE FUTURE. A FUTURE WHERE EVERYBODY KNOWS IT.
AND... AND THEY LEAVE YOU ALONE.
THEY... THEY DO?
WELL, NO, THEY KILL YOU BY PUTTING AN ARROW IN YOUR HEAD, BUT...
THEY DO. EVEN BETTY KNOWS, AND SHE MARRIES YOU ANYWAY.
AND YOU HAVE KIDS.
YOU GET A HAPPY-EVER-AFTER, HULK. YOU AND BANNER COEXIST, AND YOU'RE BOTH ACCEPTED. I SWEAR.
YOU'RE... THAT'S...

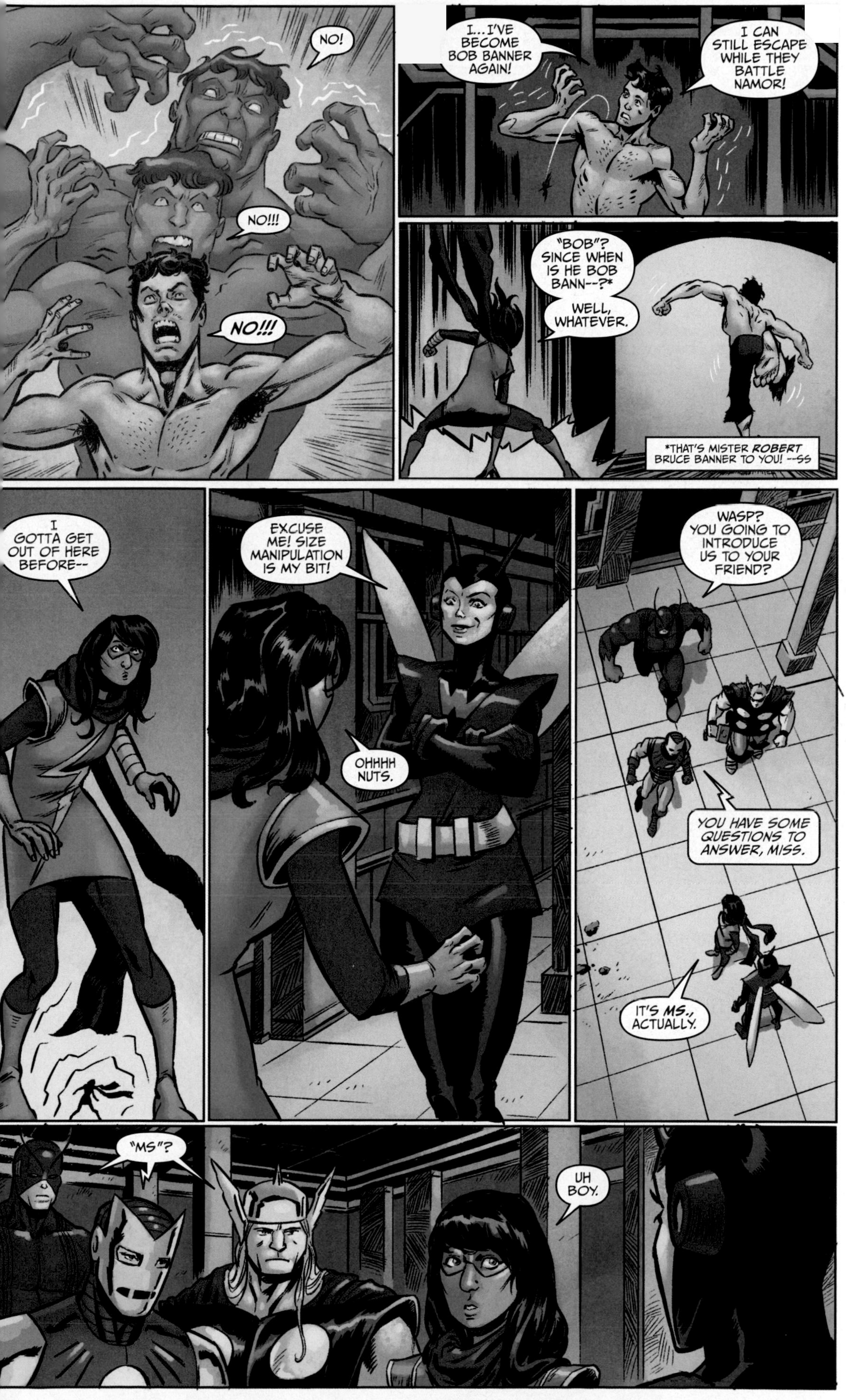
NO!
NO!!!
NO!!!
I...I'VE BECOME BOB BANNER AGAIN!
I CAN STILL ESCAPE WHILE THEY BATTLE NAMOR!
"BOB"? SINCE WHEN IS HE BOB BANN--?*
WELL, WHATEVER.
*THAT'S MISTER ROBERT BRUCE BANNER TO YOU! --SS
I GOTTA GET OUT OF HERE BEFORE--
EXCUSE ME! SIZE MANIPULATION IS MY BIT!
OHHHH NUTS.
WASP? YOU GOING TO INTRODUCE US TO YOUR FRIEND?
YOU HAVE SOME QUESTIONS TO ANSWER, MISS.
IT'S MS., ACTUALLY.
"MS"?
UH BOY.

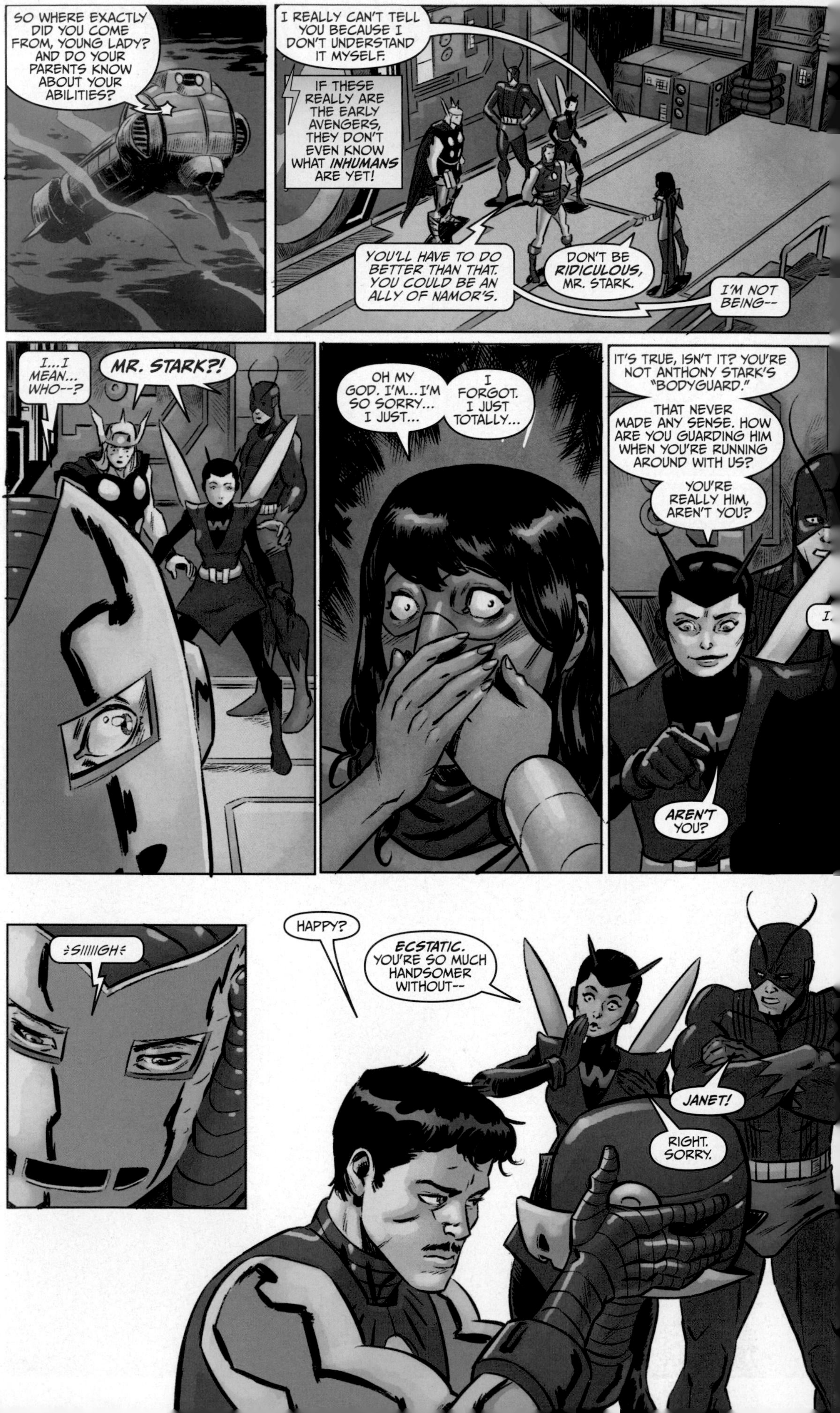

SO WHERE EXACTLY DID YOU COME FROM, YOUNG LADY? AND DO YOUR PARENTS KNOW ABOUT YOUR ABILITIES?
I REALLY CAN'T TELL YOU BECAUSE I DON'T UNDERSTAND IT MYSELF.
IF THESE REALLY ARE THE EARLY AVENGERS, THEY DON'T EVEN KNOW WHAT INHUMANS ARE YET!
YOU'LL HAVE TO DO BETTER THAN THAT. YOU COULD BE AN ALLY OF NAMOR'S.
DON'T BE RIDICULOUS, MR. STARK.
I'M NOT BEING--
I...I MEAN... WHO--?
MR. STARK?!
OH MY GOD. I'M...I'M SO SORRY... I JUST...
I FORGOT. I JUST TOTALLY...
IT'S TRUE, ISN'T IT? YOU'RE NOT ANTHONY STARK'S "BODYGUARD."
THAT NEVER MADE ANY SENSE. HOW ARE YOU GUARDING HIM WHEN YOU'RE RUNNING AROUND WITH US?
YOU'RE REALLY HIM, AREN'T YOU?
AREN'T YOU?
SIIIIGH
HAPPY?
ECSTATIC. YOU'RE SO MUCH HANDSOMER WITHOUT--
JANET!
RIGHT. SORRY.

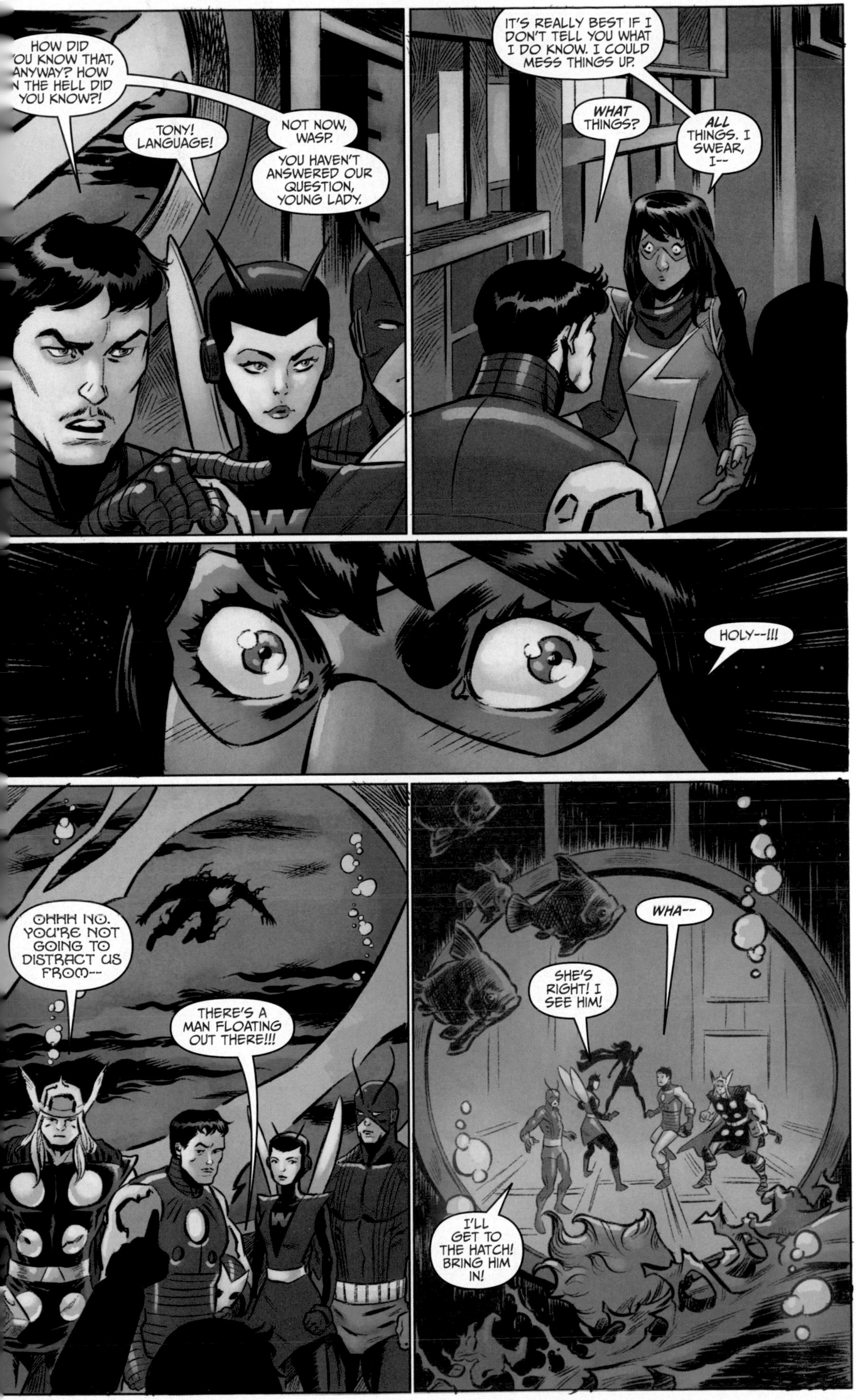
HOW DID YOU KNOW THAT, ANYWAY? HOW IN THE HELL DID YOU KNOW?!
TONY! LANGUAGE!
NOT NOW, WASP.
YOU HAVEN'T ANSWERED OUR QUESTION, YOUNG LADY.
IT'S REALLY BEST IF I DON'T TELL YOU WHAT I DO KNOW. I COULD MESS THINGS UP.
WHAT THINGS?
ALL THINGS. I SWEAR, I--
HOLY--!!!
OHHH NO. YOU'RE NOT GOING TO DISTRACT US FROM--
THERE'S A MAN FLOATING OUT THERE!!!
WHA--
SHE'S RIGHT! I SEE HIM!
I'LL GET TO THE HATCH! BRING HIM IN!

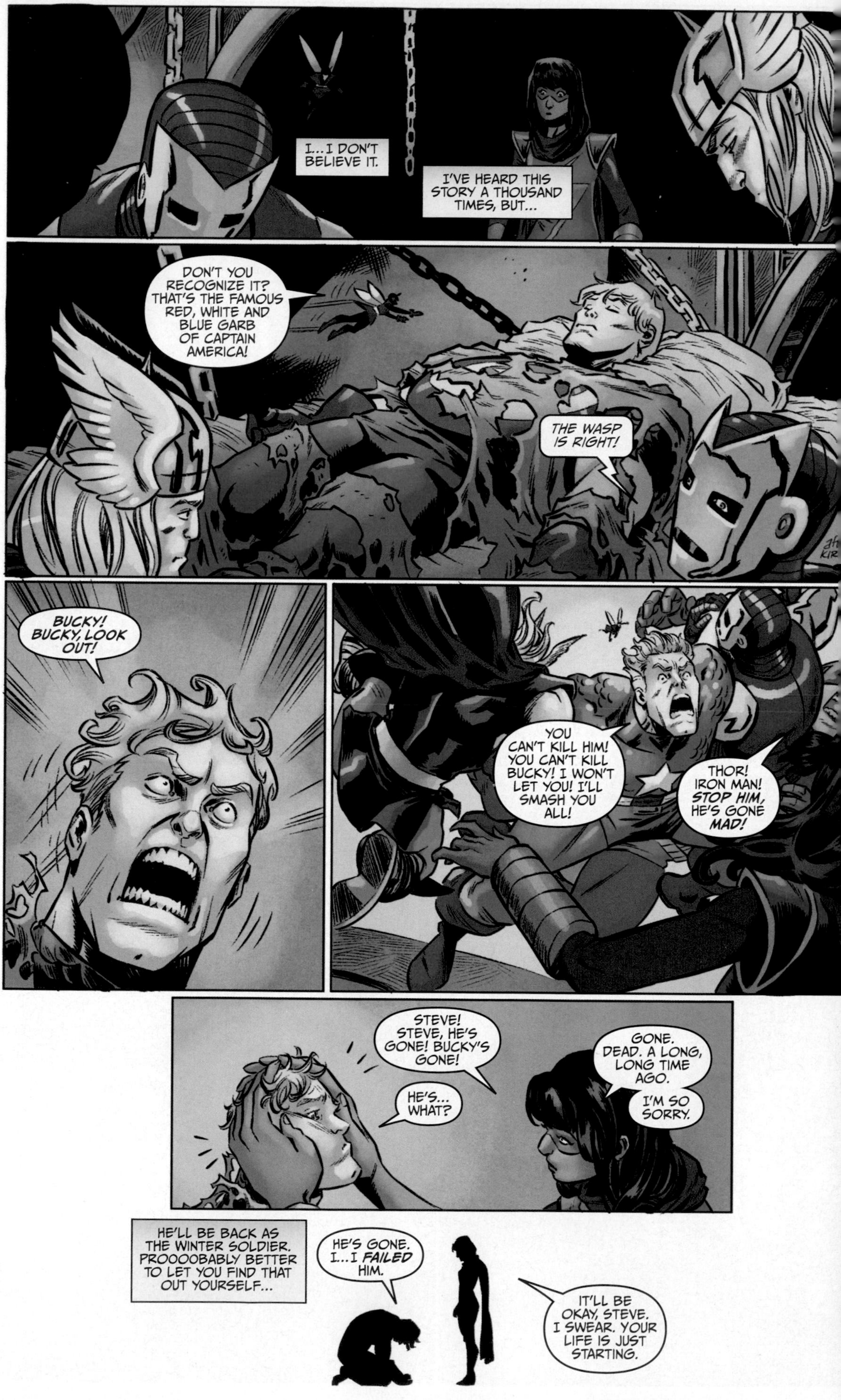
I...I DON'T BELIEVE IT.
I'VE HEARD THIS STORY A THOUSAND TIMES, BUT...
DON'T YOU RECOGNIZE IT? THAT'S THE FAMOUS RED, WHITE AND BLUE GARB OF CAPTAIN AMERICA!
THE WASP IS RIGHT!
BUCKY! BUCKY, LOOK OUT!
YOU CAN'T KILL HIM! YOU CAN'T KILL BUCKY! I WON'T LET YOU! I'LL SMASH YOU ALL!
THOR! IRON MAN! STOP HIM, HE'S GONE MAD!
STEVE! STEVE, HE'S GONE! BUCKY'S GONE!
HE'S... WHAT?
GONE. DEAD. A LONG, LONG TIME AGO.
I'M SO SORRY.
HE'LL BE BACK AS THE WINTER SOLDIER. PROOOOBABLY BETTER TO LET YOU FIND THAT OUT YOURSELF...
HE'S GONE. I...I FAILED HIM.
IT'LL BE OKAY, STEVE. I SWEAR. YOUR LIFE IS JUST STARTING.

HIS NAME IS "STEVE"?

STEVE ROGERS. YEAH. PRIVATE STEVE ROGERS. THAT'S WHY HE HAD THE TATTERS OF ARMY GEAR.

HOW COULD YOU HAVE KNOWN THAT? ONLY THE TOP ARMY BRASS WERE AWARE OF MY REAL NAME.

OH, SHE KNOWS LOTS OF STUFF SHE SHOULDN'T KNOW.

AND HOW'D YOU DO THAT THING WITH YOUR ARMS AND HANDS?

I AM MS. MARVEL. AND YES, I HAVE ARMY CLEARANCE. VERY HIGH-LEVEL.

BUT YOU LOOK LIKE A CHILD!

UH--LOOKS CAN BE DECEIVING. LET'S JUST LEAVE IT AT THAT.

…O THE TOP ARMY …RASS KNOWS WHO … AM. CAN'T SAY I'M …RILLED ABOUT THAT.

YOUR SECRET'S IN GOOD HANDS. I SWEAR.

I'LL HAVE TO TAKE YOUR WORD FOR IT.

SO...STEVE, IS IT? WHY DON'T YOU TELL US HOW YOU WOUND UP A POPSICLE?

≷WHEEWWWWWW≷ OKAY, DODGED THAT. BUT NOW WHAT DO I DO?

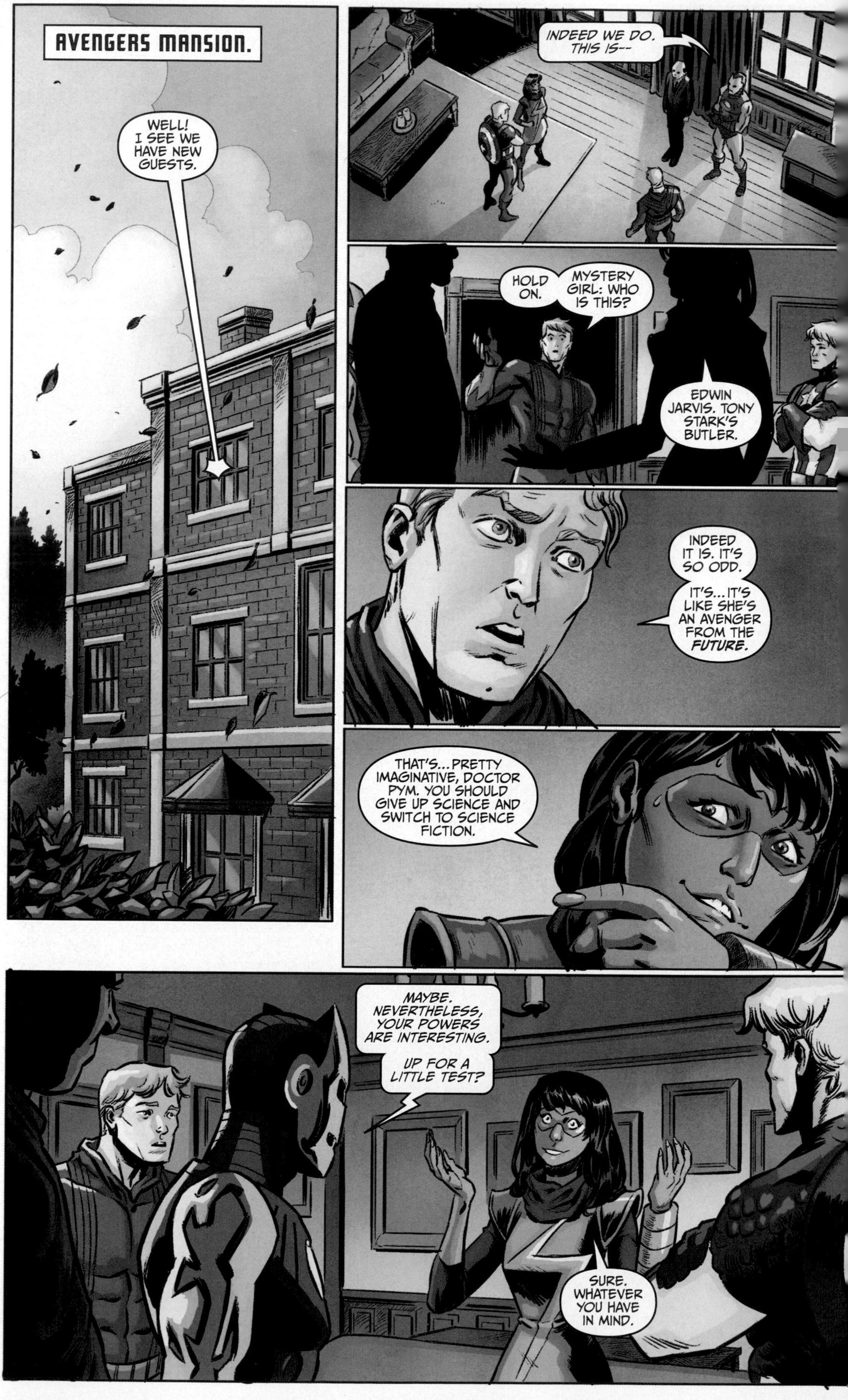
AVENGERS MANSION.
WELL! I SEE WE HAVE NEW GUESTS.
INDEED WE DO. THIS IS--
HOLD ON.
MYSTERY GIRL: WHO IS THIS?
EDWIN JARVIS. TONY STARK'S BUTLER.
INDEED IT IS. IT'S SO ODD.
IT'S...IT'S LIKE SHE'S AN AVENGER FROM THE *FUTURE.*
THAT'S...PRETTY IMAGINATIVE, DOCTOR PYM. YOU SHOULD GIVE UP SCIENCE AND SWITCH TO SCIENCE FICTION.
MAYBE. NEVERTHELESS, YOUR POWERS ARE INTERESTING.
UP FOR A LITTLE TEST?
SURE. WHATEVER YOU HAVE IN MIND.

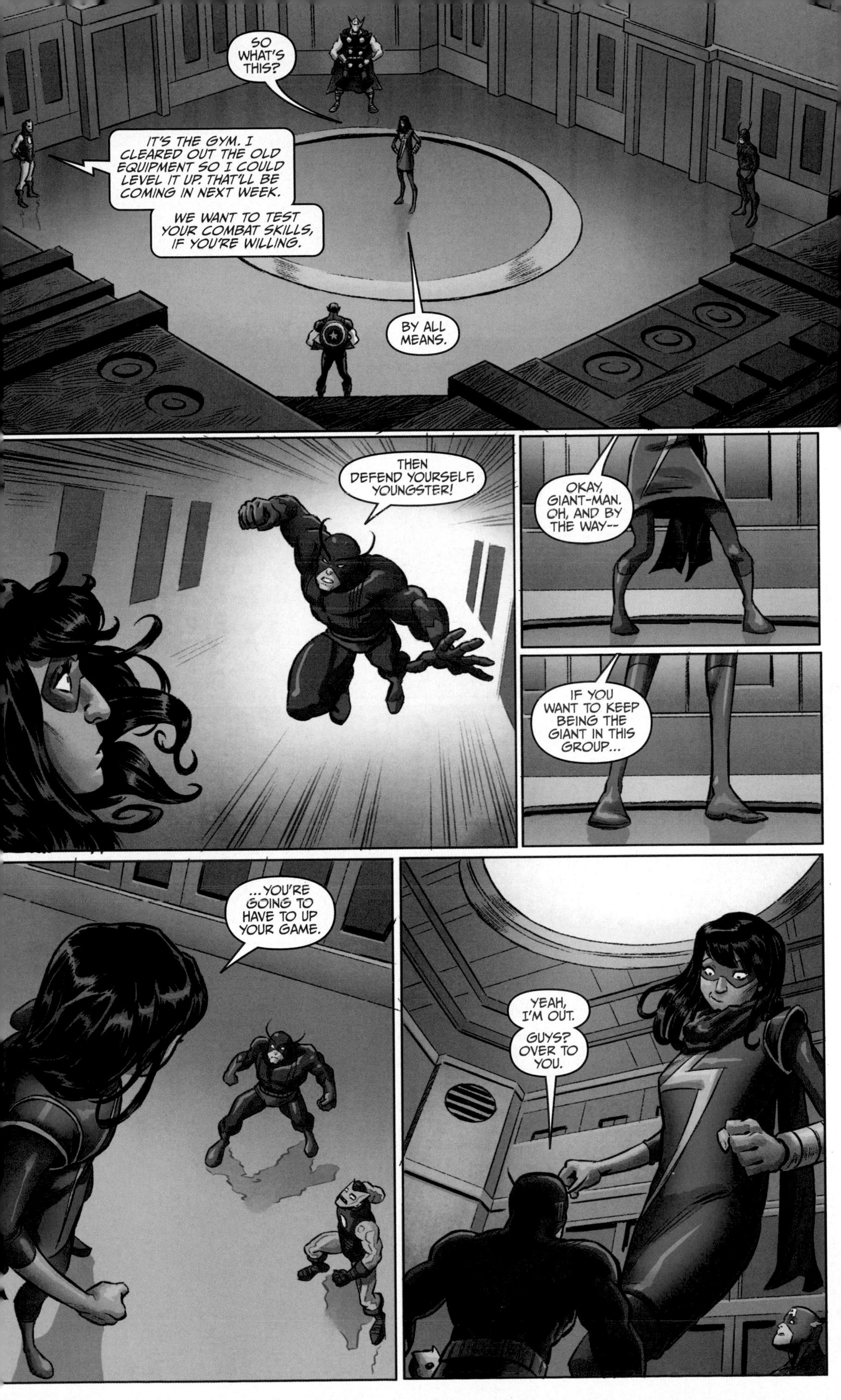
SO WHAT'S THIS?
IT'S THE GYM. I CLEARED OUT THE OLD EQUIPMENT SO I COULD LEVEL IT UP. THAT'LL BE COMING IN NEXT WEEK.
WE WANT TO TEST YOUR COMBAT SKILLS, IF YOU'RE WILLING.
BY ALL MEANS.
THEN DEFEND YOURSELF, YOUNGSTER!
OKAY, GIANT-MAN. OH, AND BY THE WAY--
IF YOU WANT TO KEEP BEING THE GIANT IN THIS GROUP...
...YOU'RE GOING TO HAVE TO UP YOUR GAME.
YEAH, I'M OUT.
GUYS? OVER TO YOU.

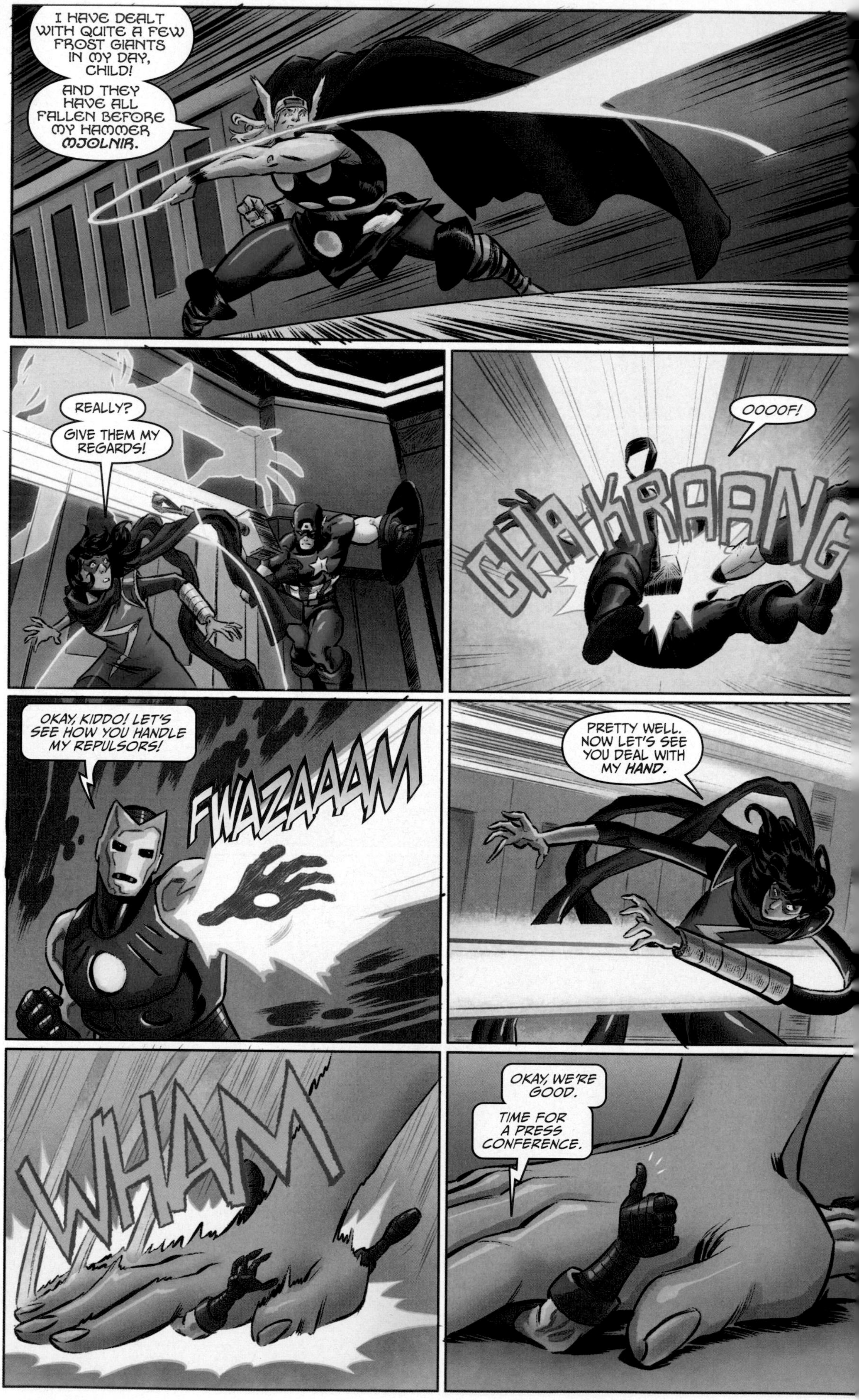
I HAVE DEALT WITH QUITE A FEW FROST GIANTS IN MY DAY, CHILD!
AND THEY HAVE ALL FALLEN BEFORE MY HAMMER MJOLNIR.
REALLY?
GIVE THEM MY REGARDS!
OOOOF!
GHA-KRAAANG
OKAY, KIDDO! LET'S SEE HOW YOU HANDLE MY REPULSORS!
FWAZAAAM
PRETTY WELL. NOW LET'S SEE YOU DEAL WITH MY HAND.
WHAM
OKAY, WE'RE GOOD.
TIME FOR A PRESS CONFERENCE.

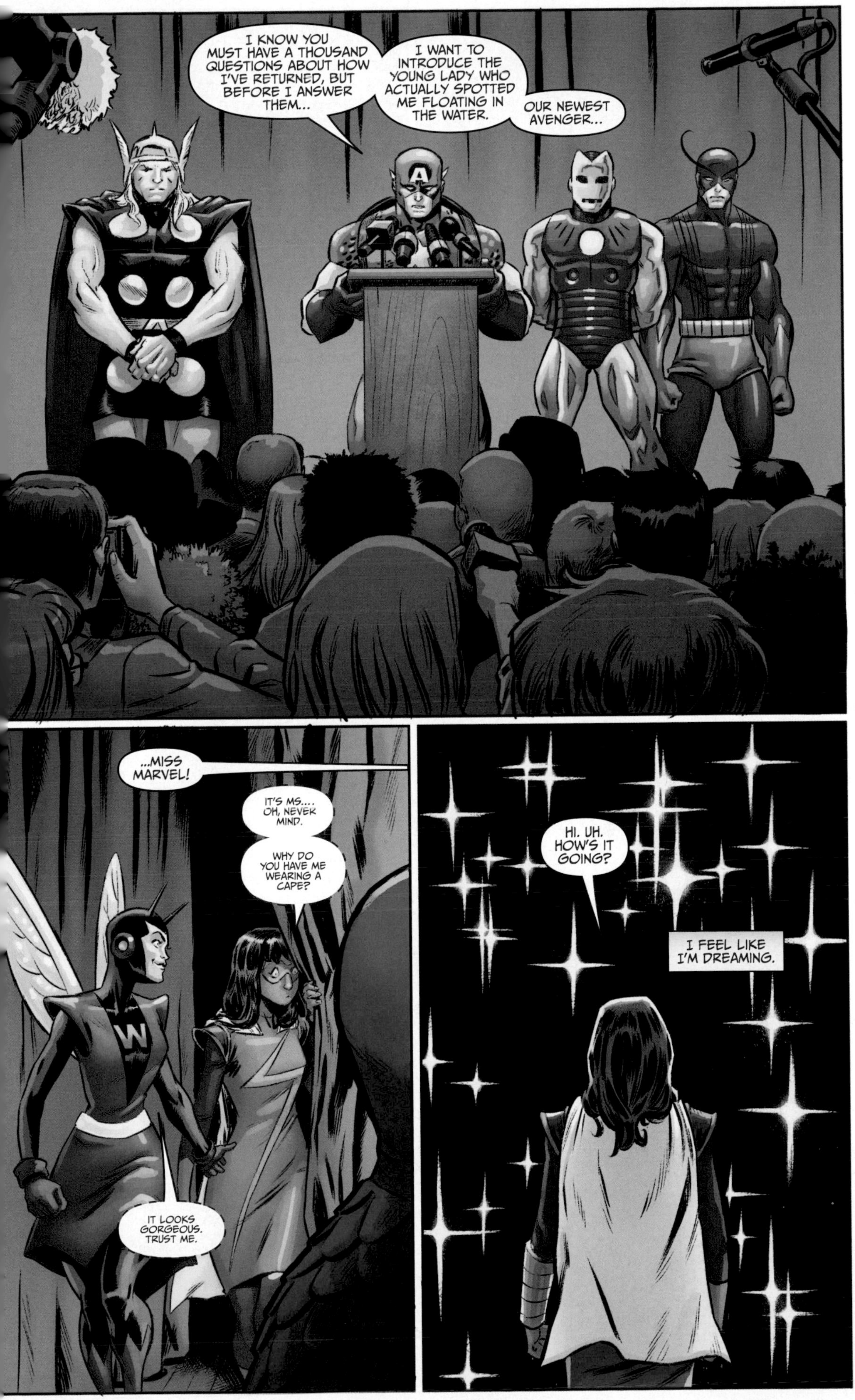
I KNOW YOU MUST HAVE A THOUSAND QUESTIONS ABOUT HOW I'VE RETURNED, BUT BEFORE I ANSWER THEM...
I WANT TO INTRODUCE THE YOUNG LADY WHO ACTUALLY SPOTTED ME FLOATING IN THE WATER.
OUR NEWEST AVENGER...
...MISS MARVEL!
IT'S MS.... OH, NEVER MIND.
WHY DO YOU HAVE ME WEARING A CAPE?
IT LOOKS GORGEOUS. TRUST ME.
HI. UH. HOW'S IT GOING?
I FEEL LIKE I'M DREAMING.

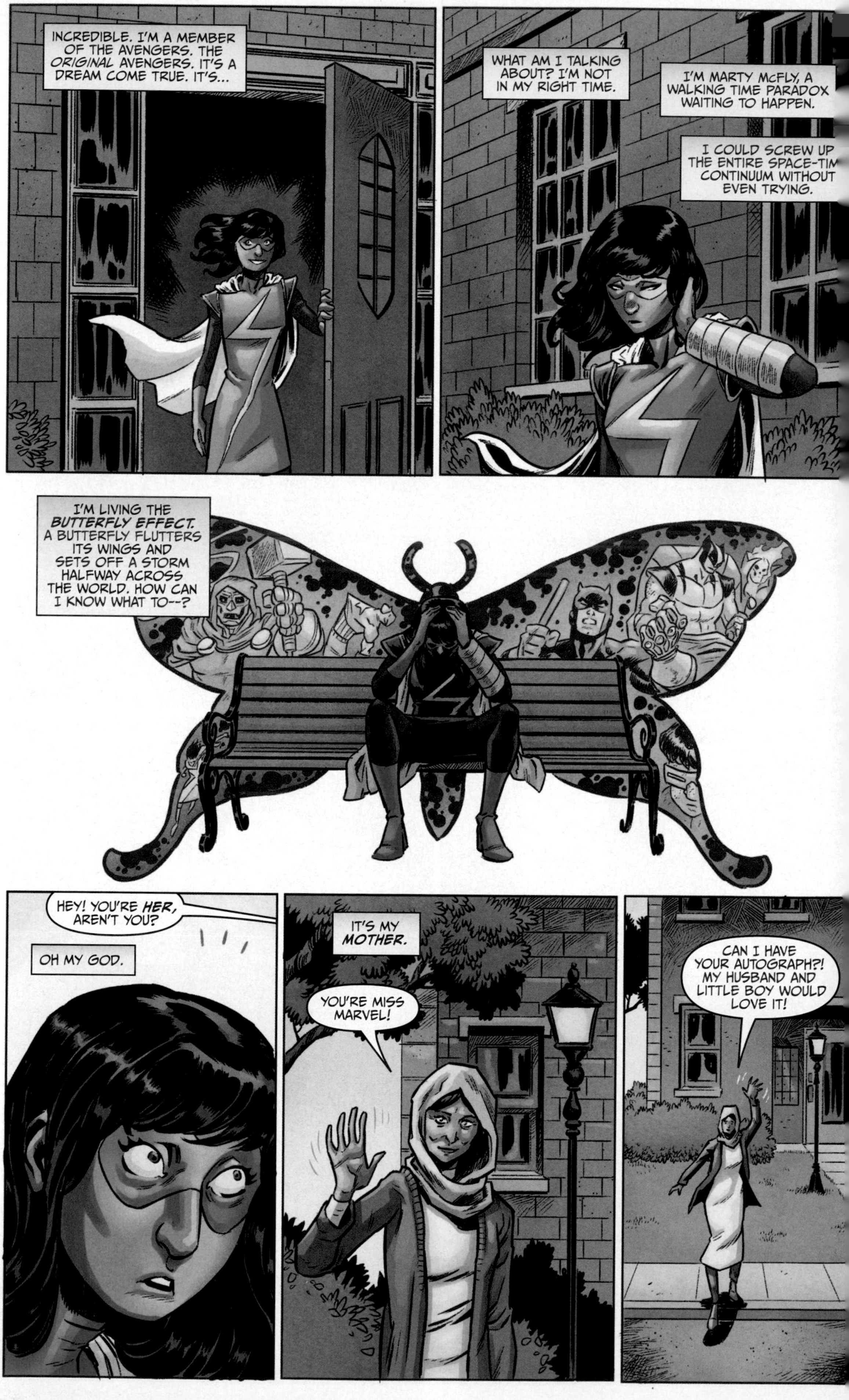
INCREDIBLE. I'M A MEMBER OF THE AVENGERS. THE ORIGINAL AVENGERS. IT'S A DREAM COME TRUE. IT'S...
WHAT AM I TALKING ABOUT? I'M NOT IN MY RIGHT TIME.
I'M MARTY McFLY, A WALKING TIME PARADOX WAITING TO HAPPEN.
I COULD SCREW UP THE ENTIRE SPACE-TIM CONTINUUM WITHOUT EVEN TRYING.
I'M LIVING THE BUTTERFLY EFFECT. A BUTTERFLY FLUTTERS ITS WINGS AND SETS OFF A STORM HALFWAY ACROSS THE WORLD. HOW CAN I KNOW WHAT TO--?
HEY! YOU'RE HER, AREN'T YOU?
OH MY GOD.
IT'S MY MOTHER.
YOU'RE MISS MARVEL!
CAN I HAVE YOUR AUTOGRAPH?! MY HUSBAND AND LITTLE BOY WOULD LOVE IT!

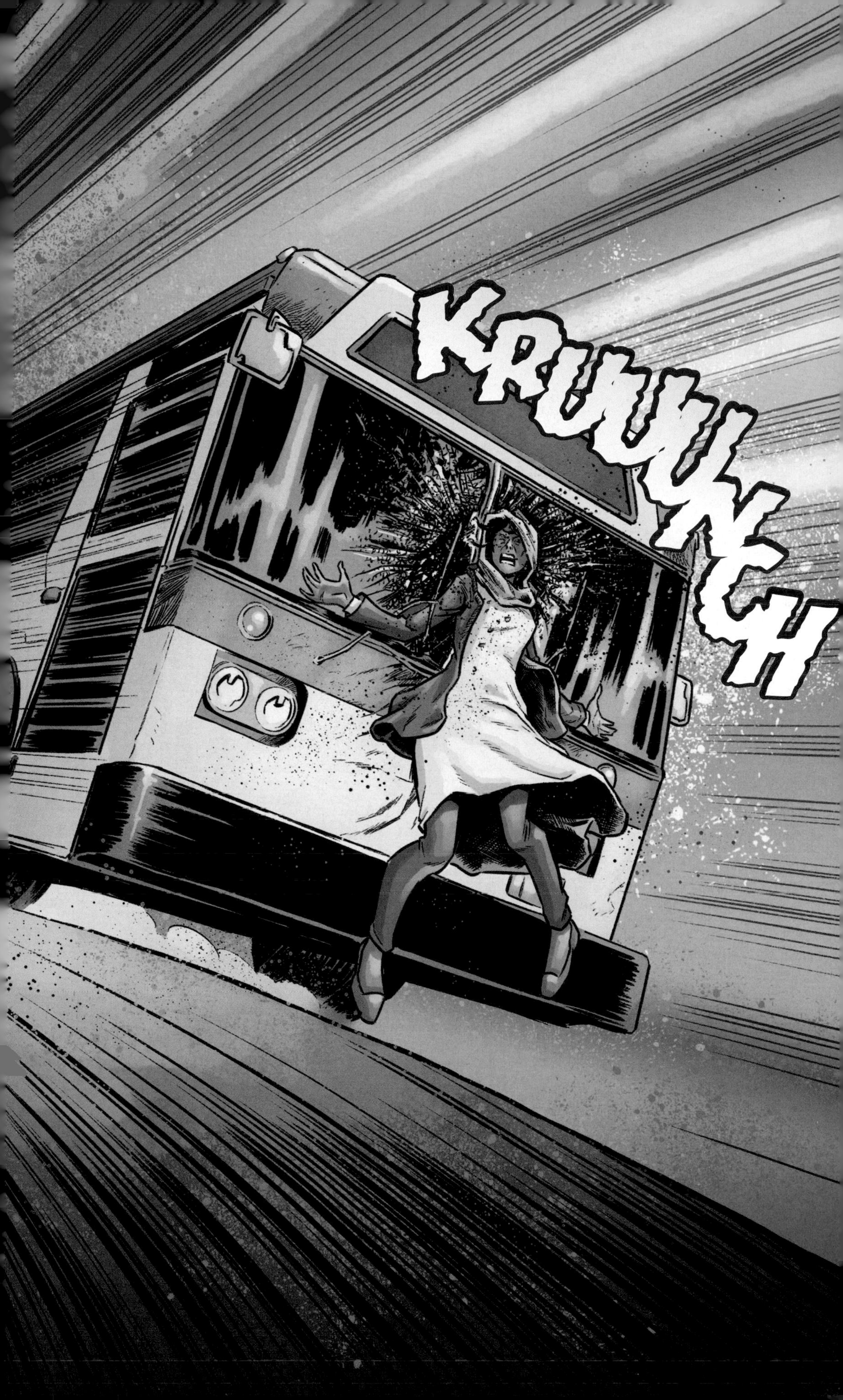
KRUUUNCH

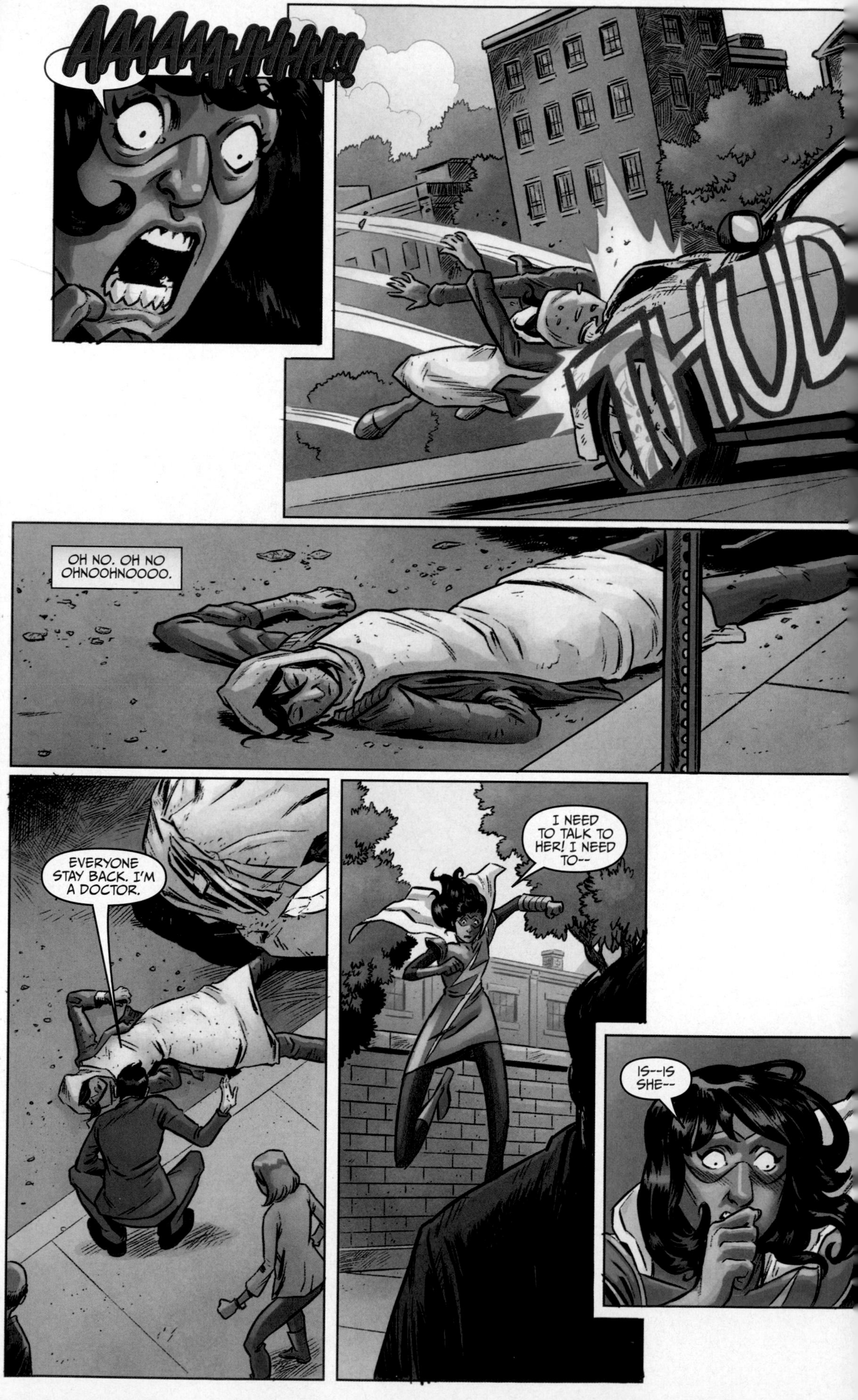
AAAAAAHHHHH!!!
THUD
OH NO. OH NO OHNOOHNOOOO.
EVERYONE STAY BACK. I'M A DOCTOR.
I NEED TO TALK TO HER! I NEED TO--
IS--IS SHE--

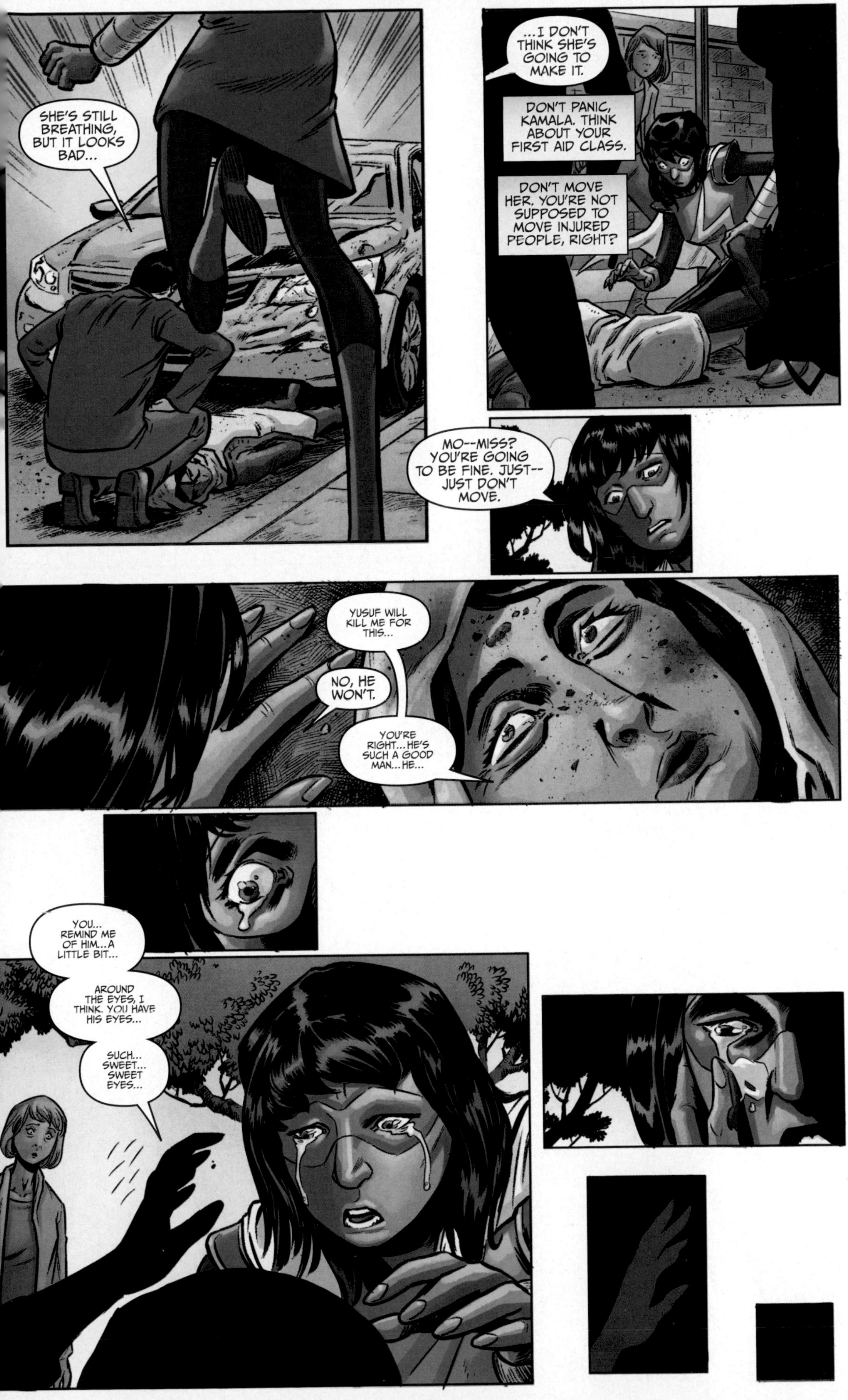
SHE'S STILL BREATHING, BUT IT LOOKS BAD...
...I DON'T THINK SHE'S GOING TO MAKE IT.
DON'T PANIC, KAMALA. THINK ABOUT YOUR FIRST AID CLASS.
DON'T MOVE HER. YOU'RE NOT SUPPOSED TO MOVE INJURED PEOPLE, RIGHT?
MO--MISS? YOU'RE GOING TO BE FINE. JUST--JUST DON'T MOVE.
YUSUF WILL KILL ME FOR THIS...
NO, HE WON'T.
YOU'RE RIGHT...HE'S SUCH A GOOD MAN...HE...
YOU... REMIND ME OF HIM...A LITTLE BIT...
AROUND THE EYES, I THINK. YOU HAVE HIS EYES...
SUCH... SWEET... SWEET EYES...

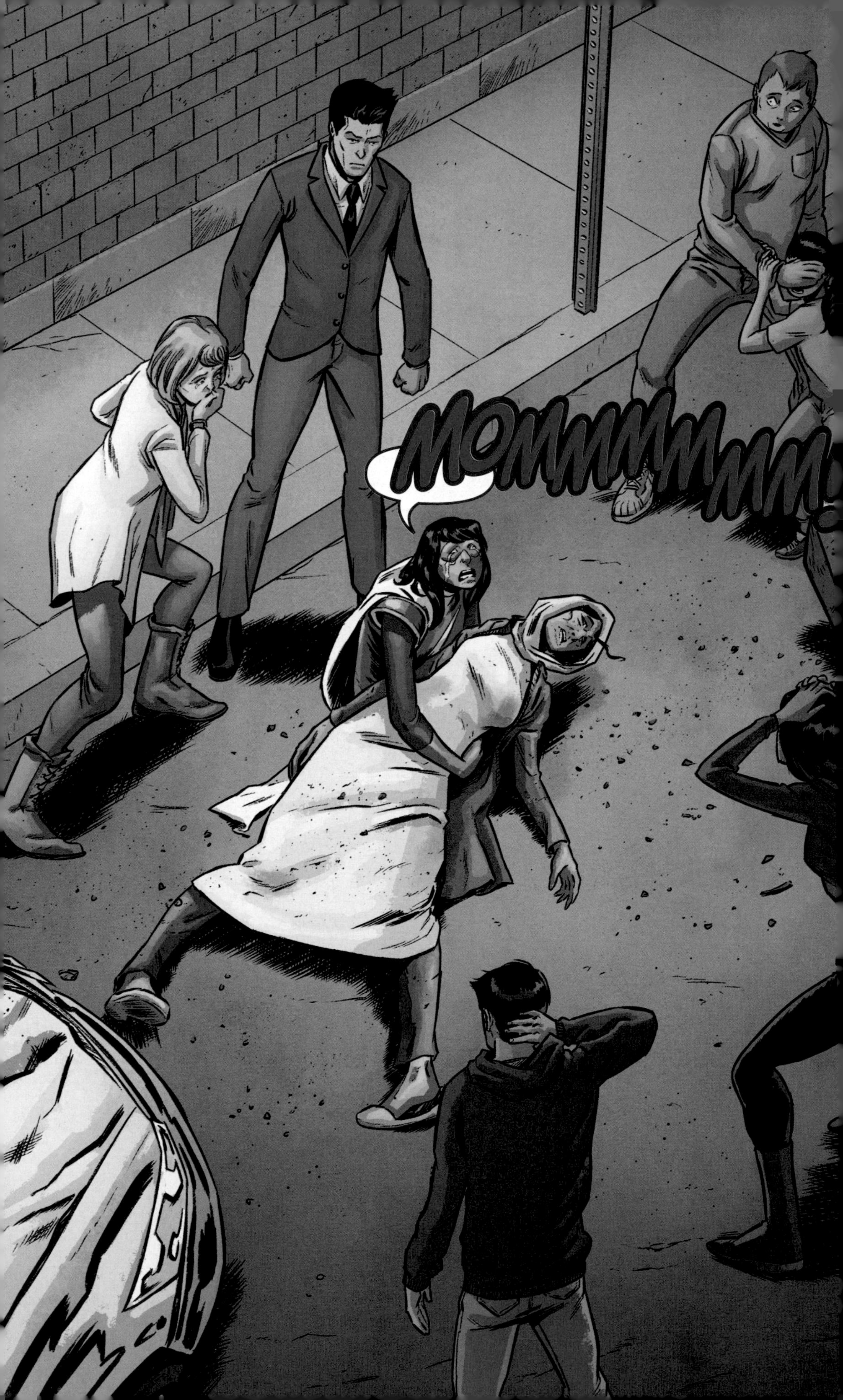
MOMMMMMMM!

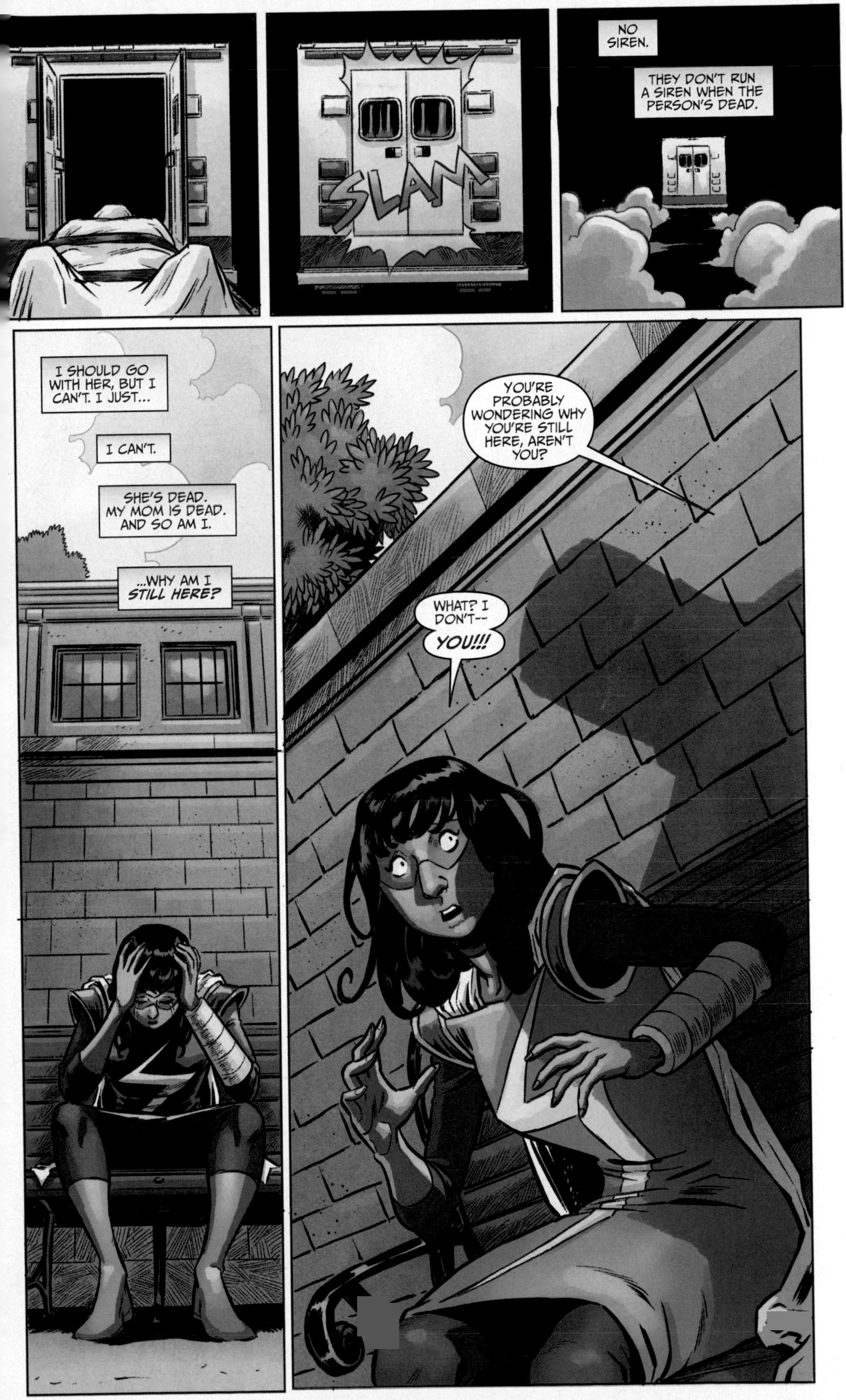
SLAM
NO SIREN.
THEY DON'T RUN A SIREN WHEN THE PERSON'S DEAD.
I SHOULD GO WITH HER, BUT I CAN'T. I JUST...
I CAN'T.
SHE'S DEAD. MY MOM IS DEAD. AND SO AM I.
...WHY AM I *STILL HERE?*
YOU'RE PROBABLY WONDERING WHY YOU'RE STILL HERE, AREN'T YOU?
WHAT? I DON'T-- *YOU!!!*

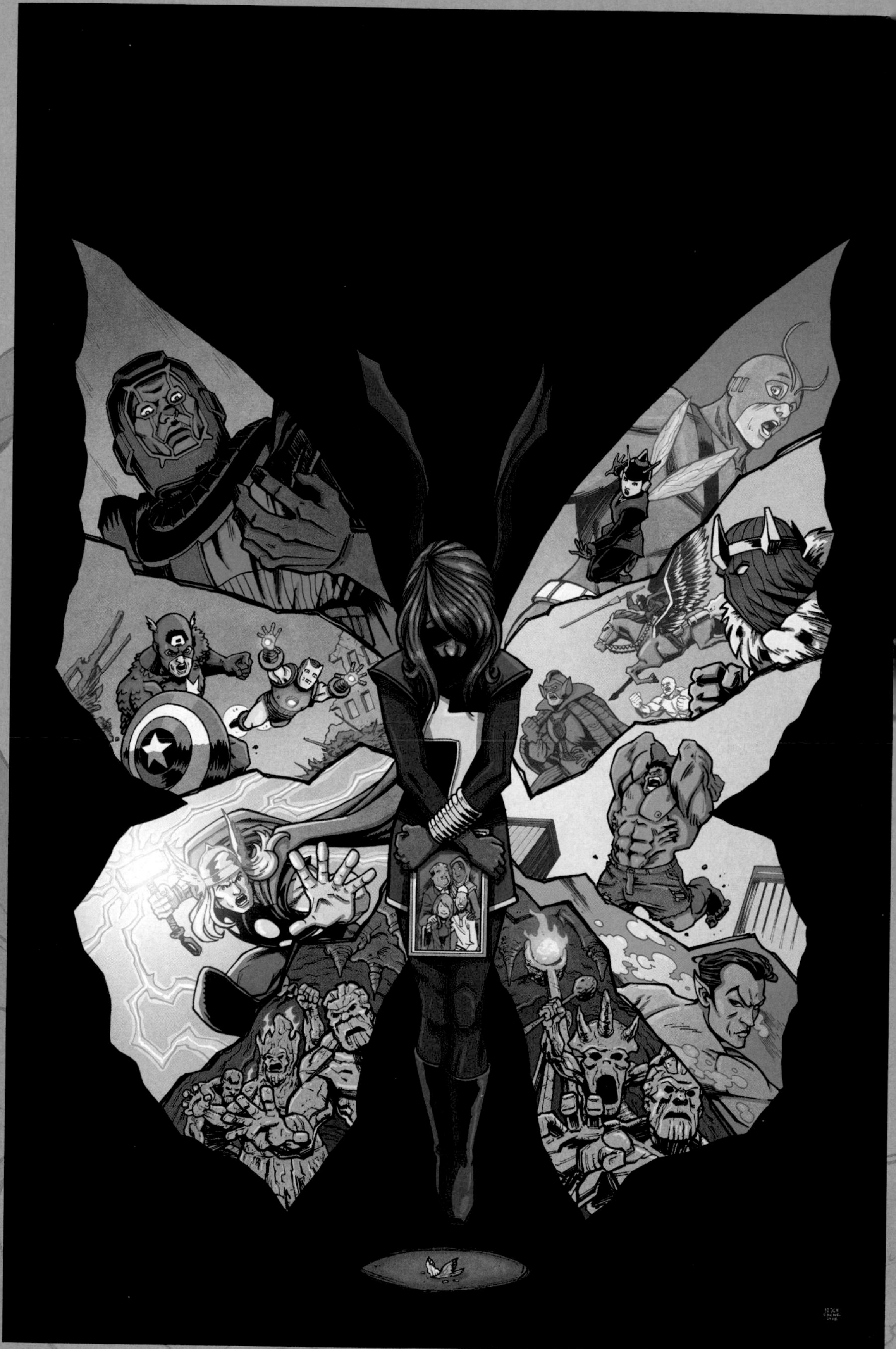

6

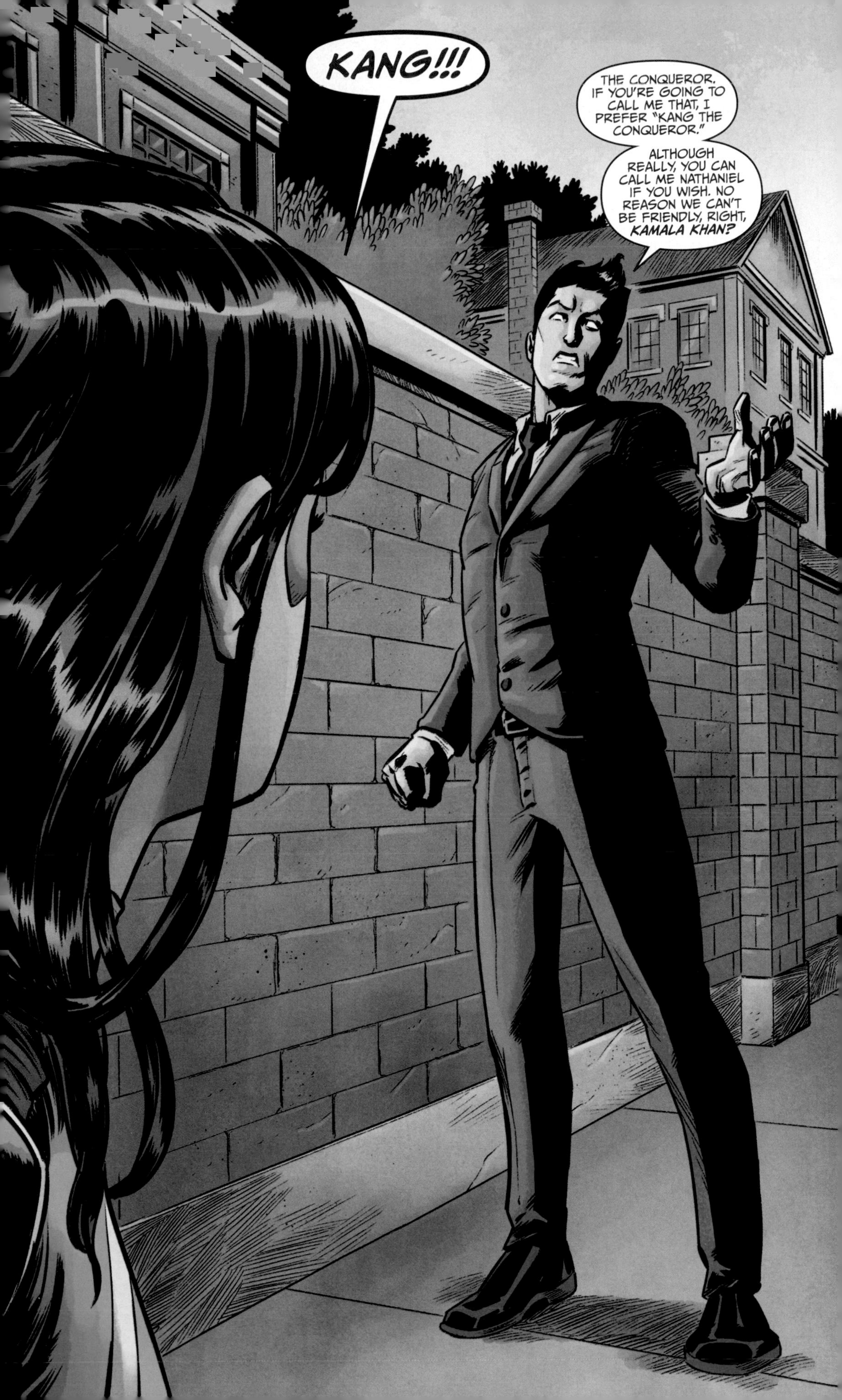
KANG!!!
THE CONQUEROR. IF YOU'RE GOING TO CALL ME THAT, I PREFER "KANG THE CONQUEROR."
ALTHOUGH REALLY, YOU CAN CALL ME NATHANIEL IF YOU WISH. NO REASON WE CAN'T BE FRIENDLY, RIGHT, KAMALA KHAN?

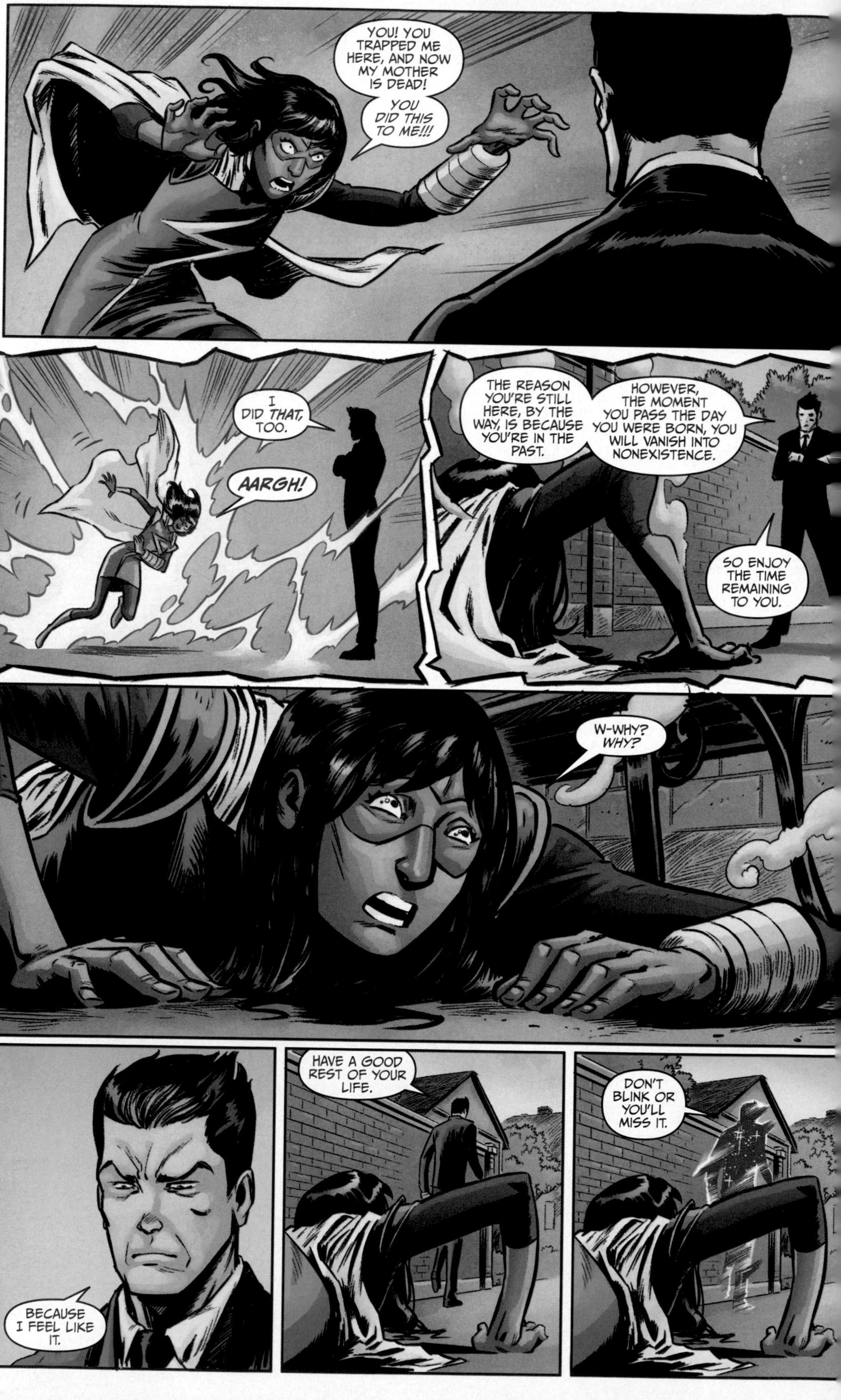

YOU! YOU TRAPPED ME HERE, AND NOW MY MOTHER IS DEAD!
YOU DID THIS TO ME!!!
I DID THAT, TOO.
AARGH!
THE REASON YOU'RE STILL HERE, BY THE WAY, IS BECAUSE YOU'RE IN THE PAST.
HOWEVER, THE MOMENT YOU PASS THE DAY YOU WERE BORN, YOU WILL VANISH INTO NONEXISTENCE.
SO ENJOY THE TIME REMAINING TO YOU.
W-WHY? WHY?
BECAUSE I FEEL LIKE IT.
HAVE A GOOD REST OF YOUR LIFE.
DON'T BLINK OR YOU'LL MISS IT.

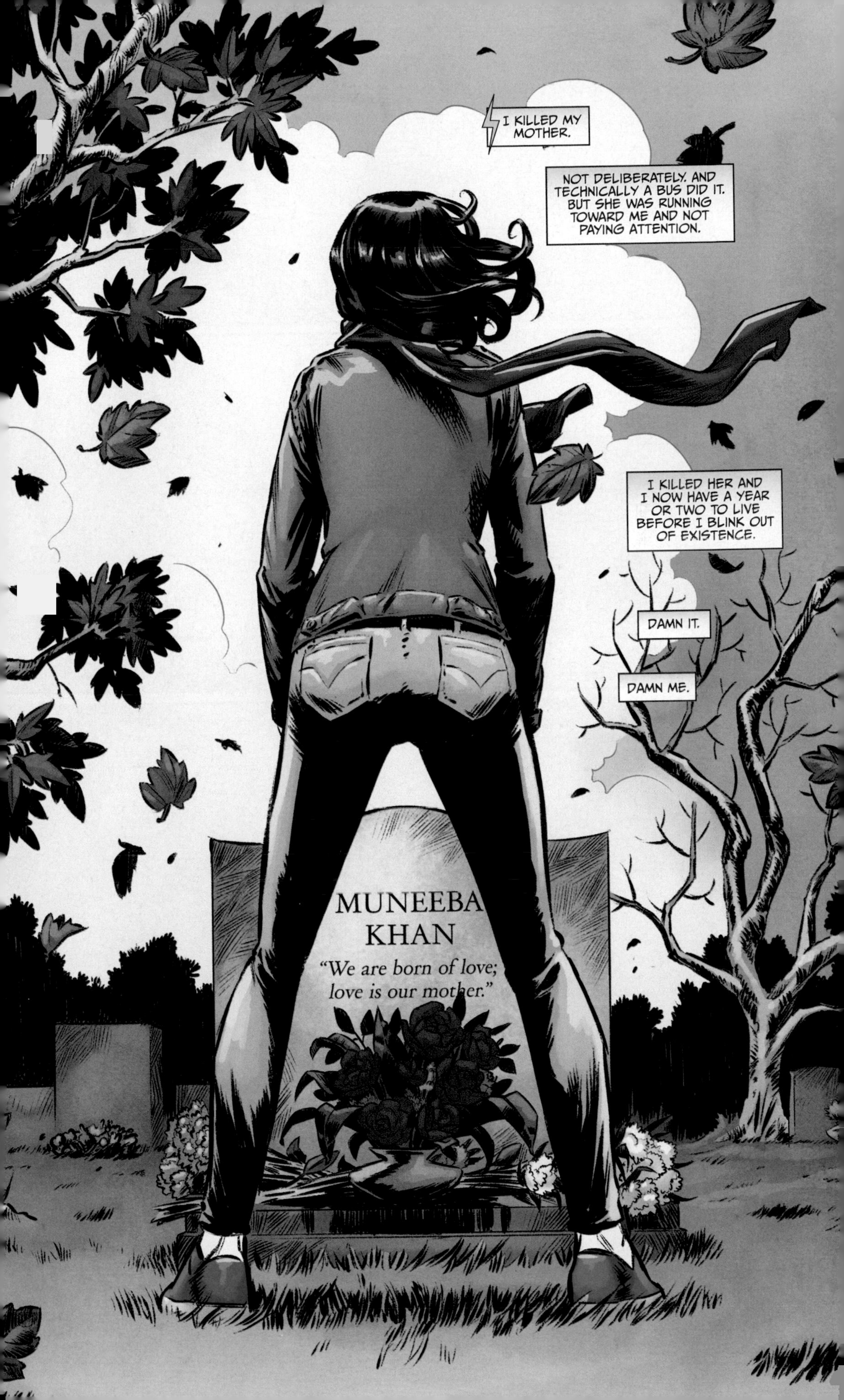
I KILLED MY MOTHER.
NOT DELIBERATELY. AND TECHNICALLY A BUS DID IT. BUT SHE WAS RUNNING TOWARD ME AND NOT PAYING ATTENTION.
I KILLED HER AND I NOW HAVE A YEAR OR TWO TO LIVE BEFORE I BLINK OUT OF EXISTENCE.
DAMN IT.
DAMN ME.
MUNEEBA KHAN
"We are born of love; love is our mother."

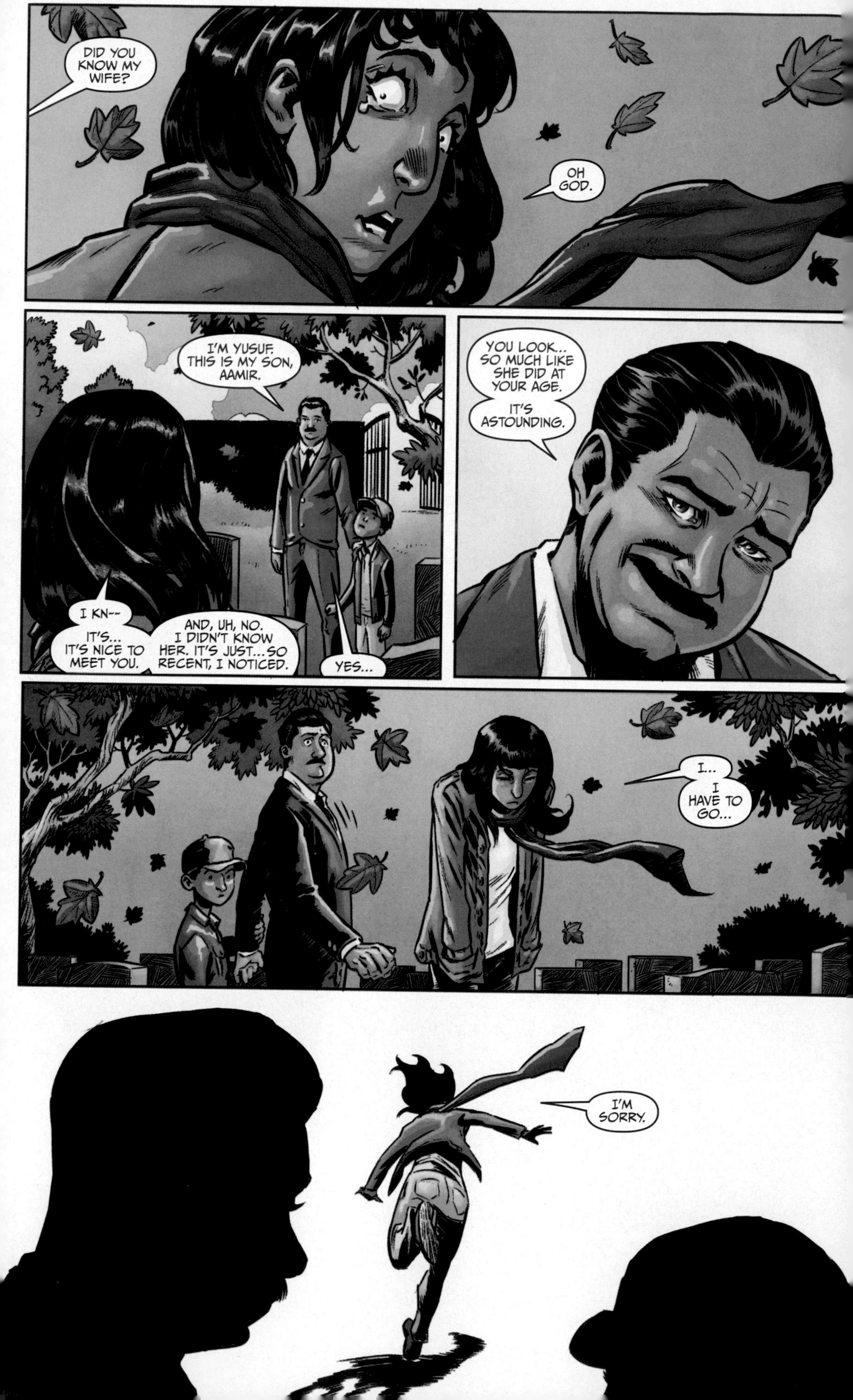
DID YOU KNOW MY WIFE?
OH GOD.
I'M YUSUF. THIS IS MY SON, AAMIR.
I KN--
IT'S... IT'S NICE TO MEET YOU.
AND, UH, NO. I DIDN'T KNOW HER. IT'S JUST... SO RECENT, I NOTICED.
YES...
YOU LOOK... SO MUCH LIKE SHE DID AT YOUR AGE.
IT'S ASTOUNDING.
I... I HAVE TO GO...
I'M SORRY.

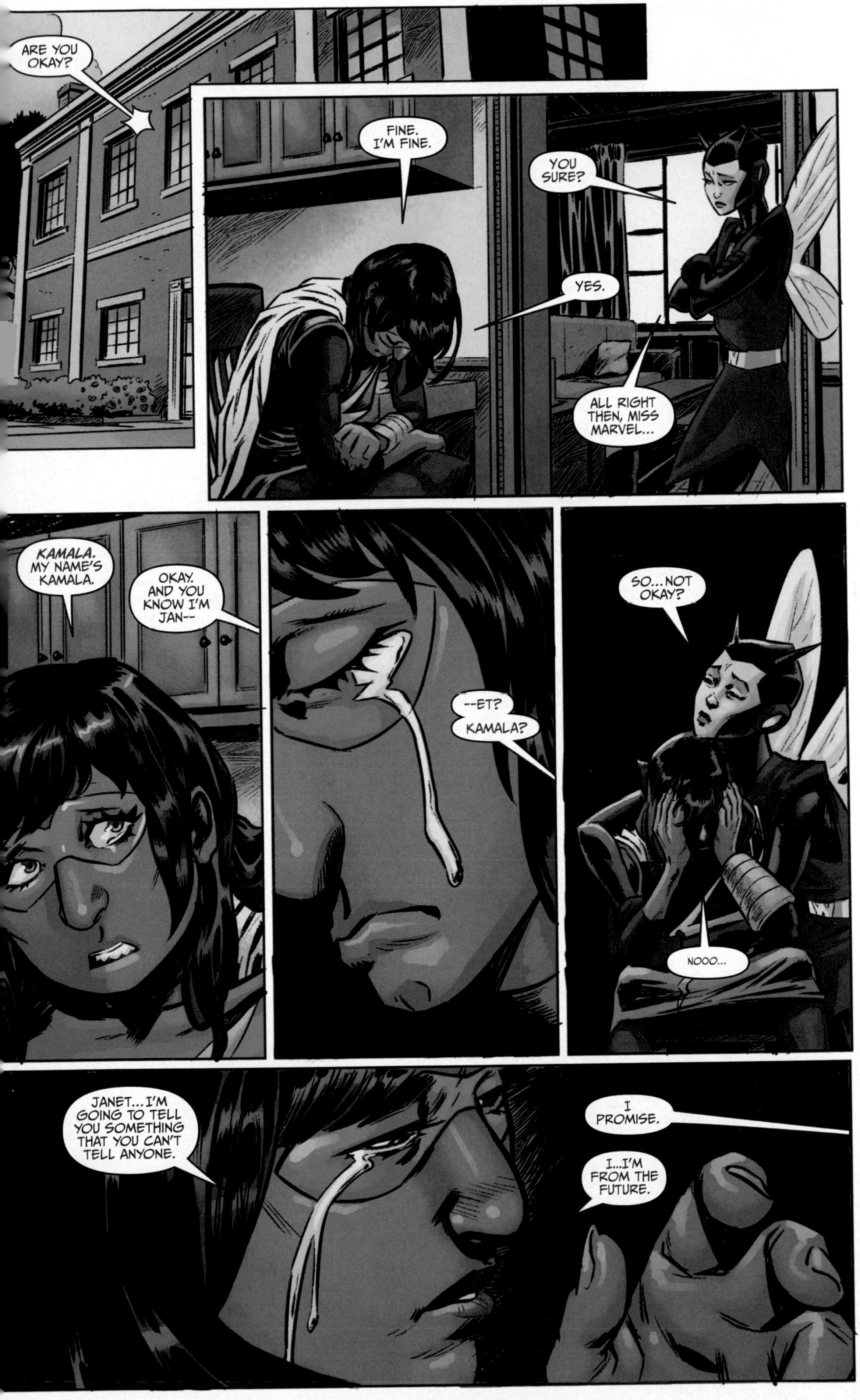
ARE YOU OKAY?
FINE. I'M FINE.
YOU SURE?
YES.
ALL RIGHT THEN, MISS MARVEL...
KAMALA. MY NAME'S KAMALA.
OKAY. AND YOU KNOW I'M JAN--
--ET?
KAMALA?
SO...NOT OKAY?
NOOO...
JANET...I'M GOING TO TELL YOU SOMETHING THAT YOU CAN'T TELL ANYONE.
I PROMISE.
I...I'M FROM THE FUTURE.

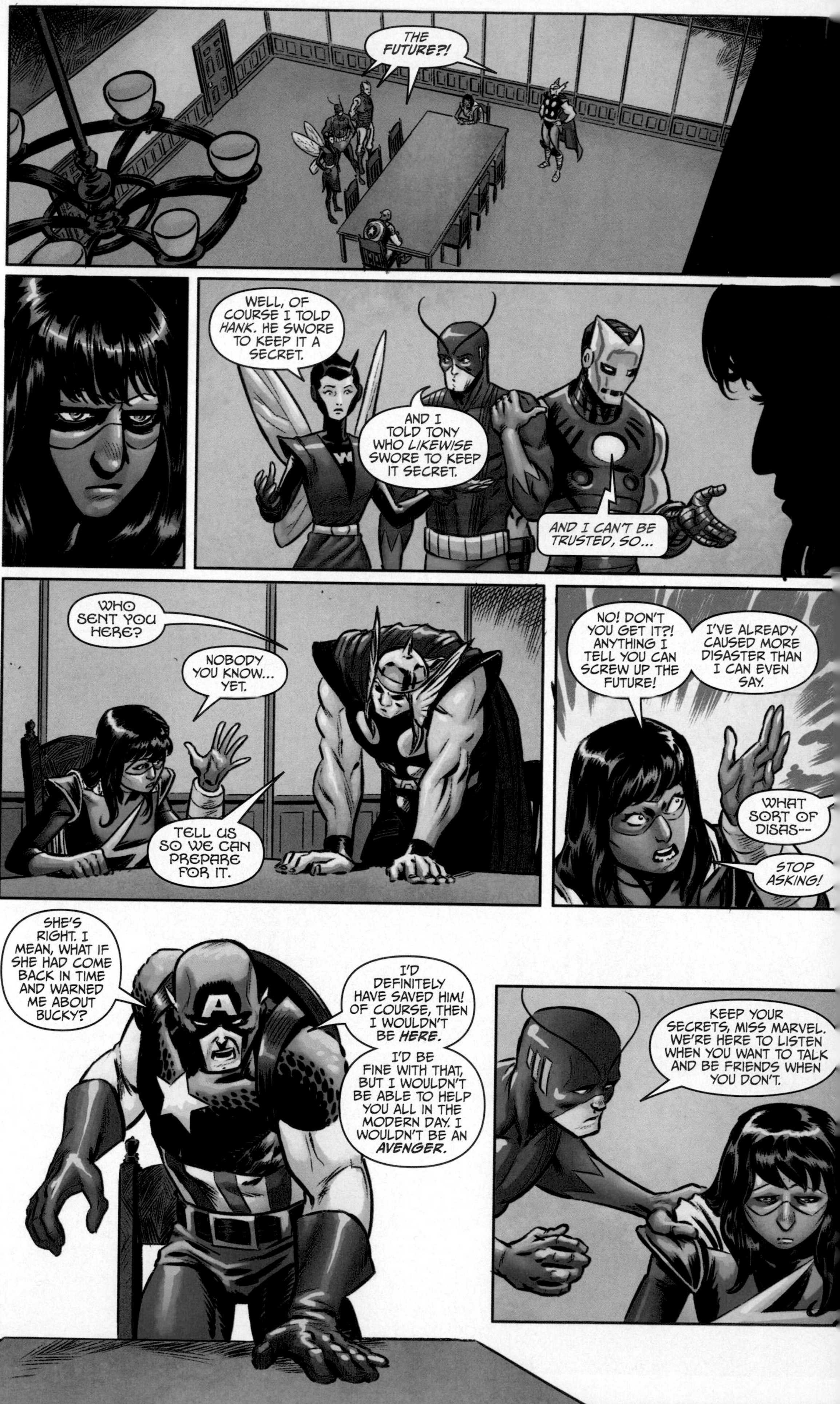
THE FUTURE?!
WELL, OF COURSE I TOLD HANK. HE SWORE TO KEEP IT A SECRET.
AND I TOLD TONY WHO LIKEWISE SWORE TO KEEP IT SECRET.
AND I CAN'T BE TRUSTED, SO...
WHO SENT YOU HERE?
NOBODY YOU KNOW... YET.
TELL US SO WE CAN PREPARE FOR IT.
NO! DON'T YOU GET IT?! ANYTHING I TELL YOU CAN SCREW UP THE FUTURE!
I'VE ALREADY CAUSED MORE DISASTER THAN I CAN EVEN SAY.
WHAT SORT OF DISAS--
STOP ASKING!
SHE'S RIGHT. I MEAN, WHAT IF SHE HAD COME BACK IN TIME AND WARNED ME ABOUT BUCKY?
I'D DEFINITELY HAVE SAVED HIM! OF COURSE, THEN I WOULDN'T BE HERE.
I'D BE FINE WITH THAT, BUT I WOULDN'T BE ABLE TO HELP YOU ALL IN THE MODERN DAY. I WOULDN'T BE AN AVENGER.
KEEP YOUR SECRETS, MISS MARVEL. WE'RE HERE TO LISTEN WHEN YOU WANT TO TALK AND BE FRIENDS WHEN YOU DON'T.

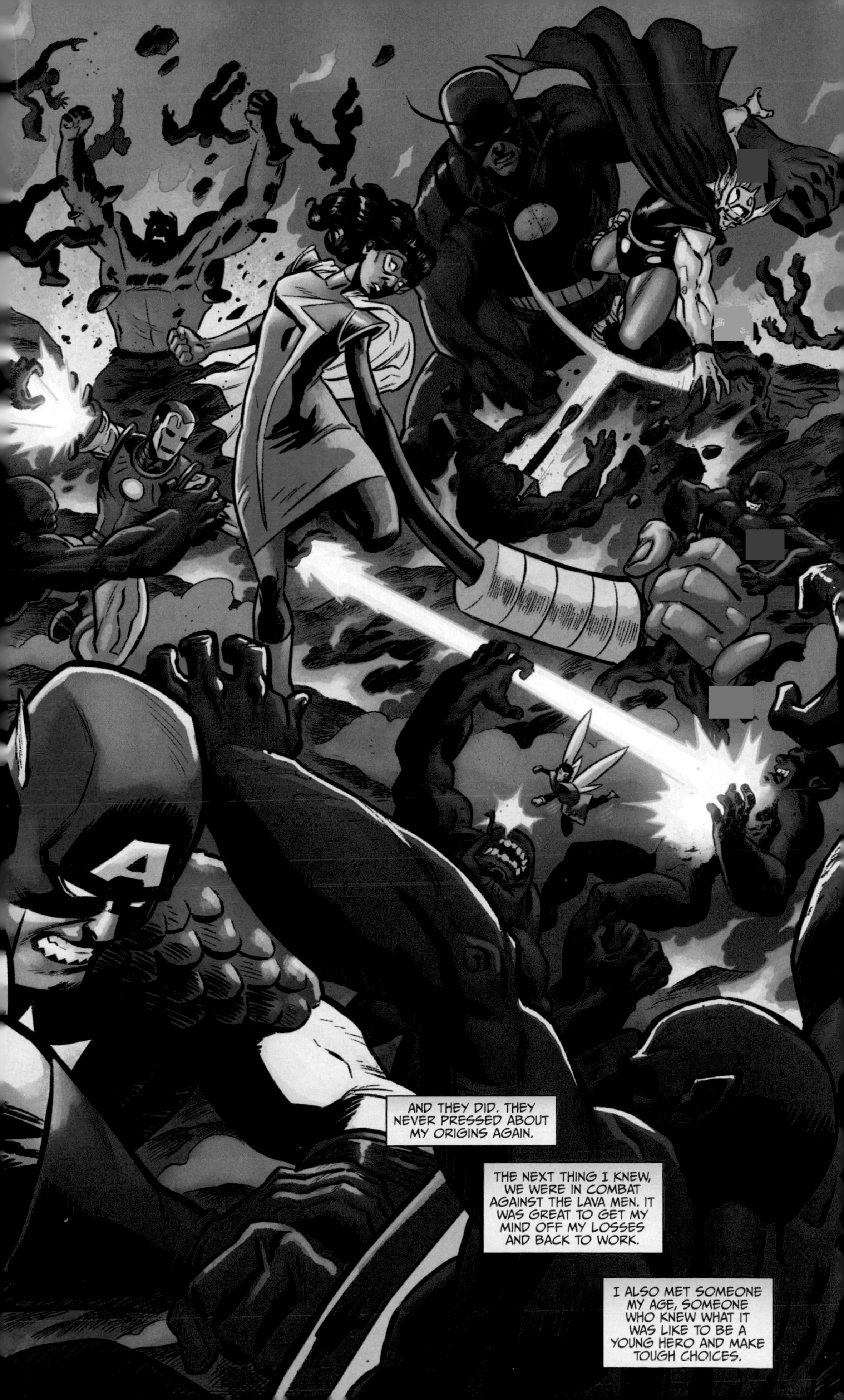
AND THEY DID. THEY NEVER PRESSED ABOUT MY ORIGINS AGAIN.
THE NEXT THING I KNEW, WE WERE IN COMBAT AGAINST THE LAVA MEN. IT WAS GREAT TO GET MY MIND OFF MY LOSSES AND BACK TO WORK.
I ALSO MET SOMEONE MY AGE, SOMEONE WHO KNEW WHAT IT WAS LIKE TO BE A YOUNG HERO AND MAKE TOUGH CHOICES.

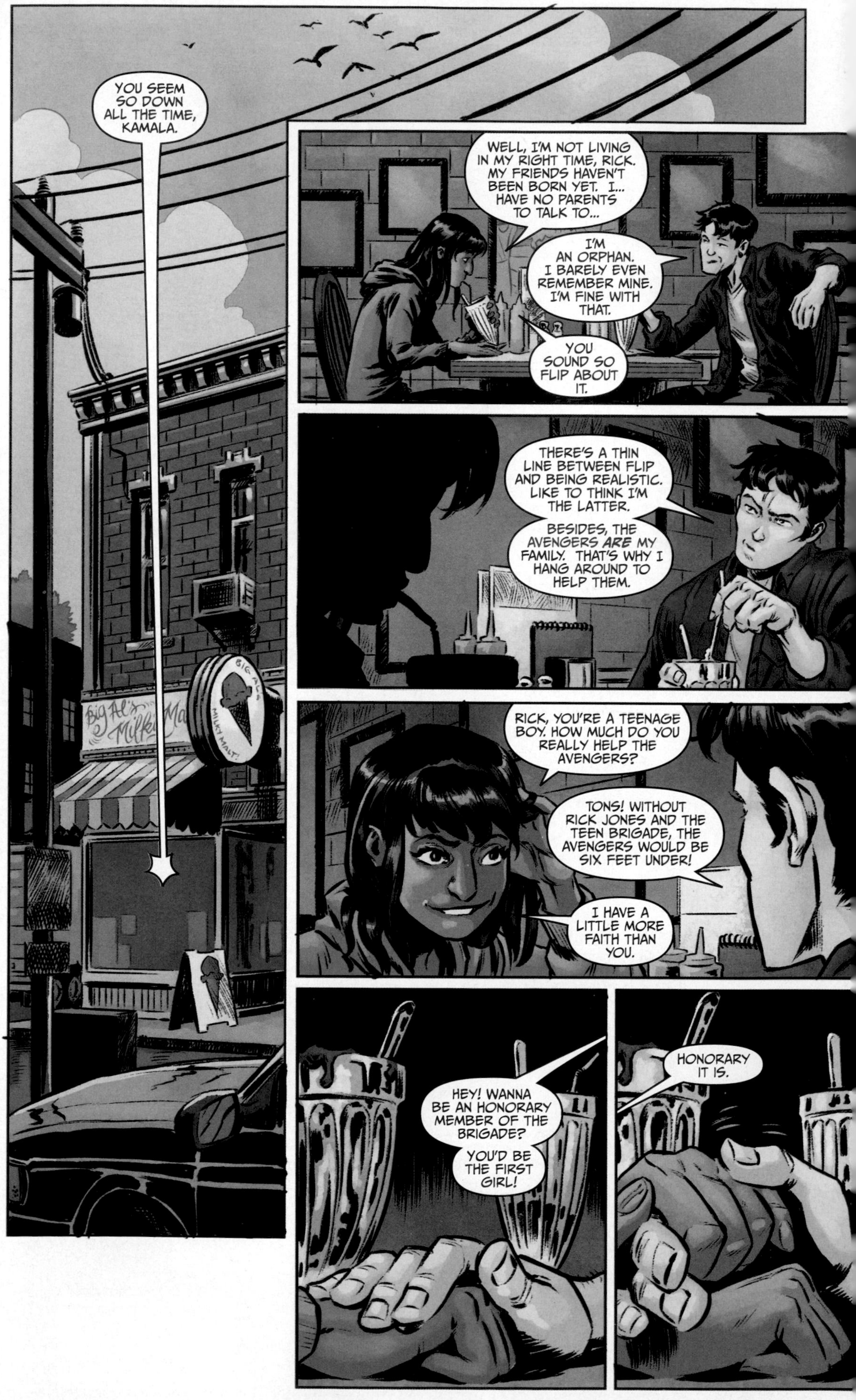

YOU SEEM SO DOWN ALL THE TIME, KAMALA.
WELL, I'M NOT LIVING IN MY RIGHT TIME, RICK. MY FRIENDS HAVEN'T BEEN BORN YET. I... HAVE NO PARENTS TO TALK TO...
I'M AN ORPHAN. I BARELY EVEN REMEMBER MINE. I'M FINE WITH THAT.
YOU SOUND SO FLIP ABOUT IT.
THERE'S A THIN LINE BETWEEN FLIP AND BEING REALISTIC. LIKE TO THINK I'M THE LATTER.
BESIDES, THE AVENGERS ARE MY FAMILY. THAT'S WHY I HANG AROUND TO HELP THEM.
RICK, YOU'RE A TEENAGE BOY. HOW MUCH DO YOU REALLY HELP THE AVENGERS?
TONS! WITHOUT RICK JONES AND THE TEEN BRIGADE, THE AVENGERS WOULD BE SIX FEET UNDER!
I HAVE A LITTLE MORE FAITH THAN YOU.
HEY! WANNA BE AN HONORARY MEMBER OF THE BRIGADE?
YOU'D BE THE FIRST GIRL!
HONORARY IT IS.

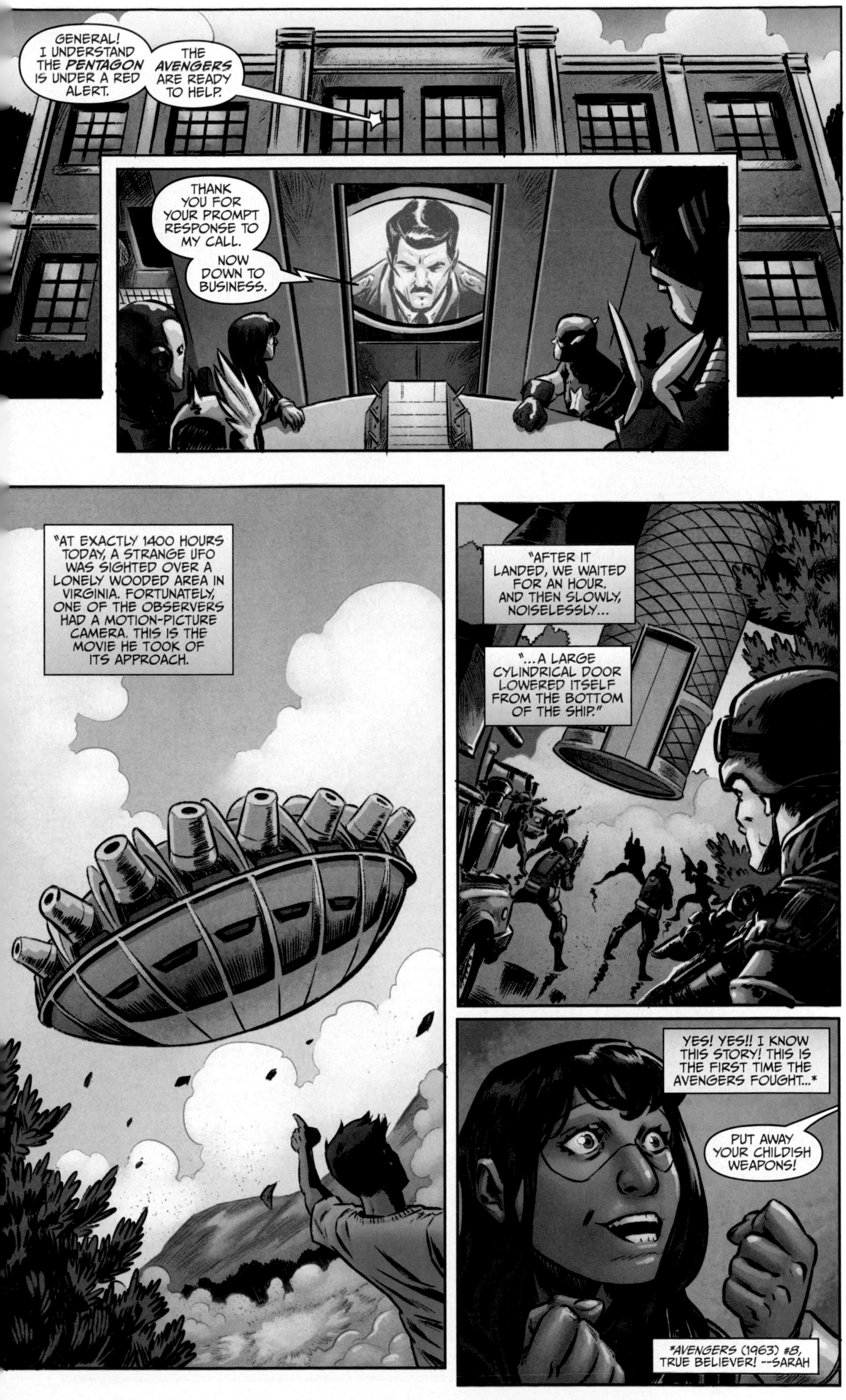
GENERAL! I UNDERSTAND THE PENTAGON IS UNDER A RED ALERT.
THE AVENGERS ARE READY TO HELP.
THANK YOU FOR YOUR PROMPT RESPONSE TO MY CALL.
NOW DOWN TO BUSINESS.
"AT EXACTLY 1400 HOURS TODAY, A STRANGE UFO WAS SIGHTED OVER A LONELY WOODED AREA IN VIRGINIA. FORTUNATELY, ONE OF THE OBSERVERS HAD A MOTION-PICTURE CAMERA. THIS IS THE MOVIE HE TOOK OF ITS APPROACH.
"AFTER IT LANDED, WE WAITED FOR AN HOUR. AND THEN SLOWLY, NOISELESSLY...
"...A LARGE CYLINDRICAL DOOR LOWERED ITSELF FROM THE BOTTOM OF THE SHIP."
YES! YES!! I KNOW THIS STORY! THIS IS THE FIRST TIME THE AVENGERS FOUGHT...*
PUT AWAY YOUR CHILDISH WEAPONS!
*AVENGERS (1963) #8, TRUE BELIEVER! --SARAH

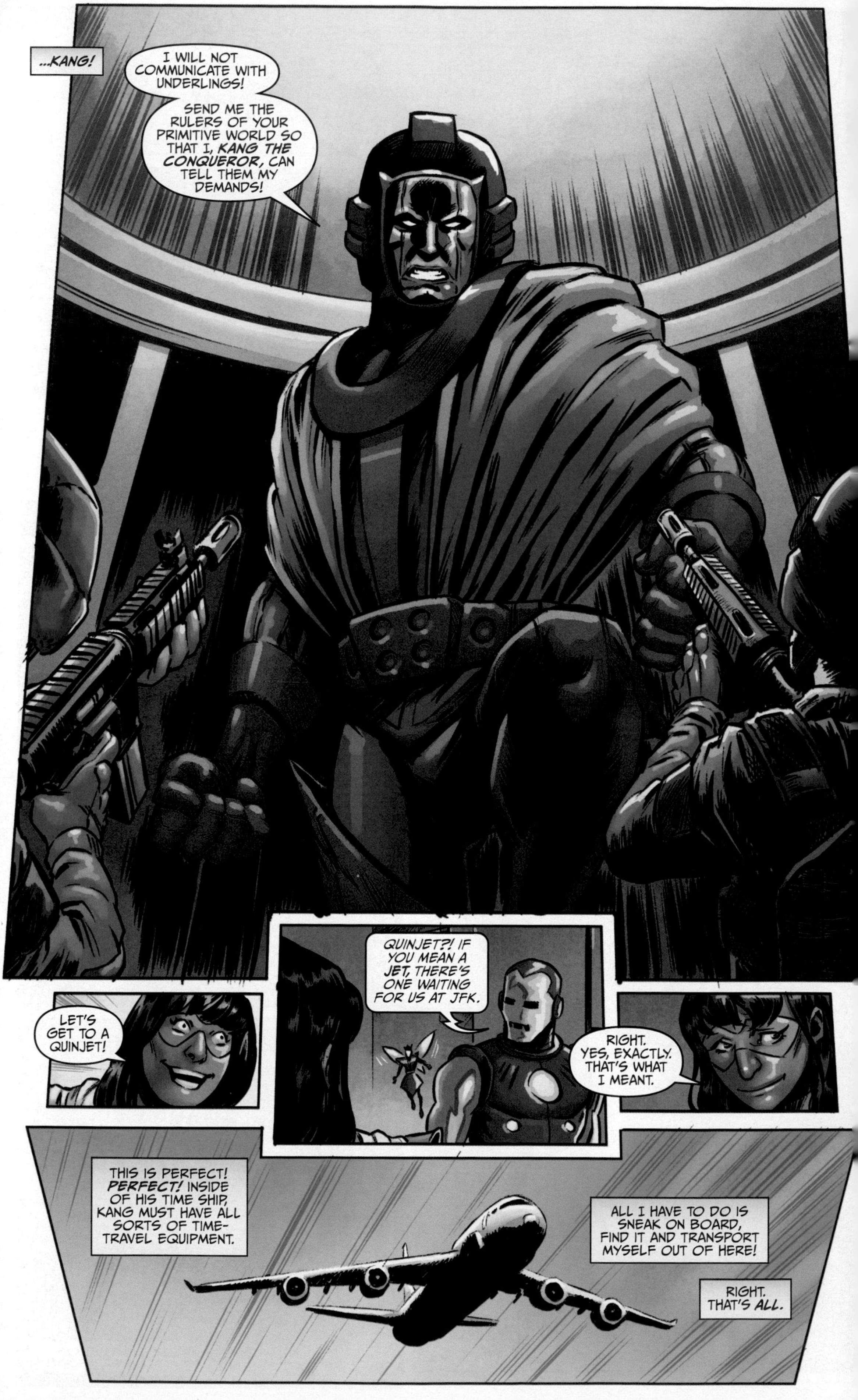
...KANG!
I WILL NOT COMMUNICATE WITH UNDERLINGS!
SEND ME THE RULERS OF YOUR PRIMITIVE WORLD SO THAT I, KANG THE CONQUEROR, CAN TELL THEM MY DEMANDS!
LET'S GET TO A QUINJET!
QUINJET?! IF YOU MEAN A JET, THERE'S ONE WAITING FOR US AT JFK.
RIGHT. YES, EXACTLY. THAT'S WHAT I MEANT.
THIS IS PERFECT! PERFECT! INSIDE OF HIS TIME SHIP, KANG MUST HAVE ALL SORTS OF TIME-TRAVEL EQUIPMENT.
ALL I HAVE TO DO IS SNEAK ON BOARD, FIND IT AND TRANSPORT MYSELF OUT OF HERE!
RIGHT. THAT'S ALL.

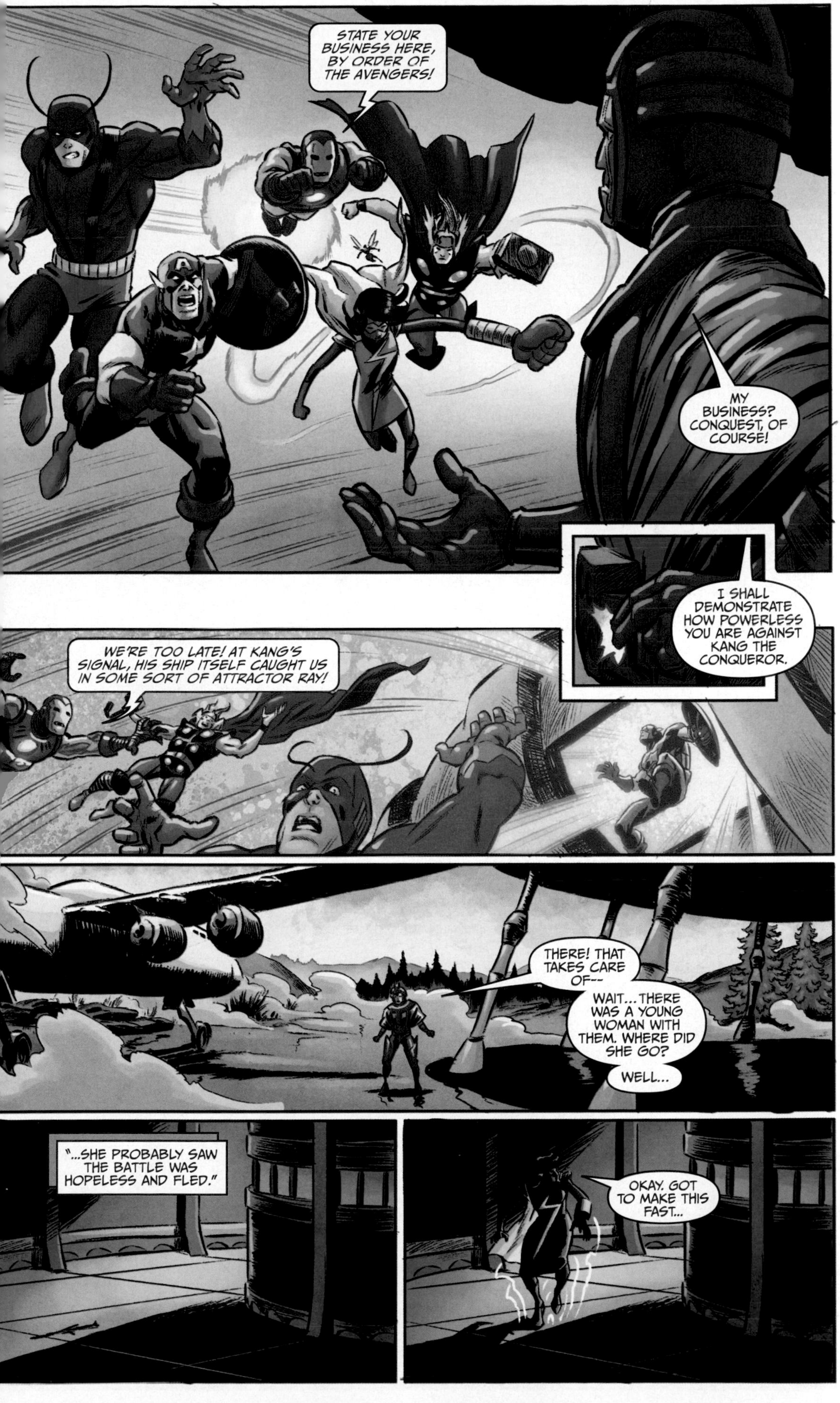
STATE YOUR BUSINESS HERE, BY ORDER OF THE AVENGERS!
MY BUSINESS? CONQUEST, OF COURSE!
I SHALL DEMONSTRATE HOW POWERLESS YOU ARE AGAINST KANG THE CONQUEROR.
WE'RE TOO LATE! AT KANG'S SIGNAL, HIS SHIP ITSELF CAUGHT US IN SOME SORT OF ATTRACTOR RAY!
THERE! THAT TAKES CARE OF--
WAIT... THERE WAS A YOUNG WOMAN WITH THEM. WHERE DID SHE GO?
WELL...
"...SHE PROBABLY SAW THE BATTLE WAS HOPELESS AND FLED."
OKAY. GOT TO MAKE THIS FAST...

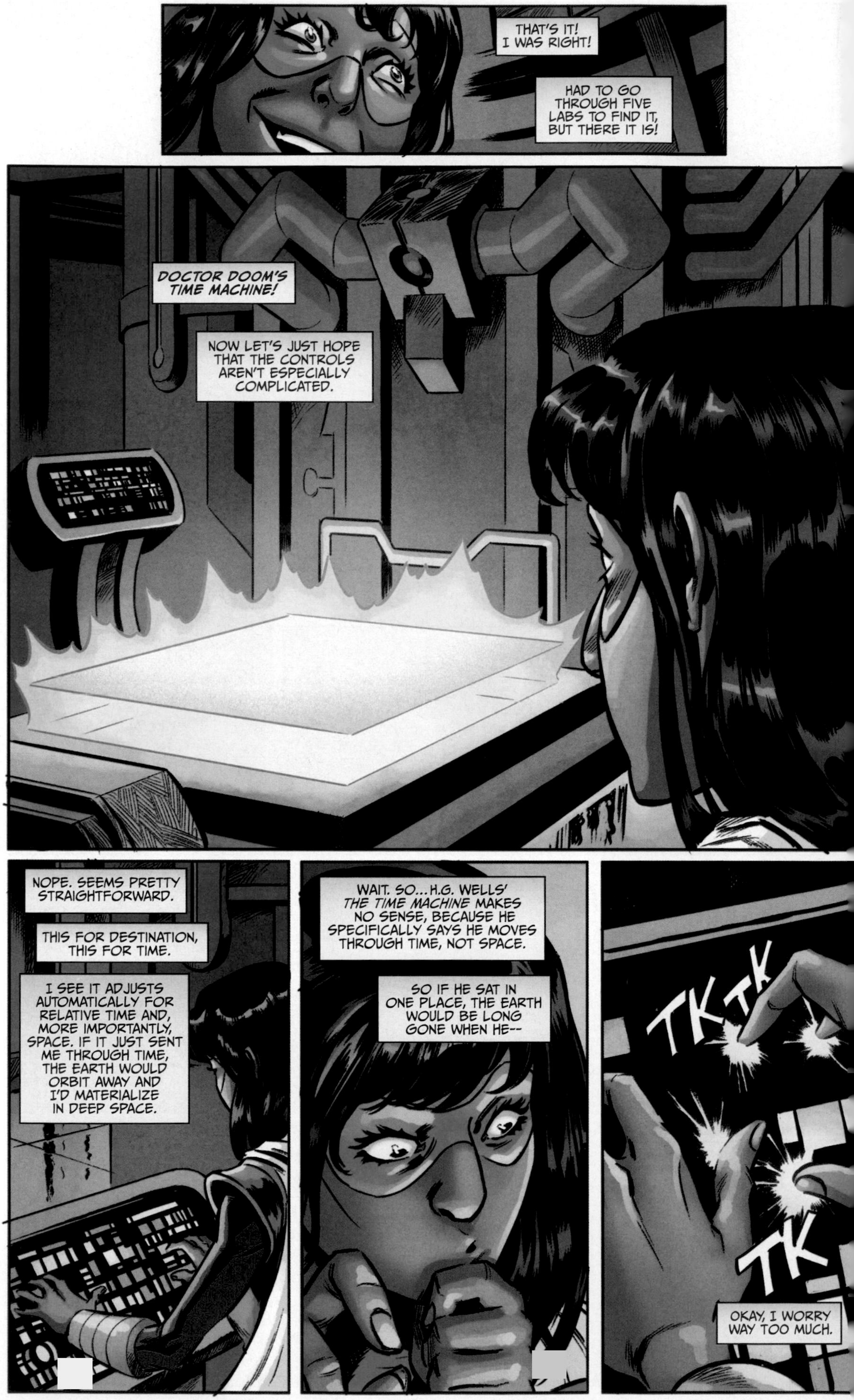
THAT'S IT! I WAS RIGHT!
HAD TO GO THROUGH FIVE LABS TO FIND IT, BUT THERE IT IS!
DOCTOR DOOM'S TIME MACHINE!
NOW LET'S JUST HOPE THAT THE CONTROLS AREN'T ESPECIALLY COMPLICATED.
NOPE. SEEMS PRETTY STRAIGHTFORWARD.
THIS FOR DESTINATION, THIS FOR TIME.
I SEE IT ADJUSTS AUTOMATICALLY FOR RELATIVE TIME AND, MORE IMPORTANTLY, SPACE. IF IT JUST SENT ME THROUGH TIME, THE EARTH WOULD ORBIT AWAY AND I'D MATERIALIZE IN DEEP SPACE.
WAIT. SO... H.G. WELLS' THE TIME MACHINE MAKES NO SENSE, BECAUSE HE SPECIFICALLY SAYS HE MOVES THROUGH TIME, NOT SPACE.
SO IF HE SAT IN ONE PLACE, THE EARTH WOULD BE LONG GONE WHEN HE--
TKTK
TK
OKAY, I WORRY WAY TOO MUCH.

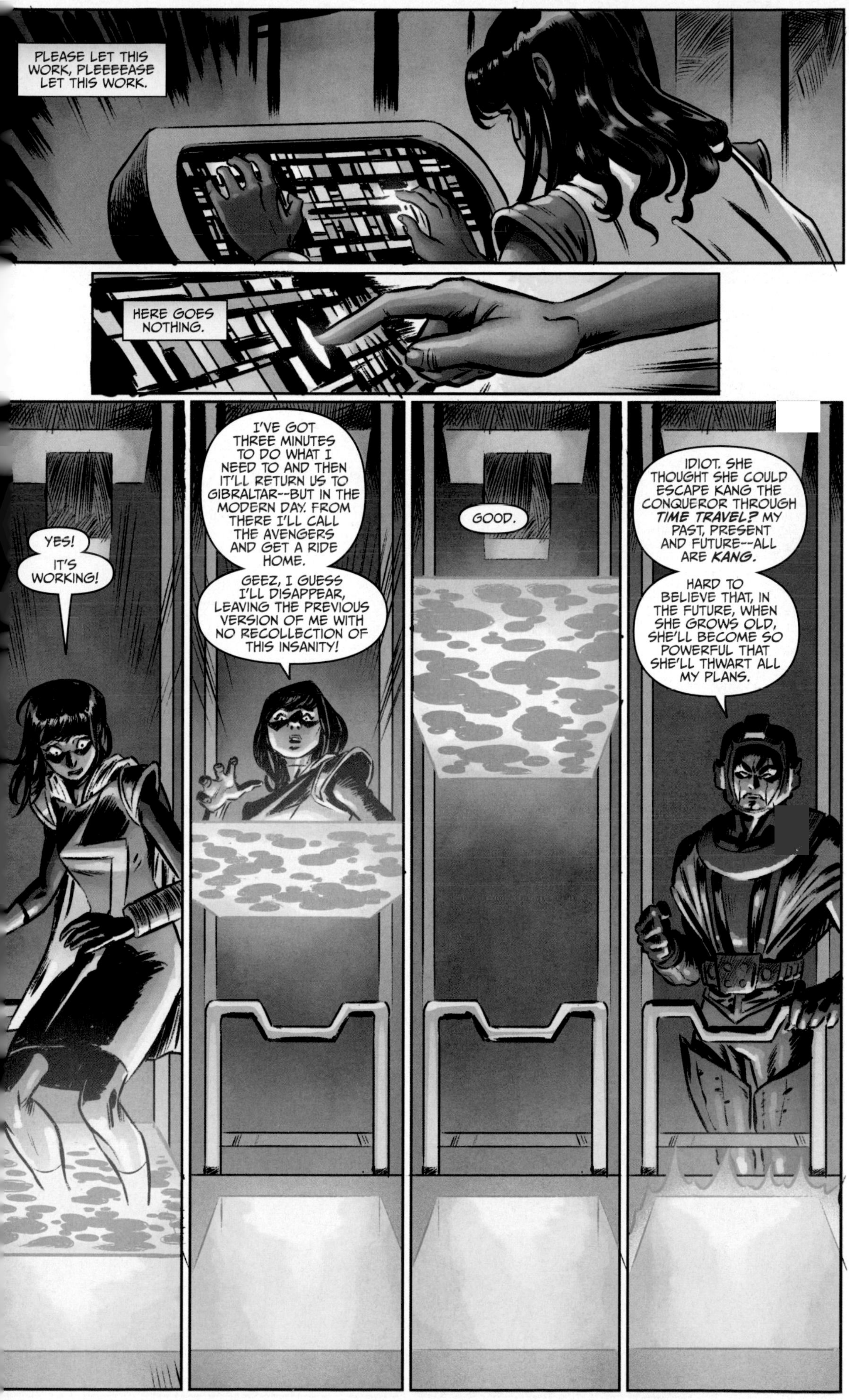
PLEASE LET THIS WORK, PLEEEEASE LET THIS WORK.
HERE GOES NOTHING.
YES!
IT'S WORKING!
I'VE GOT THREE MINUTES TO DO WHAT I NEED TO AND THEN IT'LL RETURN US TO GIBRALTAR--BUT IN THE MODERN DAY. FROM THERE I'LL CALL THE AVENGERS AND GET A RIDE HOME.
GEEZ, I GUESS I'LL DISAPPEAR, LEAVING THE PREVIOUS VERSION OF ME WITH NO RECOLLECTION OF THIS INSANITY!
GOOD.
IDIOT. SHE THOUGHT SHE COULD ESCAPE KANG THE CONQUEROR THROUGH *TIME TRAVEL?* MY PAST, PRESENT AND FUTURE--ALL ARE *KANG.*
HARD TO BELIEVE THAT, IN THE FUTURE, WHEN SHE GROWS OLD, SHE'LL BECOME SO POWERFUL THAT SHE'LL THWART ALL MY PLANS.

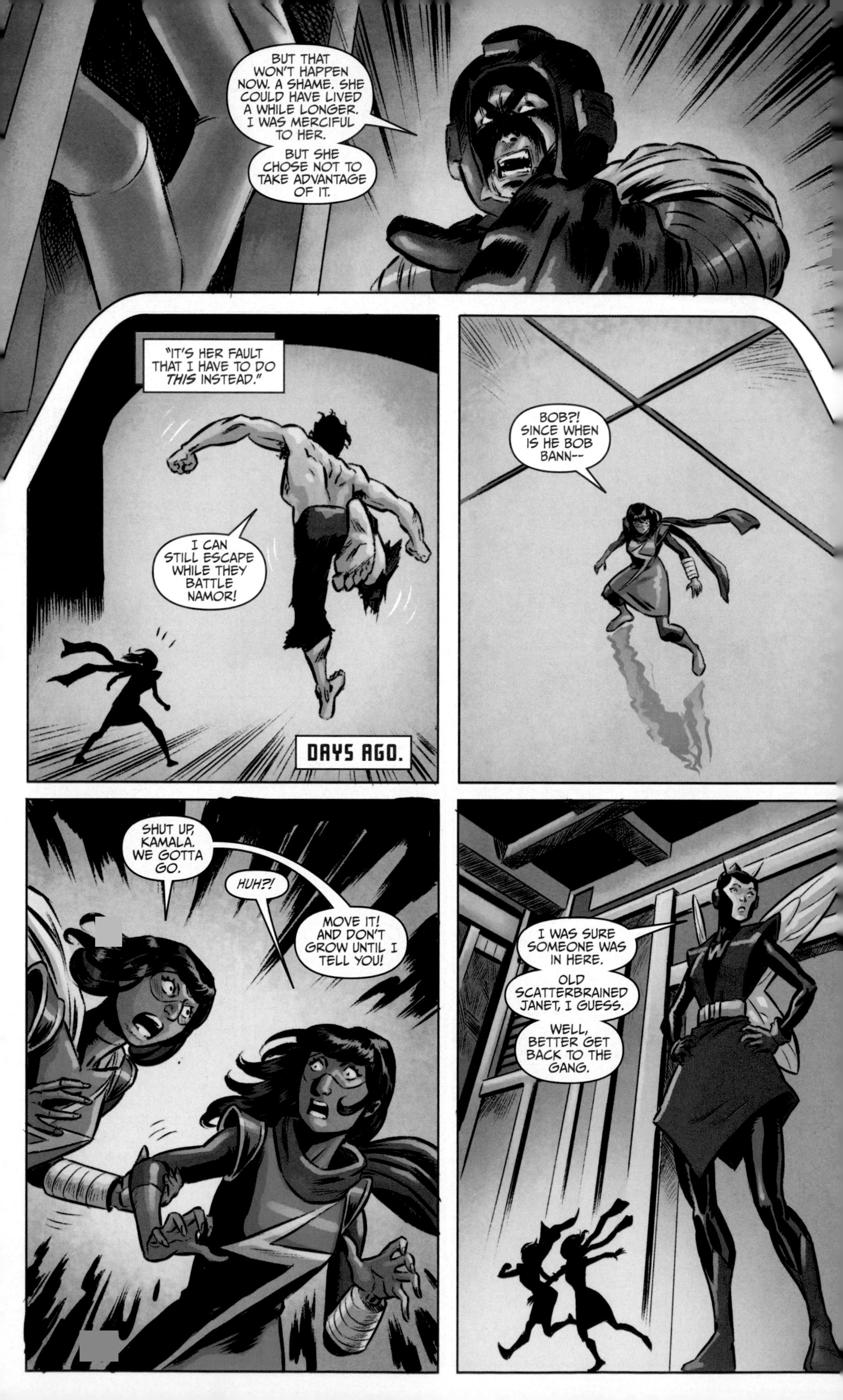

BUT THAT WON'T HAPPEN NOW. A SHAME. SHE COULD HAVE LIVED A WHILE LONGER. I WAS MERCIFUL TO HER.
BUT SHE CHOSE NOT TO TAKE ADVANTAGE OF IT.
"IT'S HER FAULT THAT I HAVE TO DO *THIS* INSTEAD."
I CAN STILL ESCAPE WHILE THEY BATTLE NAMOR!
DAYS AGO.
BOB?! SINCE WHEN IS HE BOB BANN--
SHUT UP, KAMALA. WE GOTTA GO.
HUH?!
MOVE IT! AND DON'T GROW UNTIL I TELL YOU!
I WAS SURE SOMEONE WAS IN HERE.
OLD SCATTERBRAINED JANET, I GUESS.
WELL, BETTER GET BACK TO THE GANG.

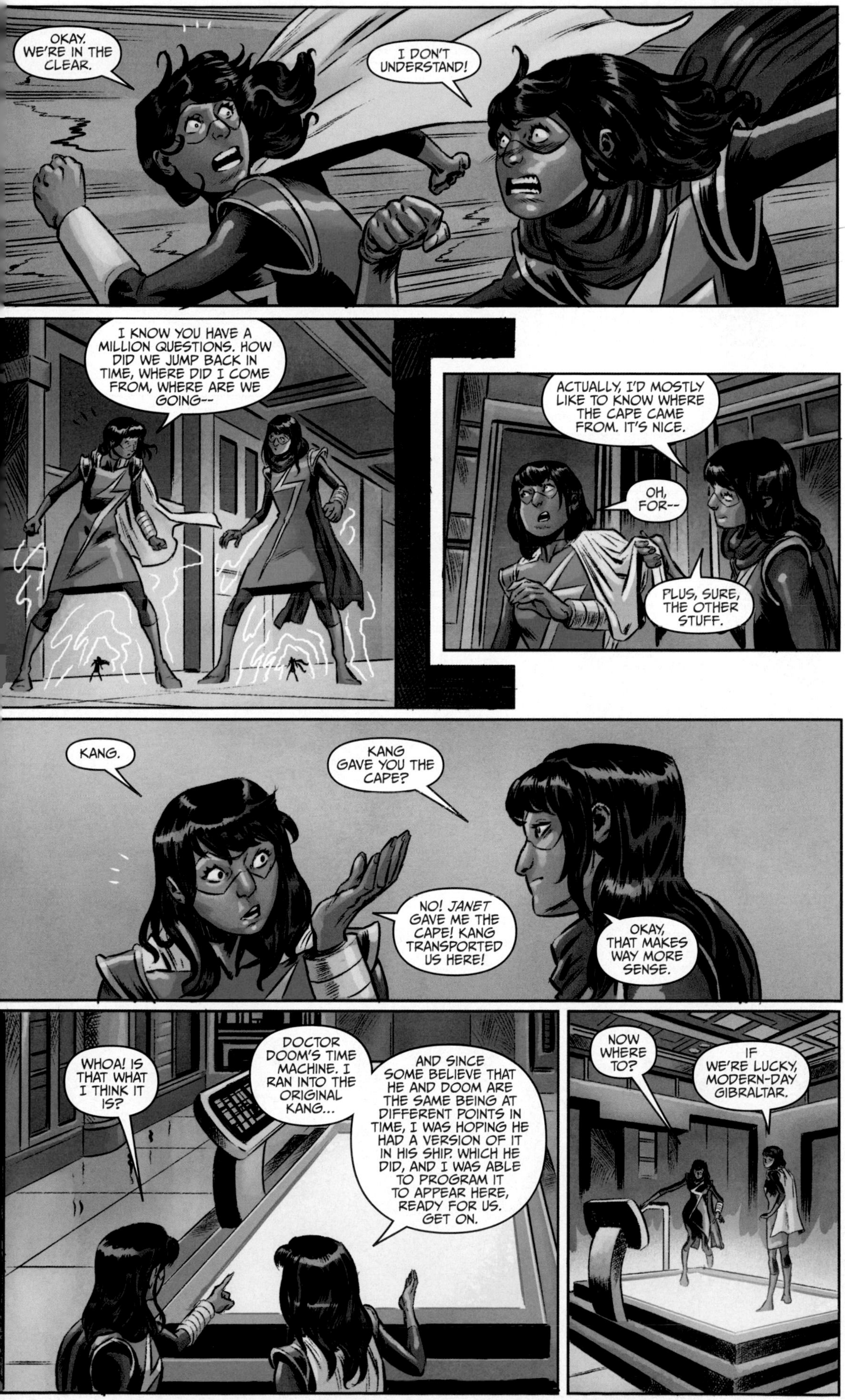
OKAY. WE'RE IN THE CLEAR.
I DON'T UNDERSTAND!
I KNOW YOU HAVE A MILLION QUESTIONS. HOW DID WE JUMP BACK IN TIME, WHERE DID I COME FROM, WHERE ARE WE GOING--
ACTUALLY, I'D MOSTLY LIKE TO KNOW WHERE THE CAPE CAME FROM. IT'S NICE.
OH, FOR--
PLUS, SURE, THE OTHER STUFF.
KANG.
KANG GAVE YOU THE CAPE?
NO! JANET GAVE ME THE CAPE! KANG TRANSPORTED US HERE!
OKAY, THAT MAKES WAY MORE SENSE.
WHOA! IS THAT WHAT I THINK IT IS?
DOCTOR DOOM'S TIME MACHINE. I RAN INTO THE ORIGINAL KANG...
AND SINCE SOME BELIEVE THAT HE AND DOOM ARE THE SAME BEING AT DIFFERENT POINTS IN TIME, I WAS HOPING HE HAD A VERSION OF IT IN HIS SHIP. WHICH HE DID, AND I WAS ABLE TO PROGRAM IT TO APPEAR HERE, READY FOR US. GET ON.
NOW WHERE TO?
IF WE'RE LUCKY, MODERN-DAY GIBRALTAR.

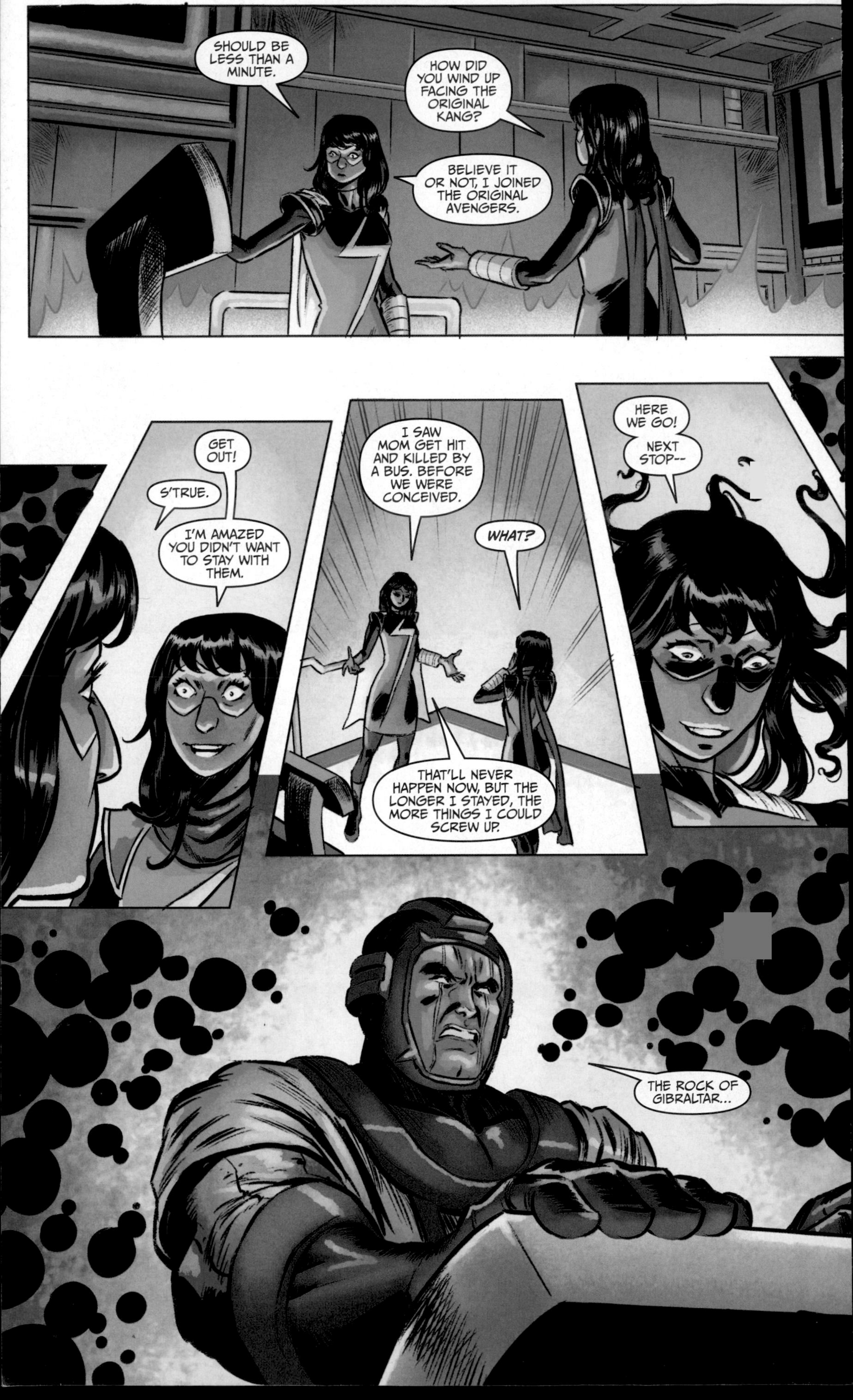
SHOULD BE LESS THAN A MINUTE.
HOW DID YOU WIND UP FACING THE ORIGINAL KANG?
BELIEVE IT OR NOT, I JOINED THE ORIGINAL AVENGERS.
GET OUT!
S'TRUE.
I'M AMAZED YOU DIDN'T WANT TO STAY WITH THEM.
I SAW MOM GET HIT AND KILLED BY A BUS. BEFORE WE WERE CONCEIVED.
WHAT?
THAT'LL NEVER HAPPEN NOW, BUT THE LONGER I STAYED, THE MORE THINGS I COULD SCREW UP.
HERE WE GO!
NEXT STOP--
THE ROCK OF GIBRALTAR...

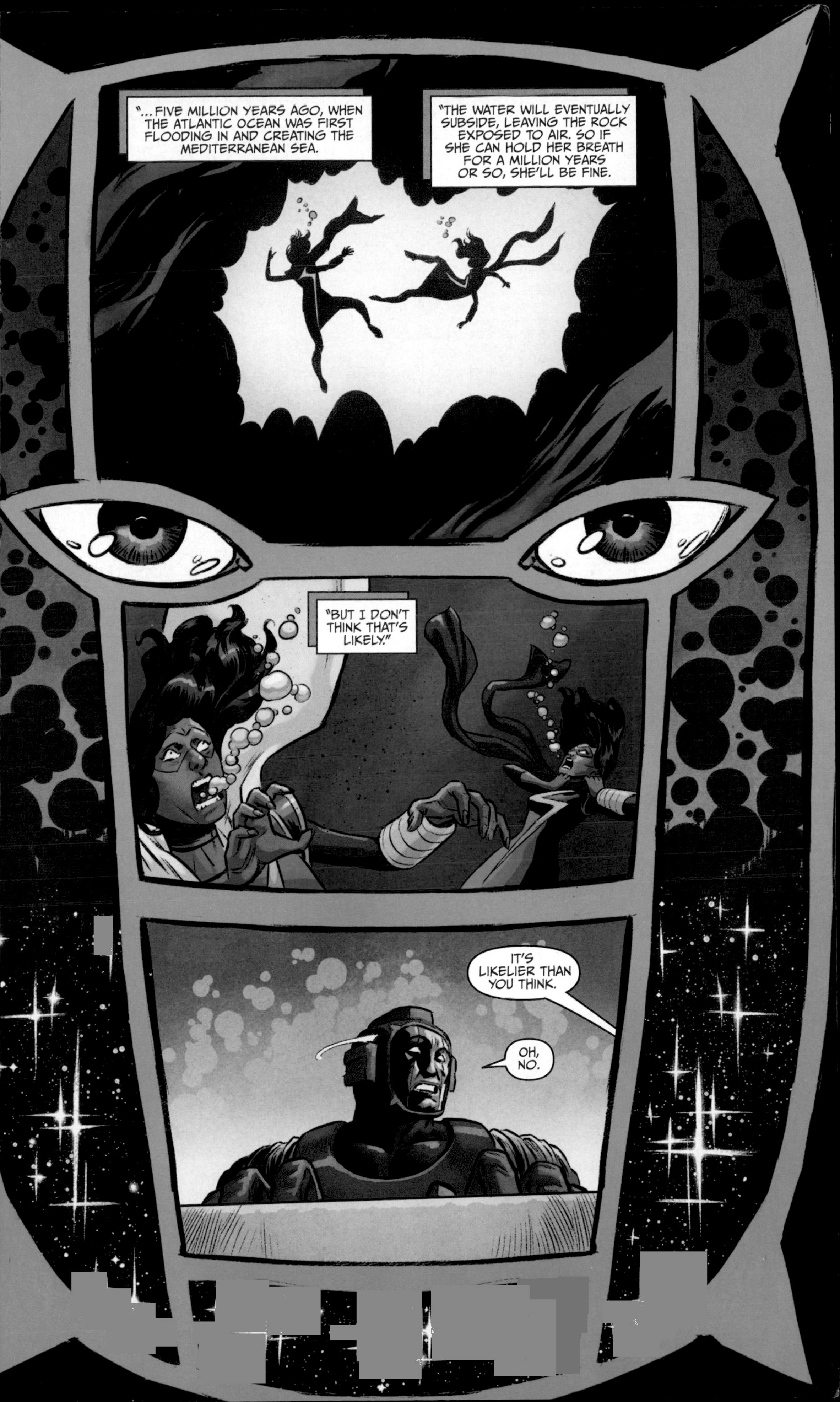
"...FIVE MILLION YEARS AGO, WHEN THE ATLANTIC OCEAN WAS FIRST FLOODING IN AND CREATING THE MEDITERRANEAN SEA.
"THE WATER WILL EVENTUALLY SUBSIDE, LEAVING THE ROCK EXPOSED TO AIR. SO IF SHE CAN HOLD HER BREATH FOR A MILLION YEARS OR SO, SHE'LL BE FINE.
"BUT I DON'T THINK THAT'S LIKELY."
IT'S LIKELIER THAN YOU THINK.
OH, NO.

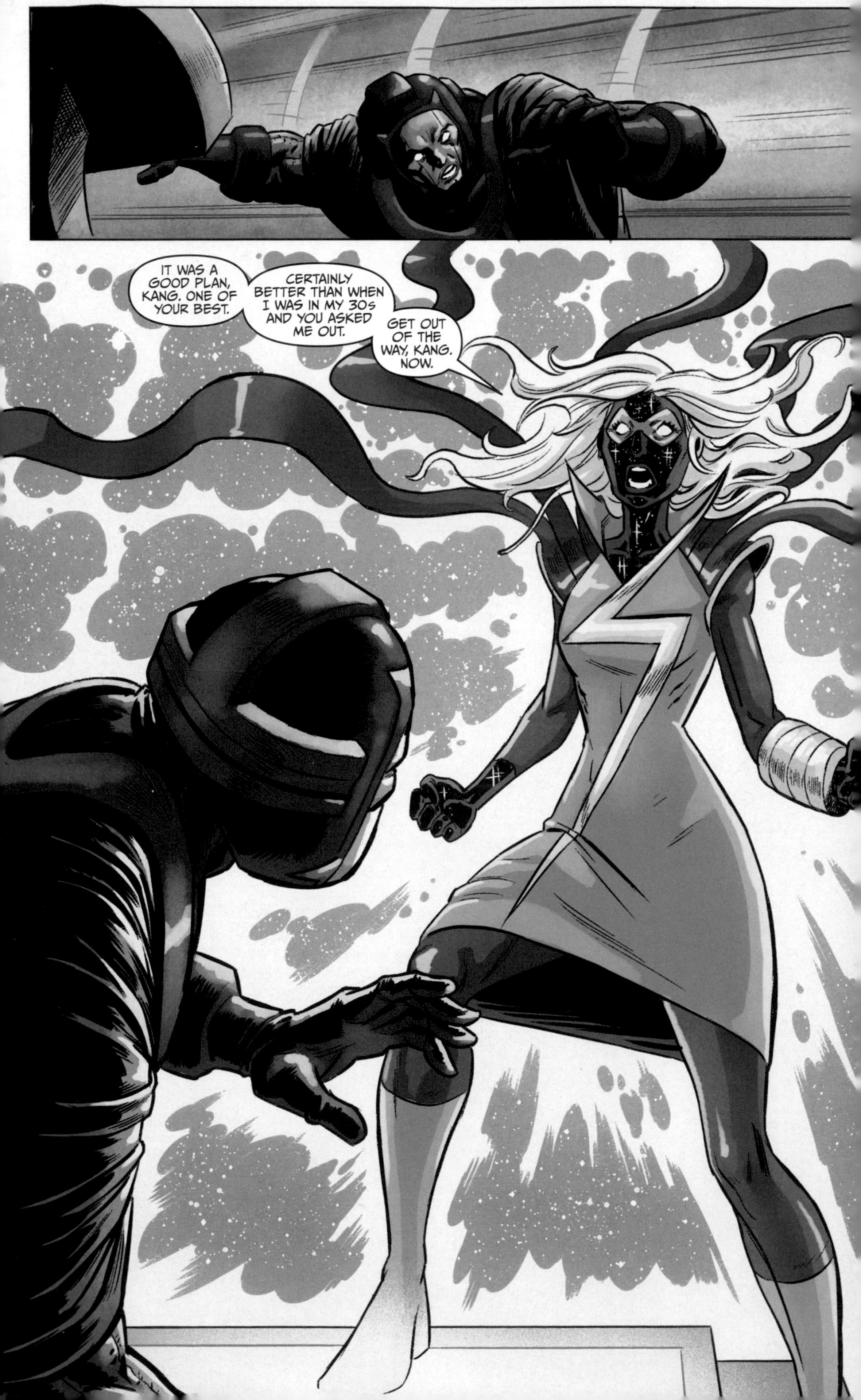
IT WAS A GOOD PLAN, KANG. ONE OF YOUR BEST.
CERTAINLY BETTER THAN WHEN I WAS IN MY 30s AND YOU ASKED ME OUT.
GET OUT OF THE WAY, KANG. NOW.

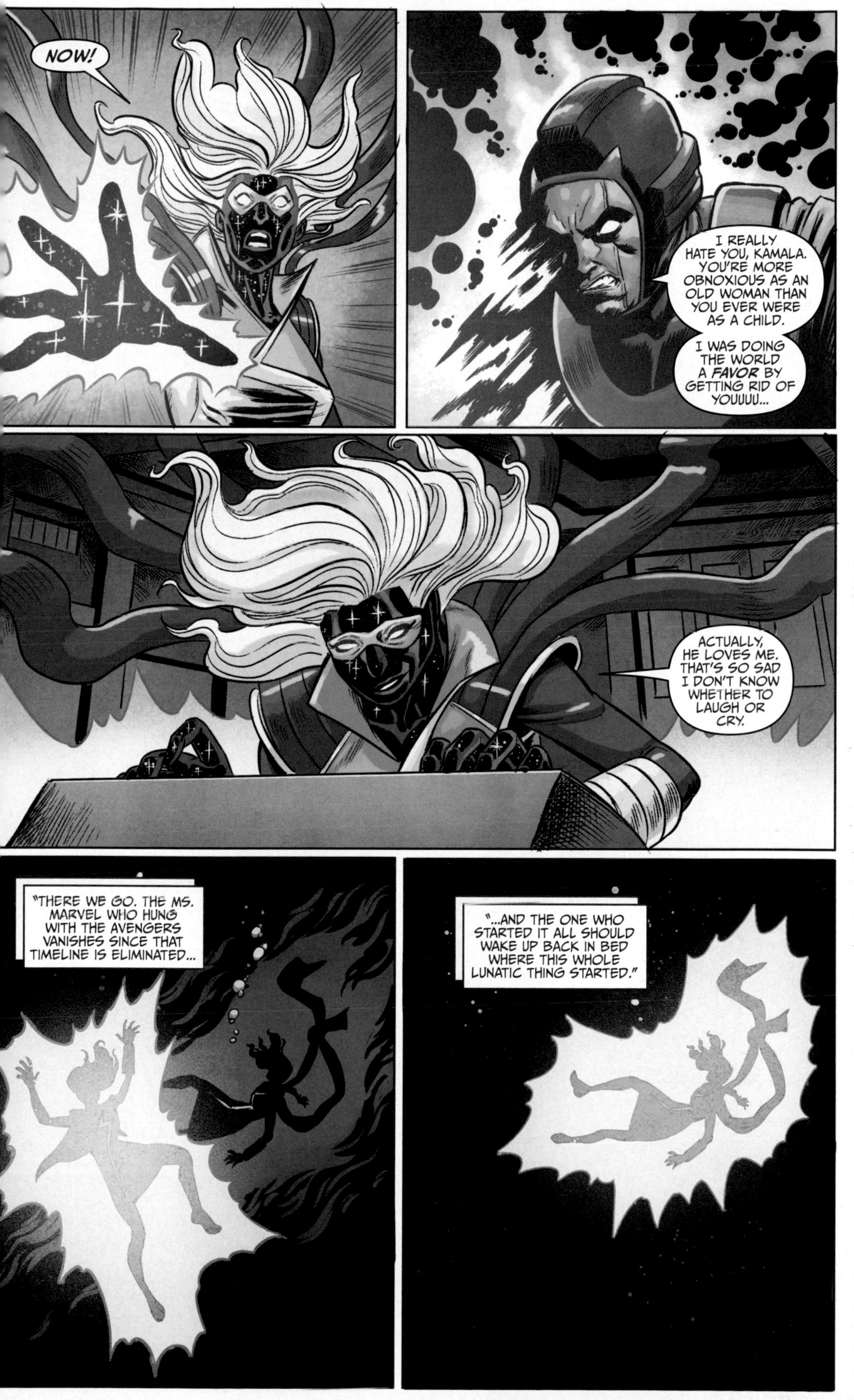
NOW!
I REALLY HATE YOU, KAMALA. YOU'RE MORE OBNOXIOUS AS AN OLD WOMAN THAN YOU EVER WERE AS A CHILD.
I WAS DOING THE WORLD A *FAVOR* BY GETTING RID OF YOUUUU...
ACTUALLY, HE LOVES ME. THAT'S SO SAD I DON'T KNOW WHETHER TO LAUGH OR CRY.
"THERE WE GO. THE MS. MARVEL WHO HUNG WITH THE AVENGERS VANISHES SINCE THAT TIMELINE IS ELIMINATED...
"...AND THE ONE WHO STARTED IT ALL SHOULD WAKE UP BACK IN BED WHERE THIS WHOLE LUNATIC THING STARTED."

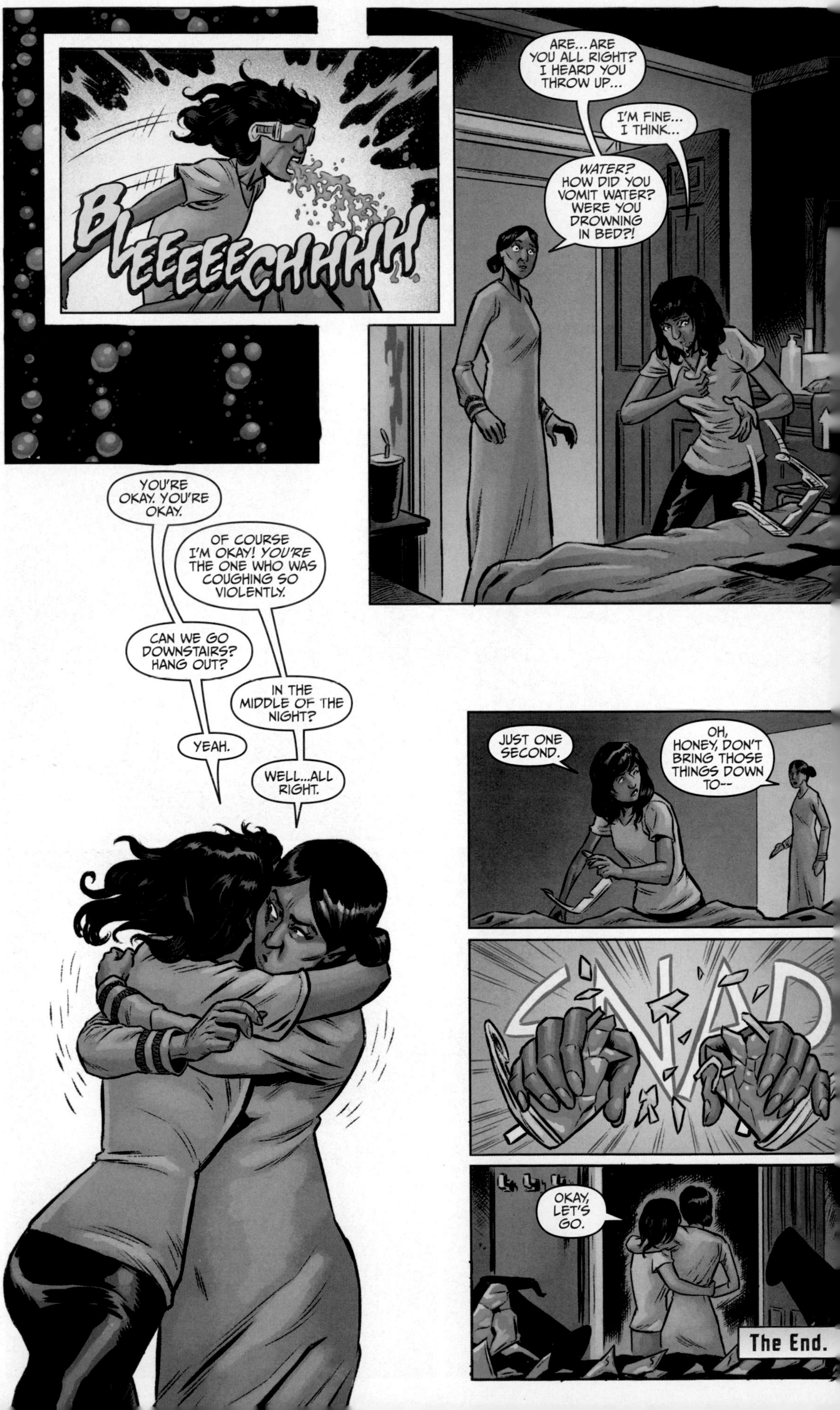

BLEEEEECHHHH
ARE... ARE YOU ALL RIGHT? I HEARD YOU THROW UP...
I'M FINE... I THINK...
WATER? HOW DID YOU VOMIT WATER? WERE YOU DROWNING IN BED?!
YOU'RE OKAY. YOU'RE OKAY.
OF COURSE I'M OKAY! YOU'RE THE ONE WHO WAS COUGHING SO VIOLENTLY.
CAN WE GO DOWNSTAIRS? HANG OUT?
IN THE MIDDLE OF THE NIGHT?
YEAH.
WELL...ALL RIGHT.
JUST ONE SECOND.
OH, HONEY, DON'T BRING THOSE THINGS DOWN TO--
SNAP
OKAY, LET'S GO.
The End.

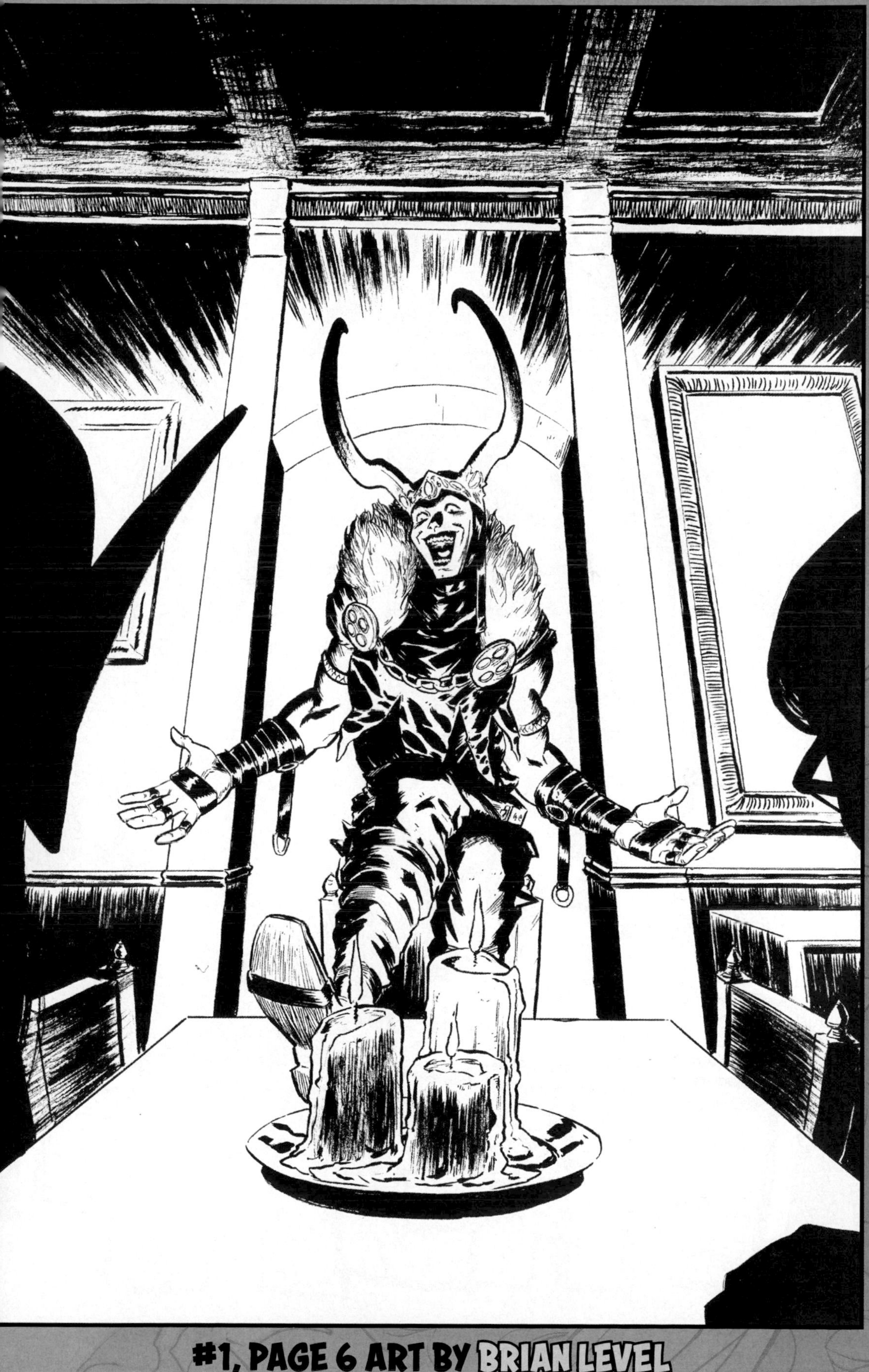

#1, PAGE 6 ART BY BRIAN LEVEL

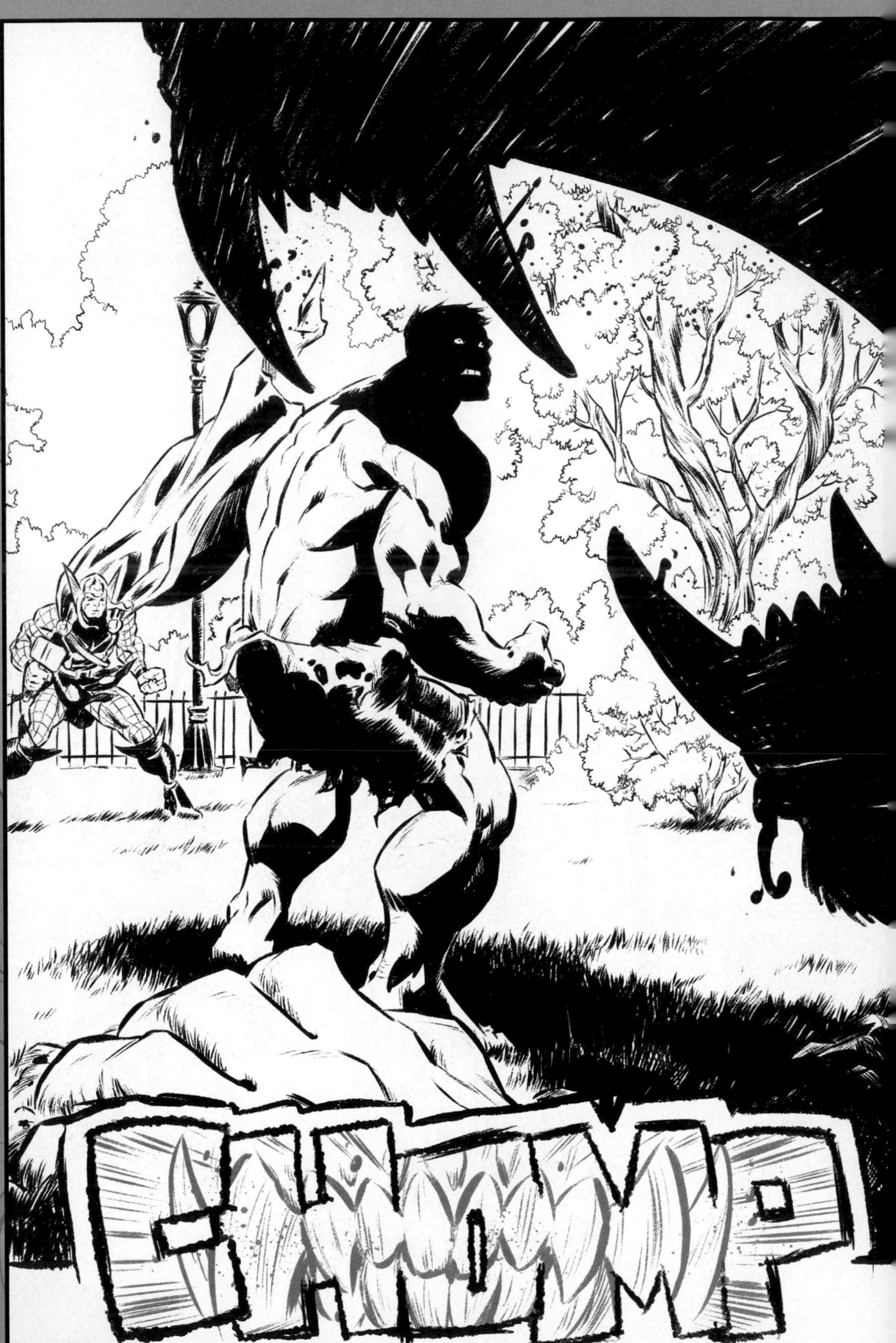
CHOMP

#2, PAGE 2 ART BY BRIAN LEVEL

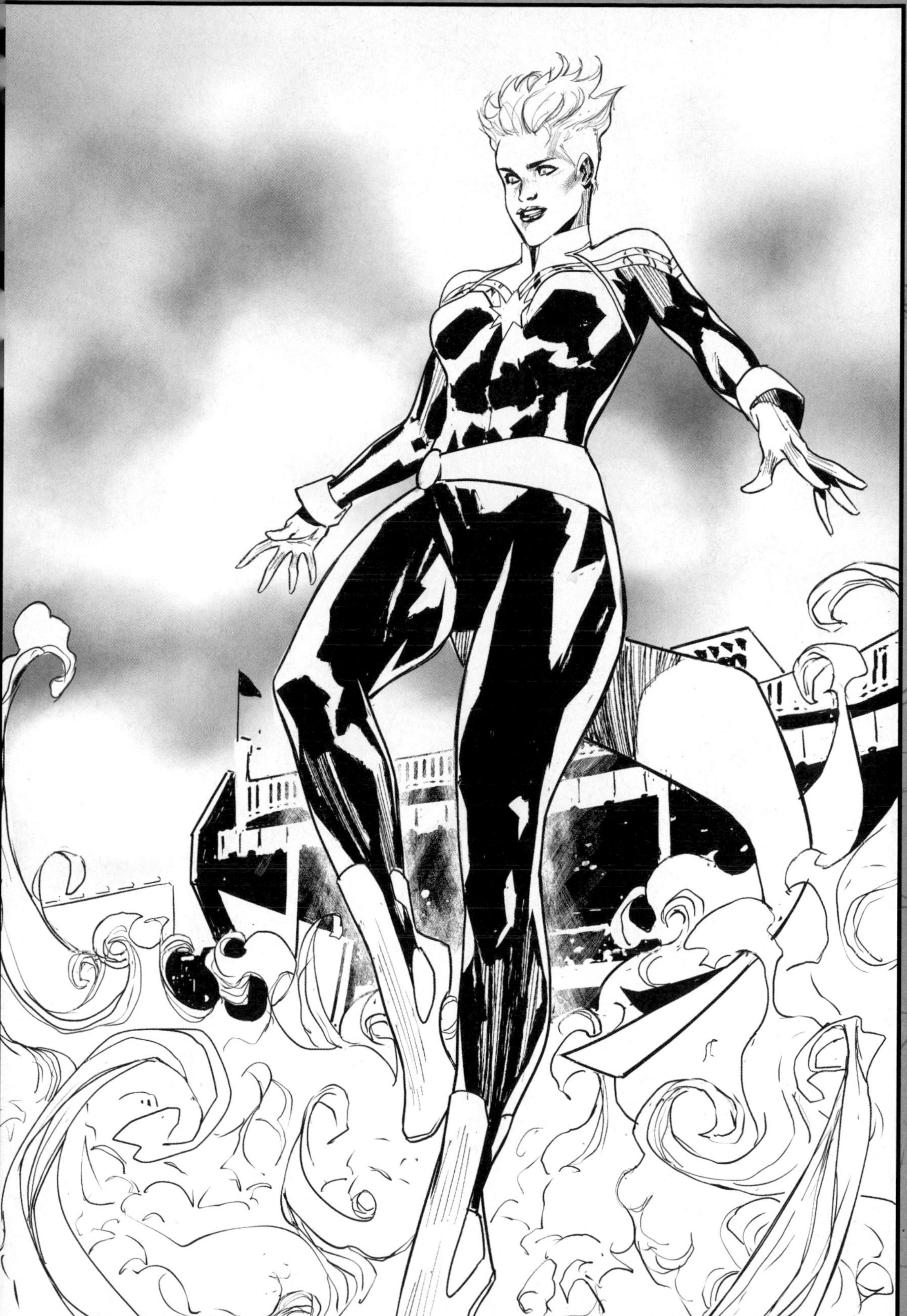

#3, PAGE 11 ART BY JUANAN RAMÍREZ

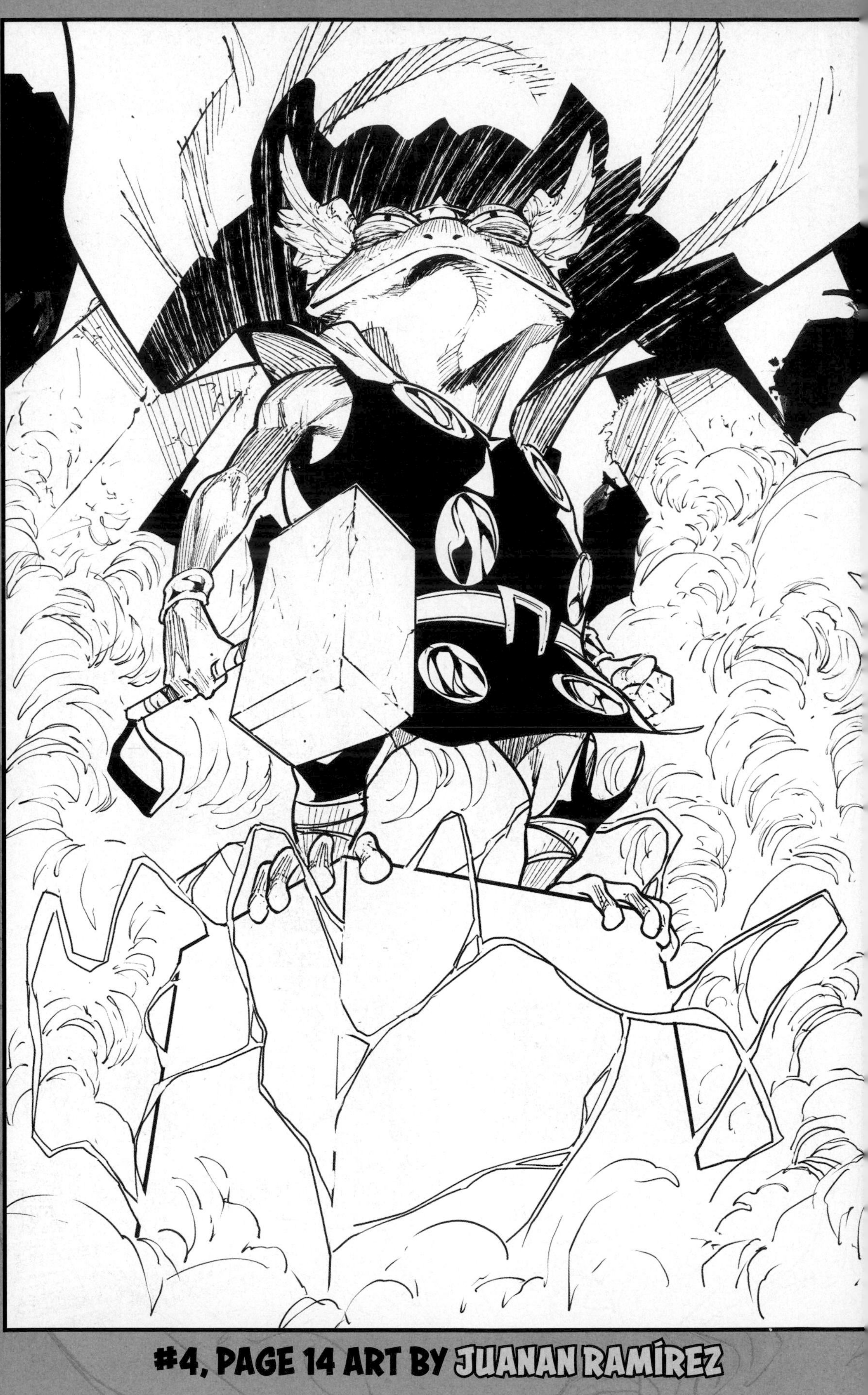

#4, PAGE 14 ART BY JUANAN RAMÍREZ

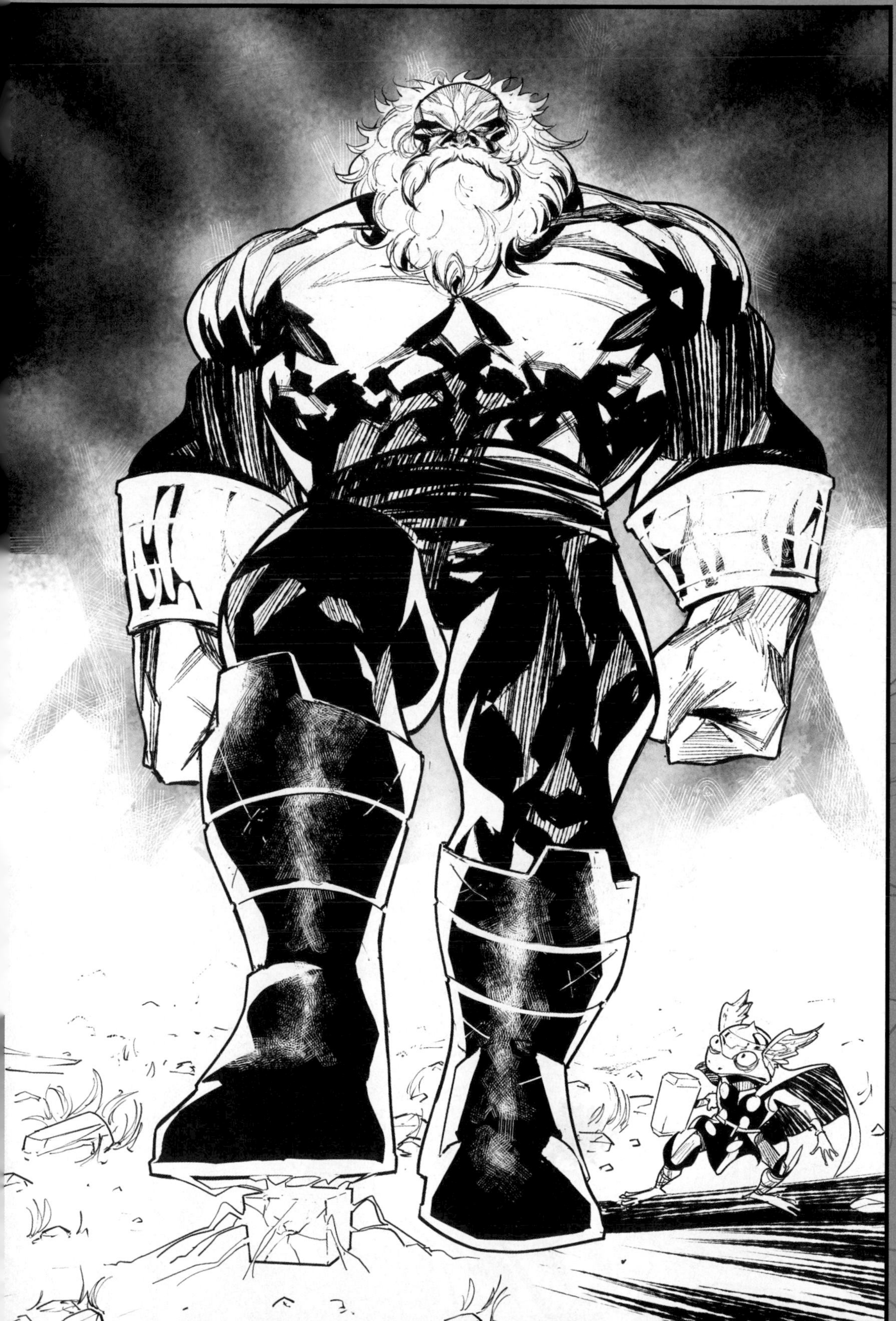

#4, PAGE 17 ART BY JUANAN RAMÍREZ

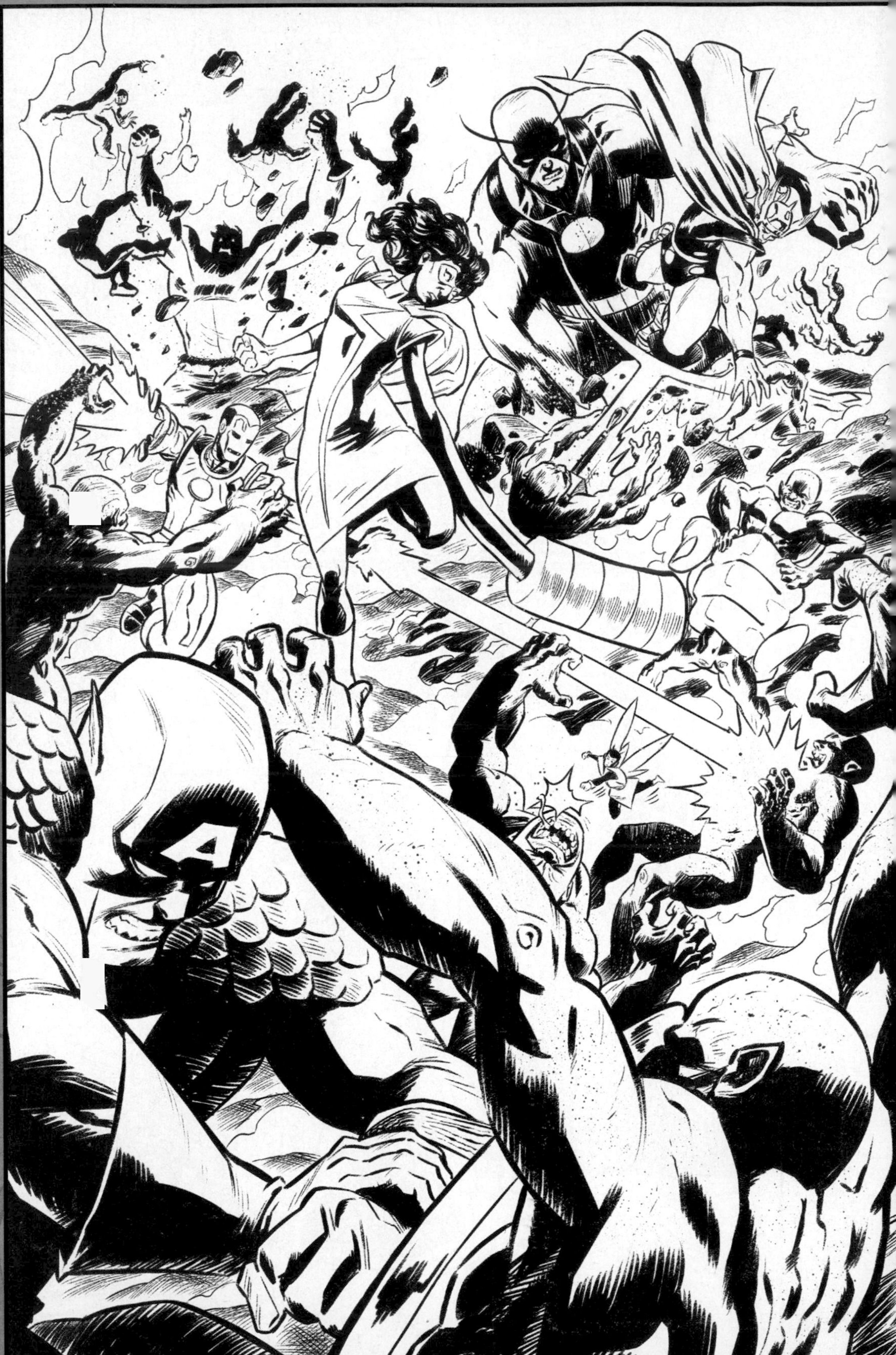

#6, PAGE 7 ART BY BRIAN LEVEL